B+T
6/86

811.52 MacLeish,
MAC   Archibald

        Collected poems,
        1917-1982

COLLECTED POEMS, 1917-1982

Also by Archibald MacLeish

Poems

> Collected Poems, 1917–1952
> Songs for Eve
> "The Wild Old Wicked Man" & Other Poems
> The Human Season
> New and Collected Poems, 1917–1976

Plays in Verse

> Panic
> The Fall of the City
> Air Raid
> The Trojan Horse
> This Music Crept by Me upon the Waters
> J.B.
> Herakles
> The Great American Fourth of July Parade
> Six Plays

Play in Prose

> Scratch

Prose

> The Irresponsibles
> The American Cause
> A Time to Speak
> A Time to Act
> American Opinion and the War
> Poetry and Opinion
> Freedom Is the Right to Choose
> Poetry and Experience
> The Eleanor Roosevelt Story
> A Continuing Journey
> Riders on the Earth
> Letters of Archibald MacLeish, 1907 to 1982
>   (edited by R. H. Winnick)

COLLECTED POEMS, 1917-1982

Archibald MacLeish

With a prefatory note
to the Newly Collected Poems
by Richard B. McAdoo

Houghton Mifflin Company · Boston   1985

Library of Congress Cataloging in Publication Data

MacLeish, Archibald, 1892–1982
Collected poems, 1917–1982.

I. Title.
PS3525.A27A17   1985   811'.52   85–14392
ISBN 0–395–39417–1
ISBN 0–395–39569–0 (pbk.)

Printed in the United States of America

P 10 9 8 7 6 5 4 3 2 1

Acknowledgment is made to the following publishers for permission to reprint some of the poems in this collection:

Duell, Sloan & Pearce, Inc., for *America Was Promises*, published by them in 1939; Random House for poems from *Actfive*, published by them in 1948; Rinehart & Company, Inc., for poems from *Public Speech*, published by them in 1936; Yale University Press for poems from *Tower of Ivory*, published by them in 1917; the Atlantic Monthly Company for the poems "The Old Men in the Leaf Smoke," "They Come No More," "What the Old Women Say," "The Patriots, 1952" ("Liberty"), "The Bed," "Where the Hayfields Were," "The Burial"; the editors of the *Atlantic Monthly*, the *New Republic*, the *North American Review*, and the *Yale Review* for certain of the poems in *The Happy Marriage*; *Saturday Review* for "Where a Poet's From," © 1967 by Saturday Review, Inc.; *The Yale Literary Magazine* for "Cummings," published by them under the title "The Sunset"; *The Atlantic* for "Hemingway," published by them under the title "The Gunshot," Copyright © 1961 by The Atlantic Monthly Company; *Equity* for the poem "Brooks Atkinson," Copyright 1960 Actor's Equity Association; *Botteghe Oscure* for the poem "How the River Ninfa Runs Through the Ruined Town Beneath the Lime Quarry"; *The New Republic*

for Ada

CONTENTS

PART TWO

PART THREE

PART SIX

PART SEVEN: NEWLY COLLECTED POEMS

PART ONE: NEW POEMS

NIGHT WATCH IN THE CITY OF BOSTON

Old colleague,
Puritan New England's famous scholar
half intoxicated with those heady draughts of God,
come walk these cobble-stones John Cotton trod,

and you, our Yankee Admiral of the Ocean Sea,
come too, come walk with me.
You know, none better, how the Bay wind blows
fierce in the soul as in the streets its ocean snows.

Lead me between you in the night, old friends,
one living and one dead, and where the journey ends
show me the city built as on a hill
John Winthrop saw long since and you see still.

*

I almost saw it once, a law school boy
born west beyond the Lakes in Illinois.
Walking down Milk Street in a summer dawn,
the sidewalks empty and the truckers gone,

I thought the asphalt turned to country lane
and climbed toward something, glimpsed and lost again —
some distance not of measure but of mind,
of meaning, Oh, of man, I could not find.

*

What city is it where the heart comes home?

*

City of God they called it on the hills of Rome
when empire changed to church and kings were crowned
to rule in God's name all the world around.

City of God!
                    Was this the city, then, of man? —
this new found city where the hope began
that Eve who spins and Adam's son who delves
might make their peace with God and rule themselves? —

this shanty city on a granite shore,
the woods behind it and the sea before,
where human hope first challenged Heaven's will
and piled a blazing beacon on a little hill? —

city where man, poor naked actor on his narrow stage,
confronted in the wilderness the God of Ages?

*

4

Lead me between you to that holy ground
where man and God contended and the hope was found.

Moses upon the Sinai in the cloud
faced God for forty days and nights and bowed;
received the Law, obedient and mute;
brought back to Israel the Decalogue of Duty.

Not so New England's prophets. When their arguments were
        done
they answered thundering skies with their own thunder:
"We have the Lord," wrote Hooker with his wild goose quill,
"We have the Lord in bonds for the fulfilling."

                    *

City of Man! Before the elms came down
no village in America, no prairie town,
but planted avenues of elms against the sky
to praise, to keep the promise, to remember by —

remember that small city of great men
where man himself had walked the earth again:
Warren at Bunker Hill who stood and died
not for a flag — there was none — but for human pride;

Emerson who prayed and quit the church,
choosing not Heaven's answer but the human search;
Thoreau who followed footprints in the snow
to find his own — the human journey he had still to go;

Holmes dissenting in a sordid age,
the Court against him and the rich man's rage —
Holmes who taught the herd how human liberty is won:
by man alone, minority of one.

*

City of Man, Oh, city of the famous dead
where Otis spoke and Adams' heart was bred:
Mother of the great Republic — mother town
before the elm trees sickened and came down . . .

*

The darkness deepens. Shrieking voices cry
below these fantasies of glass that crowd our sky
and hatred like a whirling paper in a street
tears at itself where shame and hatred meet.

*

Show me, old friends, where in the darkness still
stands the great Republic on its hill!

NATIONAL SECURITY

There are three names
in a locked file
in a secret room
on a classified stair
in the house of state.

They are not to be spoken.

The first is old,
black and gold,
cool as lacquer

smelling of plums.
This name is Cambodia.

The second is Laos,
a flexible necklace
knotted with silver
sounds like the language
of orioles.

The third is Vietnam,
a dried child
mailed to its mother
by B–52s
in a cellophane envelope.

Three names
in a locked file
in a secret room
on a classified stair
in the house of state:
not to be spoken.

Nevertheless
the names bleed.
The blood runs out
under the secret
door and down
the classified stair
to the floor of state
and over the stoop
and out on the continent:
the country is steeped in it.

Not to be spoken.

7

LONG HOT SUMMER

Never again
when the heat overwhelms us
cool elms.

The elm leaves shrivel on the twig
and the sun beats through and our time is big
with a lidless time that knows no dark,
no shadow where the heart can see,
no shade at noon where doubt can be.

The beetle of God is under the bark
and the age of the leafy trees is done:
the cities are dying one by one
of the heat and the hate and the naked sun.

Never again
when the hate overwhelms us
cool elms.

PABLO CASALS

So old, so delicate, so small
the concert master and the first
viola rose in panic at the burst
of welcoming love as though they feared he'd fall.

And when, safe-seated at his music stand,
he tapped and raised his baton, no

8

winter leaf against the winter snow
was ever veined and fragile as his hand,

and yet, before the piece was done,
Beethoven's rage so filled the room
and overflowed it that the deaf man's tomb
seemed broken open and the dying new begun.

Fragile? That fragile hand, alone
and armed with nothing but a bow,
had saved the soul of Spain.

How better know
Beethoven's courage than by courage of one's own?

A GOOD MAN IN A BAD TIME
for Jerome Weisner

Rinsing our mouths . . .

Tin cup:
limestone spring in the cool of the mint-bed.

Rinsing our mouths with praise . . .

God's will in the world if we could learn it,
test it on our lips, would taste of praise.
Why else should the world be beautiful? Why should the
leaves look as they do, the light, the water?

Rinsing our mouths with praise of a good man . . .

Nobody speaks of a good man now:
only the knave in office, public liar,
pardoned president, and all the rest.
Even the word is out of fashion: "Good!"

Rinsing our mouths with praise of a good man in a
bad time . . .

                    A time when men are scarce,
when fools forgather,
follow each other around in the fog like
sheep, bleat in the rain, complain
that Godot never comes,
that all life is a tragic absurdity, Sisyphus
sweating away at his rock and the rock
won't. "Weep," they say, "for freedom and dignity!
You're not free: it's your grandfather's itch you're scratching.
You have no dignity. You're not a man.
You're a rat in a vat of rewards and punishments.
The rewards have chosen *you*." Aye, weep!

Rinsing our mouths with praise of a good man in a
time when men are scarce, when the word
chirps like a cricket on the cellar floor,
on the damp stone, and the mind maunders.

Look at him there against the sky!
He saunters along to his place in the world's weather,
lights his pipe, hitches his pants,
talks back to accepted opinions:
Congressional committees hear him say,
"Not what you think, what you haven't thought of."

He addresses presidents. He says:
"Even now a government still has to govern:
no one is going to invent a self-governing holocaust!"

The Pentagon receives his views:
"Science," he says, "is not a substitute for thought.
Miracle drugs perhaps: not miracle wars."

Adviser to history, the papers call him.
It's the young who need competent friends, bold companions,
honest men who won't run out,
won't write off mankind, sell up the country,
quit the venture, sink the ship.

I love this man.
I rinse my mouth with his praise in a bad time.
The taste in the cup is of mint,
of spring water.

STATE FUNERAL: MARCH 31, 1969

Ten men, nine alive,
steep stone stair, the Capitol
dome above in the blowing air,
throngs below along the Drive,

and the sets switch on all over America,
children by the wood-chunk stove,
husband by the door. The woman
lays her work down, turns her chair.

11

Ten men, nine alive,
slow on the flickering screen go down
step by step the steep of stair,
no spoken word, no heard command,

and the band plays over and over
God of our Fathers Strong to Save.
The woman weeps. The flags wave.

Why does she weep? For a dead president?
The new one stands beside the stair.

Why does she weep? The trumpet says
God of our Fathers Strong to Save.

Why does she weep? O great Republic,
Lincoln's last best hope, she hears
your step upon the stone
                                    descending

THE CARRION CROW

to the memory of F. O. Matthiessen who threw himself out of a window
of the Hotel Manger in Boston in Joe McCarthy's time.

Claw at his eyes, O carrion crow.
You cannot know
what sights they saw.

Tear at his tongue, black, reeking bird.
You never heard
what words it said.

Gorge on his heart. You cannot think,
though flesh you eat and blood you drink,
what love it bore.

Christ will forgive the carrion crow
who cannot think or hear or know.
Will Christ forgive me too?

I knew.

MIDSUMMER DAWN

Listen! the sky! Vast conflagration!
Inaudible huge roaring of the sun,
too loud to hear, that sets the light on fire!

Kindle our souls, great sun, and our desire —
kindle our souls! We've loved the night
too long now. Set the dark alight,
the light ablaze, the blaze
to raging through the reek of these dim days
until our souls,
half-rotted into selves, burn clean as coals!

HANDS

We hit like a hoof.
We caress like a petal.
It's we break the loaf.
It's we lift the bottle.
The head wears the laurel.
The arm holds the bride.
But come to a quarrel
it's we will decide.

*

Two thousand years this bowl
has balanced its blue shell,
and what man's curious soul
conceived its perfect bell
no mind can now recall,
but where the dragons crawl
and where the slow curves swell
our print is on it all.

*

Some god, they said, had stayed the throw
too soon or not quite soon enough,
or fate, that fool, had willed it so
for on that toss we lost our love.
Those cubes of bone with their black eyes,
if they had turned one tumble more,
had won her for us, but, unwise,
we had not bribed the gods before,
and so, men said, we lost the throw.

We threw it though.

DOZING ON THE LAWN

I fall asleep these days too easily —
doze off of an afternoon
in the warm sun by the humming trees —
but I wake too soon:

wake too soon and wake afraid
of the blinding sun, of the blazing sky.
It was dark in the dream where I was laid:
It is dark in the earth where I will lie.

CONWAY BURYING GROUND

They set up stones to show where time has ended
first for one man, then another, on and on:
stones in rows where time has run,
run out, run out for Jane, for Mary's Joe,
but what time is, they do not know.

Only the old know time: they feel it flow
like water through their fingers when the light
ebbs from the pasture and they wade in night.
It frightens them.

Time to the old is world, is will,
turning world, unswerving will,
interval

      until

DEFINITIONS OF OLD AGE

Your eyes change.
Your handwriting changes.
You can't read what you once wrote.
Even your own thoughts sound wrong to you,
something some old idiot has misquoted.

*

When apple trees are old as you are,
over-aged and crooked grown,
something happens to their occupation.
What's the use, this late, of bearing apples?
Let the apples find a father of their own.

*

Or put it in contemporary terms: the time
when men resign from their committees,
cancel their memberships, decline
the chairmanship of the United Fund,
buy a farm in Dorset or New Fane
and still get up at seven every morning
right on time for nothing left to do but
sit and age
and look up "dying" in the yellow pages.

*

old age
level light
evening in the afternoon
love without the bitterness and so
good-night

VOYAGE TO THE MOON

Wanderer in our skies,
dazzle of silver in our leaves and on our
waters silver, O
silver evasion in our farthest thought —
"the visiting moon," "the glimpses of the moon,"

and we have found her.

                      From the first of time,
before the first of time, before the
first men tasted time, we sought for her.
She was a wonder to us, unattainable,
a longing past the reach of longing,
a light beyond our lights, our lives — perhaps
a meaning to us — O, a meaning!

Now we have found her in her nest of night.

Three days and three nights we journeyed,
steered by farthest stars, climbed outward,
crossed the invisible tide-rip where the floating dust
falls one way or the other in the void between,
followed that other down, encountered
cold, faced death, unfathomable emptiness.

Now, the fourth day evening, we descend,
make fast, set foot at last upon her beaches,
stand in her silence, lift our heads and see
above her, wanderer in her sky,
a wonder to us past the reach of wonder,
a light beyond our lights, our lives, the rising

earth,

      a meaning to us,

            O, a meaning!

HEBRIDES

Old men live in a life
as the Gaels in those ocean islands,
a croft by the sea and a wife
and sons for a while;

afterward wife and croft
and the sound of the sea and the thought of it,
children and all gone off
over the water;

even the eldest son,
even the youngest daughter,
all of them vanished and gone
by the way of the water.

A man and his wife, those two,
left on the ocean island:
they talk as the old will do
and they nod and they smile

but they think of their sons, how they laughed,
and she calls but it's not for them —

18

"she'd rather a kitten to have
than a child to remember."

You can live too long in a life
where the sons go off and the daughter
off over sea and the wife
watches the water.

SEEING
(after Simone Weill)

A lurking man in that half light,
there where eye imagines sight,
stops my heart until I see
lurking man is leaning tree.

What changed? The man? There was none. Tree?
The tree was always there. Then me?
I did not change: I came to see
and when I saw, what was could be.

FAMILY GROUP

That's my younger brother with his Navy wings.
He's twenty-three or should have been that April:
winters aged you, flying the Dutch coast.
I'm beside him with my brand-new Sam Brown belt.
The town behind us is Dunkirk. We met there
quite by accident, sheer luck.
Someone's lengthened shadow — the photographer's? —
falls across the road, across our feet.

This other's afterward —
after the Armistice, I mean, the floods,
the weeks without a word. That foundered
farmyard is in Belgium somewhere.
The faceless figure on its back, the helmet buckled,
wears what look like Navy wings. A lengthened shadow
falls across the muck about its feet.

Me? I'm back in Cambridge in dry clothes,
a bed to sleep in, my small son, my wife.

WHITE-HAIRED GIRL

Le conte de Beaumont carrying my daughter
(*C'est un amour!*) on the flat of his two
hands like an infant Buddha on a leaf —

she was four years old that August: white
hair, black eyes, exquisite.

This was on the Plage des Anges
with the Maritime Alps to the east and the Mediterranean
dazzled and dazzling in the sun.

At four she never smiled: she looked at you.

At five she was in love with Ernest.
She addressed him in grave French,
allowed him to walk with her.

Nothing he could do was wrong,
even the young black beard he had grown in Switzerland,
even the murdered birds.

                    Years later,
wakened on Conway Hill and carried down,
everything went wrong. She ran to him,
stopped, looked, screamed. It wasn't Ernest!
wasn't Ernest! wasn't . . .
                    She raced up the stair.

He knuckled his hard, small hands. "You see!"

TWO WOMEN TALKING

Jill: Naked he found her?

Jane: Naked in the fern!

Jill: The way a man might find a four-leaf clover? —
luck, you mean? No dropping of the glove —
no assignation — "Read and burn" . . .

Jane: Pure luck.

Jill: Men usually find
what's waiting for them in the mind:
it's what they dream of picking that they pluck.

Jane: Who dreams a sleeper naked on her back
deep in the fern — sweet scent of bracken?

25

Jill: That man might. His dreams go deep.
Remember what he told the little creep
who cut out pin-ups from the *Evergreen Review?* —
he'd lose his labor: he would never see
a woman naked till he'd read his Shakespeare through.

Jane: He meant that men are blind until they learn to be.

Jill: He meant that what your heart has found you'll find.
A man deep tangled in a woman's hair
might find her in a mowing almost anywhere.

Jane: He swears he'd never seen her face before
or even then. He says her heavy hair . . .

Jill: He says! You said the scent of bracken.

Jane: I suppose
you would smell bracken where a body crushed it.

Jill: Hush!
I'll never tell and no one knows.

CRITICS ON THE LAWN

Look! In the lilac bush!
No, in the *lilac* bush!
Quick as a wink in the buds of the lilac bush!

That? That's an oriole
chuckling and clucking and lilting and now
look! On the bough!

Oriole! Listen, you ass, it's a kitten
lost in the underbrush back of the wall —
miaow says the cat, miaow says the kitten.

Cat! It's a thrush in the apple orchard,
a wood thrush deep in the evening, that orison,
evening made audible.

                    No, it's him!
Dumetella carolinensis!
There he is in the leaves of the lilac bush.

That? That's a catbird — common catbird.
He knows who you are.
He knows there's a cat in the house and it's yours
and he's telling you off for it — 'ow! miaow!

Dumetella carolinensis,
slate gray, slender and delicate:
North American songbird — song
jeering and chattering, mocking its mimicry.

Dumetella! He's the one!
Never his like in the world before him —
never in England, Italy, Attica —
never a bird that could laugh at a man
like Dumetella carolinensis,
pure American mimicry, mockery,
clean as a whistle, quick as a sting.

Only a catbird!

Hear him *sing!*

NEW ENGLAND WEATHER

Hay-time when the Boston forecast
calls for haying weather, hot and fair,
Conway people stick to garden chores
and nod toward nightfall at the cemetery:

that's where Sumner Boyden's lying now
and Sumner always told the town, if Boston
promised shine you'd better count on showers
'long toward evening with your hay crop lost.

He meant, no man can tell the weather
anywhere but where he's from:
you have to have the whole of it together,
bred in your bones — the way the wind-shifts come,

how dust feels on a hayfork handle
days when there'll be thunder up for sure,
and how the swallows skim, the cattle stand,
when blue stays blue and even clover cures.

He knew the Conway signs and when the Boston
forecast didn't, team went back to stalls
and chances were, by half-past four at most
we'd hear the thunder up toward Shelburne Falls.

It wasn't luck. New England weather
breeds New Englanders: that changing sky
is part of being born and drawing breath
and dying, maybe, where you're meant to die.

IN AND COME IN

Stupid? Of course that older lot were stupid.
Any up-to-date, in poet
knows the bloody world was made for woe
and life for death and man is either dolt or dupe,

but those old locals never seemed to learn.
Emerson unlocked the tomb
and stood and stared at what had once been human,
once been his, and made that entry in his journal.

Whitman, in the stinking wards, uncovered
dead men's faces when the squad
came round at night and morning for the bodies,
but not to rage at death — to kiss them with his love.

Emily, although she said she wrote
as boys beside a graveyard whistle,
pressed no terrified finger to her wrist:
what frightened Emily was joy, the robin's note.

And later, when the word was Tragic Vision
haunting thickets of despair —
beckets of all the boredom flesh is heir to —
Frost went walking off alone in his derision.

Too ignorant to know what nightfall meant,
or why the thrush calls when the stars begin,
he told the weeping world he'd not come in
(even if asked, he said, and he hadn't been)
to mope among the hemlocks and lament.

He was out for stars, he told them, with that Yankee grin.
Stupid? Like all the rest: he didn't know.

And yet there's something *does* know in that poem.

POPULATION EXPLOSION

The fine old house with the Georgian door
stood two centuries on Beacon Hill
and would have stood two centuries more
but for the vine root in the fill,

the wisteria vine that grew and grew
till it tented the roof with grapes of flowers,
veiled the windows, choked the view,
dragged at last the whole house down,

strangling itself in the wrack, the tangle,
tendril wrestling tendril for the light.
You can hear the house and the vine still wrangling,
passing on a summer's night:

Why, says the house, did you drag us down?

Not I, says the vine, but my desire.

You *wanted* us here, a sight for the town?

All I wanted was to twine.
Love is the law of the climbing vine.

Love, says the house, is worse than a fire.

CONVERSATION IN A BELFRY

Centennial bell that will not ring,
tell me why your iron tongue
rusts in the rain, your mouth is dumb.
Why are you silent, bell?

For shame.

You are not shamed.

Not I but you.

We? With all we've done and do?
We've ruled ourselves two hundred years.
No name on earth is proud as ours.

It was your fathers' pride that ruled:
their sons are tricked and lied to, fooled
as Lincoln said no people could be —
all of them — always — for their good!

But still we're free. Ring out, O ring!

What man is free when fraud is king?

Our souls are ours: our minds our own.

While someone listens on the telephone?

This is John Adams' holy land . . .

John Adams would have seen you damned!

where Jefferson's immortal word . . .

Jefferson's immortal word
is yet to hear. It will be heard
but not by those who sell his soul.

You ring now, bell.

·
       I toll. I toll.

THE THRUSH IN THE GAELIC ISLANDS
for my Gaelic son

By the sea loch the island cattle,
auctioned off for overseas,
shriek in their frantic pens in the late
light and the thrush answers:

pure song,
perfect indifference like the will of God.

I am remembering something . . . No,
not remembering: my father told me:

Years ago in the highlands, the Hebrides,
landlords cleared the land for sheep.
There were ships on the sea, weeping children.

Afterward a man could walk
from Northbay over Barra clear to the
far side and the crofts empty,
the dogs running in and out of the open doors

and the thrush sang.

MARK VAN DOREN
AND THE BROOK

The brook beneath the water mill
is winter-bound, its stones are still,
no word at all, no syllable.

Once there were two together there
talked in the dim, the humming air:
Mark above in his desk chair,

the brook below. Old murmurers,
they talked as twilight blinds and blurs,
he of his art, she of hers.

Words out of stones she understood:
he, words from lives — how flesh and blood
are spoken and the heart construed.

Year after year they talked there; now
the brook is mute, is winter-bound,
and Mark . . .

                     no winter knows, can sound,
the silence where his voice is drowned.

THE OLD GRAY COUPLE (1)

They have only to look at each other to laugh —
no one knows why, not even they:
something back in the lives they've lived,
something they both remember but no words can say.

They go off at an evening's end to talk
but they don't, or to sleep but they lie awake —
hardly a word, just a touch, just near,
just listening but not to hear.

Everything they know they know together —
everything, that is, but one:
their lives they've learned like secrets from each other;
their deaths they think of in the nights alone.

THE OLD GRAY COUPLE (2)

She: Love, says the poet, has no reasons.

He: Not even after fifty years?

She: Particularly after fifty years.

He: What was it, then, that lured us, that still teases?

She: You used to say my plaited hair!

He: And then you'd laugh.

She: Because it wasn't plaited.
Love had no reasons so you made one up
to laugh at. Look! The old, gray couple!

He: No, to prove the addage true:
Love has no reasons but old lovers do.

She: And they can't tell.

He: I can and so can you.
Fifty years ago we drew each other,
magnetized needle toward the longing north.
It was your naked presence that so moved me.
It was your absolute presence that was love.

She: Ah, *was!*

He: And now, years older, we begin to see
absence not presence: what the world would be
without your footstep in the world — the garden
empty of the radiance where you are.

She: And that's your reason? — that old lovers see
their love because they know now what its loss will be?

He: Because, like Cleopatra in the play,
they know there's nothing left once love's away . . .

She: Nothing remarkable beneath the visiting moon . . .

He: Ours is the late, last wisdom of the afternoon.
We know that love, like light, grows dearer toward the
dark.

PART TWO

BACCALAUREATE

A year or two, and grey Euripides,
And Horace and a Lydia or so,
And Euclid and the brush of Angelo,
Darwin on man, Vergilius on bees,
The nose and dialogues of Socrates,
Don Quixote, Hudibras and Trinculo,
How worlds are spawned and where the dead gods go, —
All shall be shard of broken memories.

And there shall linger other, magic things, —
The fog that creeps in wanly from the sea,
The rotten harbor smell, the mystery
Of moonlit elms, the flash of pigeon wings,
The sunny Green, the old-world peace that clings
About the college yard, where endlessly
The dead go up and down. These things shall be
Enchantment of our hearts' rememberings.

And these are more than memories of youth
Which earth's four winds of pain shall blow away;
These are youth's symbols of eternal truth,
Symbols of dream and imagery and flame,
Symbols of those same verities that play
Bright through the crumbling gold of a great name.

TWO POEMS FROM THE WAR

Oh, not the loss of the accomplished thing!
Not dumb farewells, nor long relinquishment
Of beauty had, and golden summer spent,
And savage glory of the fluttering
Torn banners of the rain, and frosty ring
Of moon-white winters, and the imminent
Long-lunging seas, and glowing shoulders bent
To race on some smooth beach the sea-gull's wing:

Not these, nor all we've been, nor all we've loved,
The pitiful familiar names, had moved
Our hearts to weep for them; but oh, the star
The future is! Eternity's too wan
To give again that undefeated, far,
All-possible irradiance of dawn.

*

Like moon-dark, like brown water you escape,
O laughing mouth, O sweet uplifted lips.
Within the peering brain old ghosts take shape;
You flame and wither as the white foam slips

Back from the broken wave: sometimes a start,
A gesture of the hands, a way you own
Of bending that smooth head above your heart, —
Then these are vanished, then the dream is gone.

Oh, you are too much mine and flesh of me
To seal upon the brain, who in the blood
Are so intense a pulse, so swift a flood
Of beauty, such unceasing instancy.
Dear unimagined brow, unvisioned face,
All beauty has become your dwelling place.

AN ETERNITY

There is no dusk to be,
        There is no dawn that was,
Only there's now, and now,
        And the wind in the grass.

Days I remember of
        Now in my heart, are now;
Days that I dream will bloom
        White the peach bough.

Dying shall never be
        Now in the windy grass;
Now under shooken leaves
        Death never was.

from THE HAPPY MARRIAGE (1924)

First I will tell you something of these two.
He followed love as watchful as a child,
And yet unchildlike never quite beguiled
To think the thing he found the thing he knew:
She, sure of all things seen by moon or sun,
And sure that these were all her eyes could see,
Waited impatient for the victory
That should secure what was already won.

He followed love, she waited her true lover:
She waited what she need but wait to find;
He followed what pursuit could not discover
Nor time disclose nor death surprise and bind.
Over the hills, he sang, and far away —
She never knew that land nor where it lay.

♣

Well, he was drunk. That much was clear,
Or not quite clear but certain.
                                        Queer
The way a rising moon will burn
Green copper!
                        Thing you'll never learn
From books: but out of life and beer
Or beer and life you may discern
Great truths — as that a tower gleams
In moon-fire like a torch and seems
A toppling brand of burnt emprise.
No teacher else is half so wise
At demonstrating chords and themes
The singing sort of men devise.

Take Helen, — all you hear of her
In lectures is a learned slur
Of couplets solemnly undressed
To indicate the female chest,
Till Helen's lost and nothing's sure
But that she had, praise God, a breast.

And then you're drunk and out you walk
Through High Street where the shadows mock
The third dimension of thick day,
And walls chirp back the words you say;
And magically above your talk,
As lift faint mountains far away,
There lifts a sudden loveliness,
A flare of beauty, an excess
Of radiance, more sense than thought,
Like soundless music somehow caught
Back of the brain, or some impress

Of figures in a dream forgot —
And there stands Helen — there's the face
Young Marlowe saw past time and space
And would have seen again and died;
There, there the subtle breast, the side
White as white water, there the grace
Of queens and there the pride, the pride.

Helen, he said, — but was it she?
Somewhere he'd seen serenity
Drawn smooth as this across a flame
As bright to hide, and brows that tame
Eyes as unapt to secrecy, —
Nay, he had known these eyes, this same
Young breast, this throat. There was a name . . .

♣

He had used love or lust or what's between
Long, long before. When he was still a boy
Old hairy love that hugs his knees for joy
And quavers tunes, ecstatic and obscene,
Grey goatish love that whistles to the fauns,
Had whistled fever through his aching flesh
And led him giddy down his nerves' dark mesh
To lie with empresses and leprechauns.

So he had used and after in a mood
Of sluggish melancholy and vague grief,
Ruffled with such warm rifts as in a wood
A sunny wind blows over leaf by leaf,
Had longed for death that lies beneath the ground
And feels no lust and listens to no sound.

✦

And he had used love's dream of love before,
Love that hopes nothing but the hope it is,
Love that has no utterance in a kiss,
Nor eloquence in flesh, but would adore
Its perfect adoration, its desire,
As musingly in wonder as the moon
Stares back into a brook whose running rune
Burns with the imaged argent of moon-fire.

Sometimes in music when the phrase would close
And yet yearn on in silence, unfulfilled,
Once in the imperfection of a rose,
Once in an ape's face marvellously stilled,
He had imagined the perfected thing,
The hope made real, the unfolded wing.

✦

But she was both, — she was both loved and love,
She was desire and the thing desired,
She was Troy flame and she was Troy town fired,
She was hope realized and the hope thereof:
Her slender body was the instant bloom
Of lovely secrecies; the shadowed swell
Of her small breast was beauty sensible;
Her stormy hair wore wonder like a plume.

Away, his sense of her was like the sense
Of moonlight under the smooth vague of sleep;
Near, at her touch, her beauty's imminence
Was like a wave that falters at the leap
And lifts in foam a moment till it fall,
Filling with thunderous hush the interval.

✦

Passing her in the day he had but dared
To meet her eyes and in the moment's touch
Seemed to his flinching brain to dare too much
So proud she was and single and unshared.
She was another flesh than his he thought,
Another element, less earth than flame,
A different life, unnamed but for the name
Her eyes should teach him if he could be taught.

But now at midnight the remembering dark
Imaged her body naked by his side,
Her head half turned and on her mouth the mark
Of lust fed full and still unsatisfied,
And her clear eyes that had compelled his mind
Were humble now and hideously kind.

✦

Under an elm tree where the river reaches
They watched the evening deepen in the sky,
They watched the westward clouds go towering by
Through lakes of blue toward those shining beaches,
Those far enchanted strands where blowing tides
Break into light along the shallow air;
They watched how like a ship's tall lantern there
Over that silent surf the faint star rides.

Ship of a dream, he thought, — O dreamed of shore
Beyond all oceans and all earthly seas!
Now would they never call him any more,
Now would they never hurt him with unease.
She was that ship, that sea, that siren land;
And she was here, her hand shut in his hand.

47

✦

Here, O wanderer, here is the hill and the harbor,
Farer and follower, here the Hesperides.
Here wings the Halycon down through the glamorous arbor,
Here is the end of the seas.

Have you heard music at morning of far sea singing?
Have you heard singing over the water at dark?
This was the music you heard here forever reringing,
Only the thrush, O hark!

Have you seen citadels glance in the sunset, and towers?
Have you seen castles of glint and of gossamer spun?
These, only these, were the heights, these hills grown with
    flowers,
These were the gates of the sun.

There is no music but this, no loveliness other, —
Only the reaching of arms and the rose of a breast,
Only a girl's throat — beyond this earth ends and seas smother,
And the old moon fades in the west.

There is no land beyond and no shore and no ocean,
Nothing but night and the moon and the cold thin air,
Where change never comes but the stars' unchangeable motion,
Nor end but endlessness there.

✦

Things he had loved because he knew them lost,
Things he had loved and never yet had found —
The unintelligible beauty tossed
Back from a foolish dream — the smothered sound
Of laughter from a window swiftly barred
In some monk's chronicle — the ruined grace

Of carven marbles that old rains had marred —
Things he had lost and loved were in that place.

And she was like the voice of those lost things
Haunting the body that his arms held near,
And singing there of other loves as sings
The bird at evening of another year.
But now she slept and was herself and seemed
More than his love and less than he had dreamed.

♣

She was herself, not his, not anything
That might be his or he might ever own,
Or ever think, or with much thinking bring
To words that may be spoken out and known;
And that dear image he had coined of her
To spend his love, and gilded with her head,
Was but the counterfeit love's pensioner
Should hoard for all his wealth when she was dead,

And all he knew of her was something less
Than what his hand could learn against her side,
Or what his mouth remembered from the press
Of her mute mouth. She had become the bride
Of something in his sense that understood
The touch of things, the moments of the blood.

♣

They say they are one flesh:
They are two nations.
They cannot mix nor mesh:
Their conjugations
Are cries from star to star.

They would commingle,
They couple far and far —
Still they are single.

With arms and hungry hands
They cling together,
They strain at bars and bands,
They tug at tether,

Still there are walls between,
Still space divides them,
Still are themselves unseen,
Still distance hides them.

❦

Man is immortal, for his flesh is earth,
And save he lives forever — why, he dies:
Woman is mortal, for her flesh will rise
In each new generation of her birth.
She is the tree; we are the feverish
Vain leaves that gild her summer with our own,
And fall and rot when summer's overblown,
And wish eternity and have — our wish.

And man, immortal, marries his own dreams
Of immortality in flesh and blood,
And mortal woman, wiser than she seems,
Marries her man for evil or for good, —
Wherein perception sees what reason blurs:
She was not his, but he was only hers.

❦

O hide your eyes,
O turn your head away;

Are you so wise, so wise,
To watch unchanged this chemistry of clay?

It is not we,
It is another two;
Hide that you may not see
What flushed unlovely things their bodies do.

O think no grace
That I am glad of this:
I do not know your face,
It is not you but my own flesh I kiss.

Blind, blind your brow
And your too candid eyes:
You cannot love me now,
You cannot love what even love denies.

♣

This was not love but love's true negative
That spends itself in passion to be spent,
And lives no longer than the wish may live
To waste itself and then is impotent,
And fails not only but confounds in fault
What love most lives upon, the very need,
The lack, the famine, the too thirsty salt,
Till wanting want love has no will to feed.

Yet, in the glut and surfeit of desire
Desire itself was perfected and found,
And fever burned by its consuming fire
Was bare as martyrs' bones beneath the ground.
This was not love, the ever unpossessed,
But this was love of her made manifest.

✦

Love is the way that lovers never know
Who know the shortest way to find their love,
And never turn aside and never go
By vales beneath nor by the hills above,
But running straight to the familiar door
Break sudden in and call their dear by name
And have their wish and so wish nothing more
And neither know nor trouble how they came.

Love is the path that comes to this same ease
Over the summit of the westward hill,
And feels the rolling of the earth and sees
The sun go down and hears the summer still,
And dips and follows where the orchards fall
And comes here late or never comes at all.

✦

Whom do you love, she said, when you look out
So far beyond my eyes as our eyes meet?
Is she so like and yet unlike you doubt
If I'm the counterfeit or she's the cheat?
Or is she some one that I never was?
Or what I was and shall not be again?
Back of your eyes I think her image has
Not only longing and much more than pain.

She never had another's face but this,
He laughed and touched her cheek. She moved as you,
And spoke upon your tongue and used your kiss,
And knew the mysteries your wisdom knew,
And had your silence, and was called your name.

But was not I myself — was not the same!

✤

Throwing a careless pebble in the lake
She saw the clear sky crumple and the hill
Waver and reel and all the sunlight spill
In swimming circles and the willows shake,
And watching said: You say love cannot die,
But there's a lovely world has had an end.
And when he laughed and said the sky would mend
She said: And that would be another sky.

And then: Oh, yes, the image will return
Being an image — yet the sky has tumbled
However bright the sky itself may burn —
That cannot fall you say? Her fingers fumbled
Against his arm and in the touch he knew
Her heart had guessed the truth that was not true.

✤

He leans against the window-sill:
The dusk has drizzled down to rose.
Delicious damps and odors fill
The musings of his thoughtful nose.

The soft wind slides seductive touch
Along the shoulders of the oak.
My dear, I love you, dear, so much —
He cannot think of whom he spoke.

✤

The white of her Colonial
Showed patterns of a tranquil wall
Through lattices of apple trees,
And softly her serenities

53

Curled hazy blue above the backs
Of comfortable chimney stacks.
New England, not Arcadia,
She gardened her phenomena,
And tamed her asphodels to grow
To roses in a scarlet row.
New England fenced from Avalon,
The curtains of her peace were drawn
Against the peering of the moon,
And crickets shuffled down the tune
Of Pan among the lilac leaves.
From far away he saw her eaves
As shelter against every doubt,
And understood what was shut out
When doors swung back to shut him in, —
But what of that! It was no sin
To bolt with iron from the blaze
Of staring moon on empty ways
And bar the shutters to the sound
Of cloven feet on hollow ground, —
And after by the friendly stove
Sit peacefully and sup of love.

♣

No doubt he'd once had eyes to see
Through mill-stones to the mystery
That mill-stones might perhaps intend
If there were Ends beyond the end —
But now he had no plague of eyes.

There was a way of being wise
That was not wisdom: one might love
Too loftily and fall above
As well as one might fall below.

And there were things a man might know
That were not knowledge either.
                                    Truth
For instance.
                    One's ecstatic youth
Proves true what has no proof in sense:
And time strikes out the evidence
But enters judgment on the rule,
So that one's wisdom, learned fool,
Knows only that the thing is true.
But he had knowledge, for he knew
His proofs and never tried their weight
As evidence to demonstrate
The truth of anything on earth
Except themselves, and what was worth
Believing of them.
                        She was real:
He knew because his hands could feel
The bones that threatened in her wrist.
And she proved nothing but the twist
That was her way of beauty — not
Some Beauty that he had forgot
Nor Truth that now was past belief.
A woman was no lawyer's brief
Compounded to persuade the sense
Of things beyond experience
No woman's body could fulfil,
But Holy Writ that can distil
The very peace it promises.

Once he had seen the Thing That Is
In every movement of her head —

He yawned and shuffled off to bed.

♣

The humid air precipitates
In moisture on enamelled plates
And orient to opaline
The glass discolors. Crinkled green
Of lettuces grows limp and fades.
A rose bowl withering pervades
The room with sickliness and rusts
The whiteness crimson. Glutted lusts,
Renewing on a deeper nerve,
Denied, make conversation serve
Obscurer converse. Intimate,
Their meeting eyes interrogate
And being answered turn aside,
She secretly and satisfied,
He startled into discontent
By something in her quick assent,
Confided and discreetly masked,
That promised all his eyes had asked.

♣

Beside her in the dark the chime
Of ratcheted revolving time
Repeating its repeated beat
Builds complicated incomplete
Sonatas in his listening brain,
Phrase upon phrase, till the refrain
Resolves into the tick and tock
Of seconds scissored by the clock.

He thinks he has composed his dream
Of love upon as slight a theme,
And all the arduous obscure
Perfections of his overture,

Unravelled part from varied part,
Were but the drumming of his heart.

But still the clacking clockwork spins
Music of marvellous violins.

♣

Beauty is that Medusa's head
Which men go armed to seek and sever:
It is most deadly when most dead,
And dead will stare and sting forever —
Beauty is that Medusa's head.

The Pot of Earth (1925)

These (the gardens of Adonis) were baskets or pots filled with earth in which wheat, barley, lettuces, fennel, and various kinds of flowers were sown and tended for eight days, chiefly or exclusively by women. Fostered by the sun's heat, the plants shot up rapidly, but having no root they withered as rapidly away, and at the end of eight days were carried out with the images of the dead Adonis and flung with them into the sea or into springs.

Sir James G. Frazer, *The Golden Bough*

PART ONE

"For if the sun breed maggots in a dead
dog, being a god-kissing carrion, — Have you
a daughter?"
"I have, my lord."
"Let her not walk i' the sun — "

THE SOWING OF THE DEAD CORN

Silently on the sliding Nile
The rudderless, the unoared barge
Diminishing and for a while
Followed, a fleck upon the large

Silver, then faint, then vanished, passed
Adonis who had once more died
Down a slow water with the last
Withdrawing of a fallen tide.

*

That year they went to the shore early —
They went in March and at the full moon
The tide came over the dunes, the tide came
To the wall of the garden. She remembered standing,
A little girl in the cleft of the white oak tree —
The waves came in a slow curve, crumpling
Lengthwise, kindling against the mole and smoldering
Foot by foot across the beach until
The whole arc guttered and burned out. Her father
Rested his spade against the tree. He said,
The spring comes with the tide, the flood water.
Are you waiting for spring? Are you watching for the spring?
He threw the dead stalks of the last year's corn
Over the wall into the sea. He said,
Look, we will sow the spring now. She could feel
Water along dry leaves and the stems fill.
Hurry, she said, Oh, hurry. She was afraid.
The surf was so slow, it dragged, it came stumbling
Slower and slower. She tried to breathe as slowly
As the waves broke. She kept calling, Hurry! Hurry!
Her breath came so much faster than the sea —

*

One night it rained with a south wind and a warm
Smell of thawed earth and rotting straw and ditches
Sodden with snow and running full. She lay
Alone in the dark and after a long time
She fell asleep and the rain dripped in the gutter,

60

Dripped, dropped, and the wind washed over the roof
And winter melted and she felt the flow
Of the wind like a smooth river, and she saw
The moon wavering over her through the water —

And after the rain the brook in the north ravine
Ran blood-red — after the rain they found
Purple hepaticas and violets.

Stained crimson —
                    Are the waters fed
In the hill side?
                    She heard the drip, the beat
Of seas gathering underground. She heard
The moon moving under Perkins Street —
Why do you circle here, O lost sea bird?
Under the root of the pine-tree, under the stone
She heard the red surf breaking.
                              This occurred
When she was thirteen years —
                              Oh, she felt
Ill. It was horrible. She thought of one
Dead, and the weeping . . .
                          In March the snows melt
Dribbling between the shriveled roots till they brim
The soaked soil, till the moon comes, until
The moon compels them; and the surf at the sea's rim
Breaks into scarlet and the pine roots spill
Rivers of blood. There was blood upon her things.
She brought home violets enough to fill
The yellow bowl with the pattern of pigeon wings —

I am afraid of the moon. I am afraid of the moon still.

*

61

The sound of the sea breaking beyond the wall
Was surd, flat, stopped as the voice of a deaf woman.
Dead leaves tiptoed in the path.
The trees listened —
And she saw the blind moon climb through the colorless air
Through the willow branches. She could feel the moon
Lifting the numb water, and the sea fill.
She thought, The spring will come now overflowing
The clean earth. And what will the pine cone do,
The skulls and kernels that the winter gathered —
What will they do —

We are having a late spring, we are having
The snow in April, the grass heaving
Under the wet snow, the grass
Burdened and nothing blossoms, grows
In the fields nothing and the garden fallow;
And now the wild birds follow
The wild birds and the thrush is tame.
Well, there is time still, there is time.
Tomorrow there will be tomorrow
And summer swelling through the marrow
Of the cold trees.
                            Wait! Let us wait!
Let us wait until tomorrow. The wet
Snow wrinkles, it will rot,
It will molder at the root
Of the oak-tree. Wait!
                            Oh, wait, I will gather
Grains of wheat and corn together,
Ears of corn and dry barley.
But wait, but only wait. I am barely
Seventeen: must I make haste?
Tomorrow there will be a host

Of crocuses and small hairy
Snowdrops. And why, then, must I hurry?
There are things I have to do
More than just to live and die
More than just to die of living.
I have seen the moonlight leaving
Twig by twig the elms and wondered
Where I go, where I have wandered.

I have watched myself alone
Coming homeward in the lane
When I seemed to see a meaning
In my going or remaining
Not the meaning of the grass,
Not the dreaming mortal grace
Of the green leaves on the year —

And why, then, should I hear
A sound as of the sowers going down
Through blossoming young hedges in the dawn —
Winter is not done.

*

There were buds on the chestnut-trees, soft, swollen,
Sticky with thick gum, that seemed to press,
To thrust from the cold branches, to start under
The impulse of intolerable loins —
The faint sweet smell of the trees sickened her.
She walked at the sea's edge on the blank sand.

Certainly the salt stone that the sea divulges
At the first quarter does not fructify
In pod or tuber nor will the fruiterer cull
Delicate plums from its no-branches — Oh,

Listen to me for the word of the matter is in me —
And if it heats in the sun it heats to itself
Alone and to none that come after it and the rain
Impregnates it not to the slightest — Oh, listen,
You who lie on your backs in the sun, roots,
Roses among others taking the rain
Into you, vegetables, listen — the salt stone
That the sea divulges does not fructify.
It sits by itself. It is sufficient. But you —
Who was your great-grandfather or your mother's mother?

                    *

One of those mild evenings when you think
Spring is tomorrow and you can smell the earth
Smoldering under wet leaves and there's still
A little light left over the tree top
And you stand listening —
                    So she closed the gate
And walked up Gloucester Street and coming home
It was pitch dark at the railroad station they
Jostled against her Oh excuse me! excuse me!
And somebody said, laughing — she couldn't hear:
Her throat pounded — something she ran ran —
What do you want? What do you want me to do?
What can I do? Can I put roots in the earth?
Can leaves grow out of me? Can I bear leaves
Like the thorn, the lilac —
                    Why did you not come?
Why did you let me go then if you knew?

                    *

They seemed to be waiting,
The willow-trees by the wall,
Fidgeting with the sea wind in their branches,

Unquiet in the warm air.
She stood between them. She said,
You who have set your candles toward the sea
Two nights already and no sound
Only the water,
Tell me, do the dead come out of the sea?
Does the spring come from the sea?
Does the dead god
Come again from the water?

The willow-trees stirred in the wind,
Stilled,
Stirred in the wind —

She said, It may be he has come,
It may be he has come and gone, and I not knowing —
               *

Easter Sunday they went to Hooker's Grove,
Seven of them in one automobile
Laughing and singing.
                    Sea water flows
Over the meadows at the full moon,
The sea runs in the ditches, the salt stone
Drowns in the sea.
             And someone said, Look! Look!
The flowers, the red flowers,
                 Shall we go
Up through the Gorge or round by Ryan's place?
I'll show you where the wild boar killed a man.
I'll show you where the . . .
               Who is this that comes
Crowned with red flowers from the sea? Who comes
Into the hills with flowers?
              On the hill pastures

She heard a girl calling her lost cows.
Her voice hung like a mist over the grass,
Over the apple-trees.

                She bit her mouth
To keep from crying.

                  On the third day
The cone of the pine is broken, the eared corn
Broken into the earth, the seed scattered.
The bridegroom comes again at the third day.
The sowers have come into the fields sowing.
Well, at the Grove there was a regular crowd
And a band at the Casino, so they ate
Up in the woods where you could hear the music
And the dogs barking, and after lunch she lay
Out in the open meadow. She could feel
The sun through her dress —

                  Don't you want to dance?
They're all dancing — that wonderful tune —
Are you listening? Aren't you listening?

        The band
Start stuttered and
Oh, won't you?

           No —
      Just a little while. Just a little bit —
No! Oh, No! Oh, No!

                Far, far away
The singing on the mountain. She could hear
The voices singing, she could hear them come
With songs, with the red flowers. They have found him,
They have brought him from the hills —

Why, it was wonderful! Why, all at once there were leaves,
Leaves at the end of a dry stick, small, alive
Leaves out of wood. It was wonderful,

66

You can't imagine. They came by the wood path
And the earth loosened, the earth relaxed, there were flowers
Out of the earth! Think of it! And oak-trees
Oozing new green at the tips of them and flowers
Squeezed out of clay, soft flowers, limp
Stalks flowering. Well, it was like a dream,
It happened so quickly, all of a sudden it happened —

PART TWO

THE SHALLOW GRASS

The plow of tamarisk wood which is shared with black copper
And drawn by a yoke of oxen all black
Drags in the earth.
The earth is made ready with copper,
The earth is prepared for the seed by the feet of oxen
That are shod with brass.

*

They said, Good Luck! Good Luck! What a handsome couple!
Isn't she lovely though! He can't keep his
Hands off her. Ripe as a peach she is. Good Luck!
Good-bye, Good-bye —
                    They took the down express,
The five-five. She had the seat by the window —
He can't keep —
                    She sat there looking out
And the fields were brown and raw from the spring plowing,

67

The fields were naked, they were stretched out bare,
Rigid, with long welts, with open wounds,
Stripped —
                    In the flat sunlight she could see
The fields heave against the furrows, lift,
Twist to get free —
                              — his hands —
                                        Why, what's the matter?
We're almost there now, only half an hour.
We'll have our supper in our rooms. I've taken
The best room, what they call the bridal chamber —

What they call — what do they call it? —
                                        And I dressed up
All in these new things not a red ribbon
You ever had on before and mind you keep
The shoes you were married in and all to go
Into a closed room with a bed in it,
To lie in a shut chamber,
                              what they call —
Something
            the chalked letters
                              does he say
That
      I wonder
            or what —
                        She held his hand
Against her breast under the flowers. She felt
The warmth of it like the warmth of the sun driving
Downward into her heart.
                        And all those fields
Ready, the earth stretched out upon those fields
Ready, and now the sowers —

What is this thing we know that they have not told us?
What is this in us that has come to bed
In a closed room?

*

                    I tell you the generations
Of man are a ripple of thin fire burning
Over a meadow, breeding out of itself
Itself, a momentary incandescence
Lasting a long time, and we that blaze
Now, we are not the fire, for it leaves us.

I tell you we are the shape of a word in the air
Uttered from silence behind us into silence
Far beyond, and now between two strokes
Of the word's passing have become the word —
That jars on through the night;

                                        and the stirred air
Deadens,
        is still —

*

They lived that summer in a furnished flat
On the south side of Congress Street and no
Sun, but you could look into the branches
Of all those chestnut-trees, and then they had
A window-box, but the geraniums
Died leaving a little earth and the wind
Or somehow one June morning there was grass
Sprouting —
              How does your garden grow, your garden
In the shallow dish, in the dark, how does it grow?
Tomorrow we bear the milk corn to the river,
Tomorrow we go to the spring with the pale stalks:

69

Has your garden ripened?
                    She used to water them
Morning and evening and the blades grew
Yellow a sort of whitey yellowy all
Fluffy
        hairs from a dead skull
                    they say
The skulls of dead girls —
                    Won't it let you die
Even, burgeoning from your bones, your dead
Bones, from your body, not even die, not just
Be dead, be quiet?
                What is this thing that sprouts
From the womb, from the living flesh, from the live body?
What does it want? Why won't it let you alone
Not even dead?
            Why, look, you are a handful
Of fat mold breeding corruption, a pinch
Of earth for seed fall —
                How does your garden grow?

Hot nights the whole room reeked with the fetid smell
Of chestnut flowers, the live smell, the fertile
Odor of blossoms. She half drowsed. She dreamed
Of long hair fragrant with almonds growing
Out of her dead skull, she dreamed of one
Buried, and out of her womb the corn growing.

                        *

                    Construe the soundless, slow
Explosion of a summer cloud, decipher
The sayings of the wind beneath the pantry door,
Say when the moon will come, when the rain will follow —

Unless the rain comes soon the colored petals
Sheathing the secret stigma of the rose
Will fall, will wither, and the swollen womb
Close, harden, upon a brittle stalk
Seal up its summer, and the hollyhock,
The broom, the furze, the poppy will become,
Their petals fallen, all their petals fallen,
Peascods — seedboxes — haws —

It should have rained when the moon
Spilled out the old moon's shadow.
Seven days I have been waiting for the rain now,
The sound of water.
Seven days I have been walking up and down in the house.
There was nothing to do, there was nothing to do but wait,
But wait, but walk and walk
And at night hear
The patter of dry leaves on the window and wake,
And waking, think, The rain! Yes — and hear
The patter of dry leaves.
There was nothing to do, there was nothing to do but wait,
But wait, but wait, but wait, and the wind whispering
Something I couldn't understand beneath the door,
Something that I wouldn't understand.
And the grass stems
Stiffening to bear the headed grain,
The rose,
The hawthorn
Covering with bony fingers
Their swollen wombs,
The summer shriveling to husks, to shells,
Peascods, seedboxes,
The summer sucking through a withered straw
Enough stale water for a few beans,

71

For a handful of swelling peas in a sealed bladder,
For the living something in a closed womb.

*

Upon the sand
This brine, these bubbles —
The wave of summer is drowned in the salt land.
And I, the climbing tip
Of that old ivy, time,
To waver swaying over a blind wall
With all
Today to dream in,
                    and, behind,
The never-resting root
Through my live body drives
The living shoot,
The climbing ivy-tip of time.

I am a room at the end of a long journey
The windows of which open upon the night
Or perhaps
Nothing —

I am a room at a passage end where lies
Huddled in darkness one that door by door
Has come time's length through his old windy house
For this —
For what, then?

Neither.

I am a woman in a waterproof
Walking beside the river in an autumn rain.
Above the trolley bridge the market gardens

Are charnel fields where the unburied corn
Rots and the rattling pumpkin vines lift brittle fingers
Warning — of what? — and livid, broken skulls
Of cabbages gape putrid in a pond —

My face under the cold rain is cold
As winter leaves that cover up the year.
I feel the wind as the numb earth feels it.
I feel the heavy seed in the warm dark
And the spring ripening —

                         *

And what is this to be a woman? Why,
To be a woman, a sown field.
                         Let us
Attribute a significance perhaps
Not ours to what we are compelled to be
By being it:
                    as privately forestall
The seed's necessity by welcoming
The necessary seed;
                         likewise prevent
Death with the apothegm that all men die.
Yes.
        And then wake alone at night and lie here
Stripped of my memories, without the chairs
And walls and doors and windows that have been
My recognition of myself, my soul's
Condition, the whole habit of my mind —
Yes, wake, and of the close, unusual dark
Demand an answer, crying, What am I?
Ah, What! A naked body born to bear
Nakedness suffering. A sealed mystery
With hands to feed it, with unable legs,

73

With shamed eyes meaning — what? What do they mean,
The red haws out there underneath the snow,
What do they signify?

Glory of women to grow big and die
Fruitfully, glory of women to be broken,
Pierced by the green sprout, severed, tossed aside
Fruitfully —
                    Yes, all right. Yes, Yes,
But what about me —
                    What am I —
                              What do you think
I am —
          What do you take me for!

Snow, the snow —
                    When shall I be delivered?
When will my time come?

PART THREE

THE CARRION SPRING

    The flowers of the sea are brief,
    Lost flowers of the sea,
    Salt petal, bitter leaf,
    The fruitless tree —

The flowers of the sea are blown
Dead, they blossom in death:
The sea furrows are sown
With a cold breath.

I heard in my heart all night
The sea crying, Come home,
Come home. I thought of the white
Cold flowers of foam.

*

In March, when the snow melted, he was born.
She lay quiet in the bed. She lay still,
Dying.
          Under the iron rumble
Of the streets she heard the rolling
Boulders that the flood tides tumble
Climbing sea by sea the shoaling
Ledges — she could hear the tolling
Sea.
          She lay alone there.

In the morning
They came and went about her,
Moving through the room. She asked them
Whispering. They told her,
He is here. She said, Who is it,
Who is it that is born, that is here?
She said, Do you not know him?
Have you seen the green blades gathered?
Have you seen the shallow grain?
Do you know, — do you not know him?
Laugh, she said, I am delivered,
I am free, I am no longer

Burdened. I have borne the summer
Dead, the corn dead, the living
Dead. I am delivered.
He has left me now. I lie here
Empty, gleaned, a reaped meadow,
Fearing the rain no more, not fearing
Spring nor the flood tides overflowing
Earth with their generative waters —
Let me sleep, let me be quiet.
I can see the dark sail going
On and on, the river flowing
Red with the melting of the snow:
What is this thing we know? —

Under the iron street the crying
Voices of the sea. Come home,
Come to your house. Come home.
                                    She heard
A slow crying in the sea, Come home,
Come to your house —

                    *

Go secretly and put me in the ground —
Go before the moon uncovers,
Go where now no night wind hovers,
Say no word above me, make no sound.
Heap only on my buried bones
Cold sand and naked stones
And come away and leave unmarked the mound.
Let not those silent hunters hear you pass:
Let not the trees know, nor the thirsty grass,
Nor secret rain
To breed from me some living thing again,
But only earth —

Oh let my flesh be drowned
In her deep silences and never found!

*

The slow spring blossomed again, a cold
Bubbling of the corrupted pool, a frothy
Thickening, a ferment of soft green
Bubbling —
        Who knows how deep the roots drink?
They drink deep,
             And you, what do you hope?
What do you believe, walking
Alone in an old garden, staring down
Beneath the shallow surface of the grass,
The floating green? What do you say you are?
And what was she that you remember, staring
Down through the pale grass, what was she?
And what is this that grows in an old garden?

Listen, I will interpret to you. Look, now,
I will discover you a thing hidden,
A secret thing. Come, I will conduct you
By seven doors into a closed tomb.
I will show you the mystery of mysteries.
I will show you the body of the dead god bringing forth
The corn. I will show you the reaped ear
Sprouting.

     Are you contented? Are you answered?

Come.
     I will show you chestnut branches budding
Beyond a dusty pane and a little grass
Green in a window-box and silence stirred,
Settling and stirred and settling in an empty room —

77

THE SILENT SLAIN

for Kenneth MacLeish, 1894–1918

We too, we too, descending once again
The hills of our own land, we too have heard
Far off — Ah, que ce cor a longue haleine —
The horn of Roland in the passages of Spain,
The first, the second blast, the failing third,
And with the third turned back and climbed once more
The steep road southward, and heard faint the sound
Of swords, of horses, the disastrous war,
And crossed the dark defile at last, and found
At Roncevaux upon the darkening plain
The dead against the dead and on the silent ground
The silent slain —

LINES FOR A PROLOGUE

These alternate nights and days, these seasons
Somehow fail to convince me. It seems
I have the sense of infinity!

(In your dreams, O crew of Columbus,
O listeners over the sea
For the surf that breaks upon Nothing —)

Once I was waked by the nightingales in the garden.
I thought, What time is it? I thought,
Time — Is it Time still? — Now is it Time?

(Tell me your dreams, O sailors:
Tell me, in sleep did you climb
The tall masts, and before you —)

At night the stillness of old trees
Is a leaning over and the inertness
Of hills is a kind of waiting.

(In sleep, in a dream, did you see
The world's end? Did the water
Break — and no shore — Did you see?)

Strange faces come through the streets to me
Like messengers: and I have been warned
By the moving slowly of hands at a window.

Oh, I have the sense of infinity —
But the world, sailors, is round.
They say there is no end to it.

L'AN TRENTIESME DE MON EAGE

And I have come upon this place
By lost ways, by a nod, by words,
By faces, by an old man's face
At Morlaix lifted to the birds,

By hands upon the tablecloth
At Aldebori's, by the thin
Child's hands that opened to the moth
And let the flutter of the moonlight in,

By hands, by voices, by the voice
Of Mrs. Whitman on the stair,
By Margaret's "If we had the choice
To choose or not —" through her thick hair,

By voices, by the creak and fall
Of footsteps on the upper floor,
By silence waiting in the hall
Between the doorbell and the door,

By words, by voices, a lost way —
And here above the chimney stack
The unknown constellations sway —
And by what way shall I go back?

LE SECRET HUMAIN

It was not God that told us. We knew
Before, long before, long, long ago.
We knew that tonight — or tomorrow. . . . We know
Still — tomorrow. It is true that we know.

The incredulous surprise
In the faces of the dead, in dead eyes:
There was something still to happen —
There was someone that was always going to come.

And the eyes of those that sleep,
The puzzled eyes:
There are promises the silence does not keep —
And the dark has no replies.

Ah, we know
As the wind blows,
Not to the south, the north,
Not to, not ever to, but toward.

We know beyond the doors we press and open,
Beyond the smell of breakfast in the hall,
Beyond the soggy towel and the soap —
Wait! We shall know all.

We that sit and think and talk,
We that lie awake till late,
We that walk beside the river:
We can wait — Oh we can wait!

There will be little enough to forget —
The flight of crows,
A wet street,
The way the wind blows,
Moonrise: sunset:
Three words the world knows —
Little enough to forget.

It will be easy enough to forget.
The rain drips
Through the shallow clay,
Washes lips,
Eyes, brain,
The rain drips in the shallow clay,
The soft rain will wash them away —
The flight of crows,
The way the wind blows,
Moonrise: sunset:
Will wash them away
To the bare hard bones:
And the bones forget.

INTERROGATE THE STONES

Do you think
Death is an answer then?
Ah, to the How, the When,
Ah, to the hardest word.

But — have you heard
That other endless asking? Have you seen
The stale ironic question lean
At evening from a window-place
To face
The coming in of night, or stand
Where the sea breaks upon the broken land
Hour by hour listening?

Have you not seen
Old bones lie motionless between
The olives on the Tuscan hill
And still
Unanswered — still?
And do you think
Death is an answer? Do you think

The Ask no more! Oh ask
Nothing! the hand upon the mouth, the mask
With broken eyes — that thus
Death answers us?

YACHT FOR SALE

My youth is
Made fast
To the dock
At Marseilles
Rotting away
With a chain to her mast,

She that saw slaughters
In foreign waters:

She that was torn
With the winds off the Horn:

She that was beached in the bleaching environs
Of sirens:

She that rounded the Cape of Good Hope
With a rope's aid:

She's fast there
Off the Cannebière.

It's easy to see
She was frail in the knee
And too sharp in the bow —
You can see now.

IMMORTAL HELIX

Hereunder Jacob Schmidt who, man and bones,
Has been his hundred times around the sun.

His chronicle is endless — the great curve
Inscribed in nothing by a point upon
The spinning surface of a circling sphere.

Dead bones roll on.

The birthplace of Mr. William Shakespeare author
Of Timon and other poetry including
"Who sees his true love on her naked bed
Teaching the sheets" including also sonnets
"To one of one still such and ever so"
Or Lincoln's in Kentucky where they say,
From This to That: Think of it! (If they could!)
Or Dante Alighieri's — Godi Fiorenza —
Has not been found. They cannot fix their marbles
Just where the year twelve hundred sixty five
Rolled up the Arno or where time and Troy
And Stratford crossed each other. On this spot —
    Where now, where now along the great ecliptic
    Traced by a wandering planet that unwinds
    Space into hours? —
                Upon this very spot
The year of Christ one thousand five six four —
    And of Erasmus four score seventeen —
    And Leonardo one one two —
                was born —
    To P. Ovidius Naso and the queen
    Lying in Florida on a Venetian bed
    Carved with the loves of Venus —
William Shakespeare.

MOTHER GOOSE'S GARLAND

Around, around the sun we go:
The moon goes round the earth.
We do not die of death:
We die of vertigo.

MARCH

Let us think of these
Winter-stiffened trees

(Posthumously sucking pap
From the pores of a dead planet

Like the bristles on a butchered pig)
Every stalk and standing twig

Swollen with delightful sap

MISTRAL OVER THE GRAVES

Be still — listen to the wind!
Listen to the night wind slithering and splashing
In the palm trees, in the poplars —
Saying Ah, Ah, in the pine trees —
Listen to the wind! Be still!

Be still — listen to the wind.
There is no sound at all but the wind now,
No sleepless sound of old men coughing,
No knocking of little iron nails upon the stones.
Listen to the wind! Be still!

Be still — listen to the wind.
The sound of live men on the earth is the rustling
Of small mice in a windy barn.

Listen to the wind, Dead Heart, at the closed door —
Listen to the wind! Be still!

CORPORATE ENTITY

The Oklahoma Ligno and Lithograph Co
Of Maine doing business in Delaware Tennessee
Missouri Montana Ohio and Idaho
With a corporate existence distinct from that of the
Secretary Treasurer President Directors or
Majority stockholder being empowered to acquire
As principal agent trustee licensee licensor
Any or all in part or in parts or entire

Etchings impressions engravings engravures prints
Paintings oil-paintings canvases portraits vignettes
Tableaux ceramics relievos insculptures tints
Art-treasures or masterpieces complete or in sets

The Oklahoma Ligno and Lithograph Co
Weeps at a nude by Michael Angelo.

THE END OF THE WORLD

Quite unexpectedly as Vasserot
The armless ambidextrian was lighting
A match between his great and second toe
And Ralph the lion was engaged in biting
The neck of Madame Sossman while the drum
Pointed, and Teeny was about to cough
In waltz-time swinging Jocko by the thumb —
Quite unexpectedly the top blew off:

And there, there overhead, there, there, hung over
Those thousands of white faces, those dazed eyes,
There in the starless dark the poise, the hover,
There with vast wings across the canceled skies,
There in the sudden blackness the black pall
Of nothing, nothing, nothing — nothing at all.

THE FARM

Why do you listen, trees?
Why do you wait?
Why do you fumble at the breeze —
Gesticulate
With hopeless fluttering hands —
Stare down the vanished road beyond the gate
That now no longer stands?
Why do you wait —
Trees —
Why do you listen, trees?

(1750)

Ephraim Cross drives up the trail
From Worcester. Hepsibah goes pale
At sumac feathers in the pines.
The wooden wagon grunts and whines.
Blunt oxen leaning outward lurch
Over the boulders. Pine to birch
The hills change color. In the west
Wachusett humps a stubborn crest.
Ephraim takes the promised land,
Earth, rock and rubble, in his hand.

(1800)

Young sugar maples in a row
Flap awkward leaves. Ripe acres blow
In failing ripples to the blue
Of hemlocks. Ephraim's house stands true
Above the troubling of a brook.
Ephraim's gravestones seem to look
West of the Berkshires and still west.
Hepsibah's stones turn back compressed
And bitter silence toward the sea.
Between, her sons sleep patiently.

(1871)

A blind door yawing to the snow
Questions them in. They knock and go
Through the old bedroom to the back.
The kitchen door swings out a crack
Framing Aunt Aggie in her chair —
Dead as a haddock — ragged hair

Scrawled over on her shriveled eyes.
Since Monday morning, they surmise:
Last of her name she was, and best
Be lyin' up there with the rest.

(1923)

Plummets of moonlight thinning through
Deep fathoms of the dark renew
Moments of vision and deflect
Smooth images the eyes expect
To images the brain perceives.
Choked in a pine wood chafe the leaves
Of aged maples, but the moon
Remembers; and its shadows strewn
Sidelong and slantingly restore
Ephraim's trees about his door.

Why do you listen, trees?
Why do you wait?
Why do you fumble at the breeze —
Gesticulate
With hopeless fluttering hands —
Stare down the vanished road beyond the gate
That now no longer stands?
Why do you listen, trees?
Why do you listen, trees?

ELEVEN

And summer mornings the mute child, rebellious,
Stupid, hating the words, the meanings, hating
The Think now, Think, the Oh but Think! would leave
On tiptoe the three chairs on the verandah
And crossing tree by tree the empty lawn
Push back the shed door and upon the sill
Stand pressing out the sunlight from his eyes
And enter and with outstretched fingers feel
The grindstone and behind it the bare wall
And turn and in the corner on the cool
Hard earth sit listening. And one by one,
Out of the dazzled shadow in the room,
The shapes would gather, the brown plowshare, spades,
Mattocks, the polished helves of picks, a scythe
Hung from the rafters, shovels, slender tines
Glinting across the curve of sickles — shapes
Older than men were, the wise tools, the iron
Friendly with earth. And sit there, quiet, breathing
The harsh dry smell of withered bulbs, the faint
Odor of dung, the silence. And outside
Beyond the half-shut door the blind leaves
And the corn moving. And at noon would come,
Up from the garden, his hard crooked hands
Gentle with earth, his knees still earth-stained, smelling
Of sun, of summer, the old gardener, like
A priest, like an interpreter, and bend
Over his baskets.
                    And they would not speak:
They would say nothing. And the child would sit there
Happy as though he had no name, as though
He had been no one: like a leaf, a stem,
Like a root growing —

WAY-STATION

The incoherent rushing of the train
Dulls like a drugged pain

Numbs
To an ether throbbing of inaudible drums

Unfolds
Hush within hush until the night withholds

Only its darkness.
                    From the deep
Dark a voice calls like a voice in sleep

Slowly a strange name in a strange tongue.

Among

The sleeping listeners a sound
As leaves stir faintly on the ground

When snow falls from a windless sky —
A stir   A sigh

CHARTRES

I do not wonder, stones,
You have withstood so long
The strong wind and the snows.

Were you not built to bear
The winter and the wind
That blows on the hill here?

But you have borne so long
Our eyes, our mortal eyes,
And are not worn —

SIGNATURE FOR TEMPO

I

Think that this world against the wind of time
Perpetually falls the way a hawk
Falls at the wind's edge but is motionless —

Think that this silver snail the moon will climb
All night upon time's curving stalk
That as she climbs bends, bends beneath her —

Yes
And think that we remember the past time.

II

These live people,
These more
Than three dimensional
By time protracted edgewise into heretofore
People,
How shall we bury all

These time-shaped people,
In graves that have no more
Than three dimensions?
Can we dig
With such sidlings and declensions
As to coffin bodies big
With memory?
And how
Can the earth's contracted Now
Enclose these knuckles and this crooked knee
Sprawled over hours of a sun long set?

Or do these bones forget?

III

Borne
Landward on relinquishing seas,
Worn
By the sliding of water

Whom time goes over wave by wave, do I lie
Drowned in a crumble of surf at the sea's edge? —

And wonder now what ancient bones are these
That flake on sifting flake
Out of deep time have shelved this shallow ledge
Where the waves break —

NOCTURNE

The earth, still heavy and warm with afternoon,
Dazed by the moon:

The earth, tormented with the moon's light,
Wandering in the night:

La, La, The moon is a lovely thing to see —
The moon is an agony.

Full moon, moon rise, the old old pain
Of brightness in dilated eyes,

The ache of still
Elbows leaning on the narrow sill,

Of motionless cold hands upon the wet
Marble of the parapet,

Of open eyelids of a child behind
The crooked glimmer of the window blind,

Of sliding faint remindful squares
Across the lamplight on the rocking-chairs:

Why do we stand so late
Stiff fingers on the moonlit gate?

Why do we stand
To watch so long the fall of moonlight on the sand?

What is it we cannot recall?

Tormented by the moon's light
The earth turns maundering through the night.

SELENE AFTERWARDS

The moon is dead, you lovers!
                    She who walked
Naked upon the dark Ægean, she
Who under Ida in the beech groves mocked
The rutting satyrs, she who secretly,
Leaving below her the slow lifting sea,
Climbed through the woods of Latmos to the bed
Of the eternal sleeper — she is dead,

Dead, you lovers! I have seen her face.
The sun rose by St.-Etienne. She fled
Half turning back (as though the plunge of space
Over the world's rim frightened her) her head
And stared and stared at me. Her face was dead.
It was a woman's face but dead as stone
And leper white and withered to the bone.

It was a woman's skull the shriveling cold
Out there among the stars had withered dry
And its dry white was mottled with dry mould.
It was a long dead skull the caustic lye
Of time had eaten clean, and in the sky
As under the cold water of a lake
Lay crumbling year by year, white flake by flake,

Scabious, scurfy. Oh, look down, look down,
You lovers, through that water where there swing
Night shadows of the world. Look deep, deep.
        Drown
Your eyes in deepness. Look! There lies the thing
That made you love, that maddened you!
                     Oh sing,

Sing in the fields, you lovers. The low moon
Moves in the elms. It will be summer soon. . . .

NO LAMP HAS EVER SHOWN US
WHERE TO LOOK

No lamp has ever shown us where to look.

Neither the promiscuous
And every-touching moon
                                nor stars
Either with their not much caring
                                nor
Lights to seaward and far off
Not meant for us,
                        nor, say, the flash
From darkened promontories that
Goes out, leaving an afterward
Of trees no more
                        nor even
The whole sun —
                        No —
                                Within
The buried staring eyes of one
A long time dead, long drowned, there stands
Still fixed upon impenetrable skies
The small, black circle of the sun.

"LE SEUL MALHEUR EST QUE
JE NE SAIS PAS LIRE"

In the doorway of the Bar
Du Bon Port at Saint Tropez
Sharp against the light
The old sailor in the fez

Stands face upward to the stars.
Is it I then, only I,
I who have such need to know,
I alone that cannot read?

ANCESTRAL

The star dissolved in evening — the one star
The silently
            and night O soon now, soon
And still the light now
                and still now the large
Relinquishing
           and through the pools of blue
Still, still the swallows
            and a wind now
                  and the tree
Gathering darkness:
           I was small. I lay
Beside my mother on the grass, and sleep
Came —

slow hooves and dripping with the dark
The velvet muzzles, the white feet that move
In a dream water
                    and O soon now soon
Sleep and the night.

                    And I was not afraid.
Her hand lay over mine. Her fingers knew
Darkness, — and sleep — the silent lands, the far
Far off of morning where I should awake.

GRAZING LOCOMOTIVES

Huge upon the hazy plain
Where bloom the momentary trees,
Where blows immensely round their knees
The grass that fades to air again,

Slow and solemn in the night
Beneath the slender pole by pole
That lifts above their reach each sole
Enormous melon of the light,

Still sweating from the deep ravines
Where rot within the buried wood
The bones of Time that are their food,
    Graze the great machines.

SOME ASPECTS OF IMMORTALITY

The alley between the elm trees ends
In nothing, abruptly, as a life ends.

Down that straight avenue I stare
At the final blank, the abyss of air.

A nursemaid with a carriage steers
Across the vista, pushes, nears
The brink, goes over, disappears.

Too ignorant, think I, for fears!

VOYAGE EN PROVENCE

The birds in the gardens of Avignon
Were words without songs.

At Arles in the Arena the doves were
Voices of old women.

My heart, have we not heard

The birds at Avignon and in the roofs
Of Arles cool doves?

MEMORIAL RAIN

for Kenneth MacLeish

Ambassador Puser the ambassador
Reminds himself in French, felicitous tongue,
What these (young men no longer) lie here for
In rows that once, and somewhere else, were young . . .

    All night in Brussels the wind had tugged at my door:
    I had heard the wind at my door and the trees strung
    Taut, and to me who had never been before
    In that country it was a strange wind, blowing
    Steadily, stiffening the walls, the floor,
    The roof of my room. I had not slept for knowing
    He too, dead, was a stranger in that land
    And felt beneath the earth in the wind's flowing
    A tightening of roots and would not understand,
    Remembering lake winds in Illinois,
    That strange wind. I had felt his bones in the sand
    Listening.

*   . . . Reflects that these enjoy*
Their country's gratitude, that deep repose,
That peace no pain can break, no hurt destroy,
That rest, that sleep . . .

                At Ghent the wind rose.
    There was a smell of rain and a heavy drag
    Of wind in the hedges but not as the wind blows
    Over fresh water when the waves lag
    Foaming and the willows huddle and it will rain:
    I felt him waiting.

*   . . . Indicates the flag*
Which (may he say) enisles in Flanders plain

This little field these happy, happy dead
Have made America . . .

                                        In the ripe grain
    The wind coiled glistening, darted, fled,
    Dragging its heavy body: at Waereghem
    The wind coiled in the grass above his head:
    Waiting — listening . . .

            . . . Dedicates to them
This earth their bones have hallowed, this last gift
A grateful country . . .

                                Under the dry grass stem
    The words are blurred, are thickened, the words sift
    Confused by the rasp of the wind, by the thin grating
    Of ants under the grass, the minute shift
    And tumble of dusty sand separating
    From dusty sand. The roots of the grass strain,
    Tighten, the earth is rigid, waits — he is waiting —

    And suddenly, and all at once, the rain!

MAN!

> FREE
> > To the World
> > > THE PATENT PROPAGATIVE,
> The Cause of Causes in the Handy Case,
> Tomorrow in Tubes, Eternity in Cartons,
> One hundred billion lives in each Container,
> Cities, Nations, Continents even, Planets,
> New hopes, New hungers, New despairs, New Christs,
> Ages, Eras, Centuries, Ends, Beginnings,
> > LIFE
> > > LIFE in the vial with the Safety Catch,
> > > LIFE in the Perpendicular Decanter,
> The insulated, thermo-static, safe
> In every clime and climate, weather-proofed,
> Perfected, folding Holder decorated
> With fancy hair and finished in the likeness
> Of the Inventor. His face on every package.
> None genuine without the photograph.
> Free! Death's cure, Grave's simple, Time's elixir,
> The drug for darkness, Night's mandragora —
> > FREE
> > > To the World
> > > > For nothing. . . .

HEARTS' AND FLOWERS'

> The delicate lepidopteran tongue
> Uncurls,
> Invades, insinuous penetrant,

Through vulnerable whorls,
The cloven stigma of that fluctuant,
   That palpable among
   Impalpable soft flowers, sea
Anemone
Whose labial perianth
Closes.

Neither amaranth
Nor Venus-roses,
Themselves within themselves that sheathe
The velvet anther,
   Queens who feel in their embraces breathe
   The silken belly of the languid panther,
Thus —
No, nor convolvulus
That under
Gradual fingers of the evening yields.

Deep down beneath the ocean summer thunder
Thrills without sound in the slow muculent fields
The trembling tentacles of the voluptuous

Polyp.

AGAINST ILLUMINATIONS

Avoid, you strollers in the dark street,
You side by side touching at knee and shoulder,
You going your own way your own ways together
And who knows where, avoid these shafts of light,

These oblongs out of doorways, the thin jet
Under the window shade, beneath the shutter,
The match flame squirting at the dark, the glimmer
Between bent fingers where the old men sit —

Avoid the gas-light on the winding stair.
She who climbs beside you is not there.

ARS POETICA

A poem should be palpable and mute
As a globed fruit,

Dumb
As old medallions to the thumb,

Silent as the sleeve-worn stone
Of casement ledges where the moss has grown —

A poem should be wordless
As the flight of birds.

*

A poem should be motionless in time
As the moon climbs,

Leaving, as the moon releases
Twig by twig the night-entangled trees,

Leaving, as the moon behind the winter leaves,
Memory by memory the mind —

A poem should be motionless in time
As the moon climbs.

*

A poem should be equal to:
Not true.

For all the history of grief
An empty doorway and a maple leaf.

For love
The leaning grasses and two lights above the sea —

A poem should not mean
But be.

SKETCH FOR A PORTRAIT OF
MME. G—— M——

"Her room," you'd say — and wonder why you'd called it
Hers, as though she hadn't seven others
Not counting the reception room beside
The front door in red paper with a view
Of Paris in a bottle and real snow
Made out of something else and through the window
The railroad cutting where the trains went by
To Marly-le-château-du-roy: but somehow
Whether you came to dinner or to see
The last Picasso or because the sun
Blazed on her windows as you passed or just

Because you came, and whether she was there
Or down below in the garden or gone out
Or not come in yet, somehow when you came
You always crossed the hall and turned the doorknob
And went in; — "Her room" — as though the room
Itself were nearer her: as though the room
Were something she had left for you to see —
The room triangular with morning sunlight,
The room half-globed and low above the lamps,
The room oblique and leaning to the fire.
And yet it was not hers, not hers by title,
Nor hers because she'd had the walls redone
In rose to match the color of her dresses,
Nor hers because Le Bal du Comte Orgel
Lay on a chair and she had picked the flowers,
Nor merely hers because she lived in it.
No one, — not the most precisely careless
Distributor of household knick-knacks, boxes,
Candlesticks, pillows, receptacles for ashes
Or photographs of children, — could have fixed
Its fine proportions in that attitude
Of gratified compliance worn by salons
Whose white-and-gold has settled into home;
And other men and women must have left
The touch of hands there — say, for one, old Gounod
Who'd written Mireille in the room and played
The airs from Baucis on the grand piano
And wasn't, you would understand, a man
To leave his mortal habitation empty
No matter how the doors had closed on him.
And yet you'd say, "Her room," as though you'd said
Her voice, Her manner, meaning something else
Than that she owned it; knowing it was not
A room to be possessed of, not a room

To give itself to people, not the kind
Of room you'd sit in and forget about,
Or sit in and look out from. It reserved
Something that in a woman you would call
Her reticence by which you'd mean her power
Of feeling what she had not put in words —
Which, in the room, was more perhaps the windows
And what there was beyond them that you saw
Only in shadows on the floor and ceiling
Than anything the room itself contained.
Sometimes toward twilight when the windows seemed
Faintly to let the half-light ebb away
And through that lapsing and last fall of day
The ancient dark a moment showed itself
And then was darkness — in that moment — then —
The room, made probable, made real, became
As strangely visible as if it were
The shape of something she was thinking of.

And there were afternoons when the snow fell
Softly across the wind and in the mirrors
The snow fell softly, flake on flake, the vague
Reflected falling in the long dim mirrors,
Faint snow across the image of the wind, —
And there were afternoons when the room remembered,
When her life passed in the mirrors of the room.

THE HAMLET OF A. MACLEISH (1928)

No man living but has seen the king his father's ghost. None alive that have had words with it. Nevertheless the knowledge of ill is among us and the obligation to revenge, and the natural world is convicted of that enormity . . .

In the old time men spoke and were answered and the thing was done clean in the daylight. Now it is not so.

1

From these night fields and waters do men raise,
Sailors from ship, sleepers from their bed,   *Elsinore.*
Born, mortal men and haunted with brief days,   *A platform*
Their eyes to that vast silence overhead.   *before the*
They see the moon walk slowly in her ways   *castle.*
And the grave stars and all the dark outspread.
They raise their mortal eyelids from this ground:
Question it . . .

        What art thou . . .

                And no sound.

2

Ha, but the sun among us . . .

Ha, but the great sun
Shouts in the shouldering leaves and the grasshoppers
Scatter before him. Ho, but his brass
Voice is the voice of the beater of horses.
He roars from the splashed sea driving the
Nude girls through the surf, striking their
Golden rumps with the hand flat, deriding
Shyness with lewd words. He is loud
In the blown blue sky as the laughter of
Fed kings under arbors

The same: a room of state. He is reproved his melancholy by the uncle-father.

Ha, but the sun among us . . . wearers of
Black cloths, bearers of secrets!
The jay jeer of the sun in the ear of our
Pain . . . and the nudge of the blunt pink
Thumb troubling the pride of despair in us . . .

Ha, but the sun in our air

We stand in the still earth and the sun comes
Swelling among us with large light, with the
Browsing of bees about him, with flattering
Tree sound. He is tall. He reveals the
Dark to us (He is informed in these matters)
"Behold!" he mouths in the gilt twigs.
He advises our souls with the blabbed loose
Light over water. He declaims the spangles of
Glass in the high ways. He reproves us with
Shining. Ho, he repeats the proverbs of
Brisk leaves to enliven the laugh in us.
He lays his hands on our sex to persuade us of
Happiness under the sea noon

How is it that the clouds still hang on thee?

Why seems it so — particular — with thee?

Seems, Madam! . . .

Ha, we are preached by the
Loud mouth, by the blooming of brightness.
We are admonished with flares. "Get over it!"
"Cease," he instructs us, "to feel the emotions of
Misery! Be bright boys! Console yourselves!"

Ah, but the sun in our sky!

I shall in all my best obey you . . .

Only
We have these dreams!
Only —
the old have announced us the
Irremediable woe, the ill
Long done, lost in the times before memory.

3

But men have known   *The same. Horatio,*
The secret a long time. Men, forgotten,   *Bernardo,*
                              Marcellus. He is
Few, keepers of lean goats on the mountains, *informed of the*
Knew in the old time the standing before   *apparition seen*
    us of   *upon the wall.*
Strangeness under the clear air . . .

There have been men a long, long time that knew this.

113

The words come to us
Far off, faint in our ears, confused. They have told us of
Signs seen by night and the vanishing signals.
They have told how the lights change. They have told of the
     ominous
Stir over the leaves and the showing among them of
Mysteries hiding a dark thing . . .

Now is Bleheris speaking in the book.   *Horatio:* " . . . *till*
I am beside the fire. The old page   *I may deliver . . .*
Wrinkles with light. A log falls. The wind   *This marvel to*
Swings from tree to tree in the wet night.   *you . . .* "
Now is Bleheris speaking:
                         . . . and all that day
Seaward and down from ridge to ridge and the
Pines oak and the oaks birch and the birch trees
Pine again rooting in coarse sand, the horse track
Swallowed behind, the jays ahead of me screaming,
And I by the ridge rode on: and the wind changed with
Flaws from westward, cold in the sun, and a sound
Echoing surf from the leaves: and the steep land
Fell and I saw the sea.
And by the sea was a ship but no man in her.
And sail was set on the ship and I led the beast by a
Rock's bridge and I cut rope and the wind was
Off shore smelling at first of the furze root,
Afterward cold: and the boom jibed over and
She moved, wind in the sail top, rolling to the long
Swell, the land against the wind, the skystain
Spilling from trough to trough of the dead waves.
And she cleared the lee with the light and the wind freshened
     and
Night came. Thence north until dawn and at dawn
Hills and a morning tower in the sun:

114

Then nothing. And the wind held all that day
Heaping the wave tops westward, and all night
The wind was with us but the second morning
Hauled south and drove her, the lee rail
Free by a strake, the wake washed out by the sea-scud.
And all that day I held her and at dark
Luffed to have reefed her but she went about,
Heeled and came up half foundered running off
East by north with the wind aft and the waves
Taking her stern, the lift logged with the bilge water.
That was the third night and the morning stormy,
Rain and the wind gone east, the geer wet,
The bow sheer down with water. And I slept
And woke past sunset and I saw the sky
Gold, and against it black, and the black, land:
And the scud blew over it blurring the golden light.
And all that night the surf was through the sea mist:
The pine tops combing through the fog at dawn.
And I struck the sea with the oars but the ship lifted,
Grinding on gravel, and the bow fell off
Waiting the seventh wave and leaned and rode with it
Beam-on high on the beach and the wave drew
Down and she held the shingle. And I rode
And climbed through rock-scrub inland to a marsh
And past the marsh a forest and till night
Tunneled in tree-dark riding and saw neither
Glebe nor fence, fallow nor cow track, only
Dog foot, wolf, nor birds but three birds silent,
Nor any live thing other but the bat,
Nor sound but bat's sound nor the whine of flies.
And the sun went down, red among beech trees, leaving
High in the east, red, and no stars, and after
Wind again, rain behind it, the first few
Drops and the storm gust, thunder and the flash

Casting no shadow. And I rode and there was
One light lingered through the shut of dark.
That light I followed. And I found a door:
And past the door a church nave: and the church
Empty, the sill moss growing on the stone:
And one bare chapel. And I saw the light
Bright in that chapel. And I saw a cup
Crimson and burning and a flame of candles
Burning before it. And I knew that cup.
I knelt there thanking Jesus Christ.

                           And the wind
Sucked at the dead air and the water dripped
And the candle flame fell limp in the heavy dark   *"In the dead*
And stiffened smoking and the moving leaves   *waste and*
                                                    middle of the
Flapped in the window. So the night passed half   *night . . . "*
And I awake still staring at the cup
Forefeeling terror heard the beast go back,
Rear and a hoof ring striking, and looked up
And saw come inward at that window place,
Come from the plunging darkness into light,
Loose fingers groping, cropped, no arm there, grey,
The nails gone, shriveled, a dead hand, and droop
And close about the vessel. And the flame
Leapt and the night had all. Then silence. Then,
Loud till the stone shook, lamentable, long   *" . . . both in*
                                                    time, Form of
As all the dead together, a great cry   *the thing, each*
Shrieking with laughter: afterward the sound   *word made*
The horse made breathing. And I rose and ran   *true and good,*
                                                    The appari-
And mounted, leaning for the door, the stench   *tion comes."*
Of death, of flesh rot, choking me, rode out,
Spurred, and the wet leaves cold against my face,
Came to a clearing in the wood and reined
And saw the storm had passed there and the sky all
Clean, the stars out . . .

. . . peace! I pray you all
If you have hitherto concealed this sight . . .

the page
Wrinkles with light. A log falls. The wind
Swings from tree to tree in the wet night.

It may be then we are deceived in this.
It may be this is other than we think
And in our sleep . . . or secretly . . . or by
The sudden blade of pain . . .
it may well be
The thing is evil and these seeming soft
Familiar gestures, these half signs, this shy
Withheld warm look the earth has after day,
This green, this ever blue, these stars — these stars —
Are false and to deceive us. It may be

4

Night after night I lie like this listening.
Night after night I cannot sleep. I wake
Knowing something, thinking something has happened.
I have this feeling a great deal. I have
Sadness often. At night I have this feeling.   *The platform.*
Waking I feel this pain as though I knew
Something not to be thought of, something unbearable.
I feel this pain at night as though some   *The King his*
Terrible thing had happened. At night the sky   *father's ghost*
    appears to him.
Opens, the near things vanish, the bright walls
Fall, and the stars were always there, and the dark
There and the cold and the stillness. I wake and stand
A long time by the window. I always think
The trees know the way they are silent. I always

Think some one has spoken, some one has told me.
Reading the books I always think so, reading
Words overheard in the books, reading the words
Like words in a strange language. I always hear
Music like that. I almost remember with music . . .
This is not what you think. It is not that. I swim
Every day at the beach under the fig tree.
I swim very well and far out. The smell
Of pine comes over the water. The wind blurs
Seaward. And afternoons I walk to the phare.
Much of the time I do not think anything;
Much of the time I do not even notice.
And then, speaking, closing a door, I see
Strangely as though I almost saw now, some
Shape of things I have always seen, the sun
White on a house and the windows open and swallows
In and out of the wallpaper, the moon's face
Faint by day in a mirror; I see some
Changed thing that is telling, something that almost
Tells — and this pain then, then this pain. And no
Words, only these shapes of things that seem
Ways of knowing what it is I am knowing.
I write these things in books, on pieces of paper.
I have written "The wind rises . . ." I have written "Bells
Plunged in the wind . . ." I have written "Like
Doors . . ." "Like evening . . ."
It is always the same: I cannot read what the words say.
It is always the same: there are signs and I cannot read them.
There are empty streets and the blinds drawn and the sky
Sliding in windows. There are lights before
Dawn in the yellow transoms over the doors.
There are steps that pass and pass all night that are always
One, always the same step passing . . .
I have traveled a great deal. I have seen at Homs

The cranes over the river and Isfahan
The fallen tiles in the empty garden, and Shiraz
Far off, the cypresses under the hill.
It is always the same. I have seen on the Kazvin road
On the moon grey desert the leafless wind,
The wind raging in moon-dusk. Or the light that comes
Seaward with slow oars from the mouth of Euphrates.
I have heard the nightingales in the thickets of Gilan,
And at dawn, at Teheran, I have heard from the ancient
Westward greying face of the wandering planet
The voices calling the small new name of god,
The voices answered with cockcrow, answered at dusk
With the cry of jackals far away in the gardens.
I have heard the name of the moon beyond those mountains.
It is always the same. It is always as though some
Smell of leaves had made me not quite remember;
As though I had turned to look and there were no one.
It has always been secret like that with me.
Always something has not been said. Always
The stones were there, the trees were there, the motionless
Hills have appeared in the dusk to me, the moon
Has stood a long time white and still in the window.
Always the earth has been turned away from me hiding
The veiled eyes and the wind in the leaves has not spoken . . .

As now the night is still. As the night now
Stands at the farthest off of touch and like
A raised hand held upon the empty air
Means and is silent.
                    Look! It waves me still . . .
    I say Go on! Go on!
                            As the whole night now
Made visible behind this darkness seems
To beckon to me . . .

5

Where wilt thou lead me? Speak . . .

We who have followed the clouds by day and by darkness
The march of the wandering fires, we who have watched
Bird signs in the sky, we who have questioned
The doubtful flares, who have seen the gestures before us
Of rain in the faint hills, who have heard the stammering
Voices of thunder cry out to us, we who have come now
A long road in the earth and the touching upon us
Of leaves like fingers on closed eyes and the taste of the
Air strange in our nostrils,
                    where wilt thou lead us?
Where, at what extreme confine, wilt thou turn,

Mark me!
    I will.

*Another part of the
platform: the truth
revealed: he swears
to be revenged.*

    and speak! . . . and at these ears, Oh
At these mortal ear-pits speak to us?

Where wilt thou lead us? When wilt thou turn to us?
Not now? Not at this farthest verge? Not even
Here where the walls end and the ruinous tower
Leans with its uninhabitable black
Long builded stones above the ultimate sea?
We are alone now. There are none to hear.
I say we are alone upon this place.
Not even those are with us that in times
Past from the leaves of future-telling oaks,
From lowing heifers with all flowery horns,
From dolphin-ridden surf, from the deep pool
Spoke and would comfort us, the shining heel,
The seal-like swimming in the lovely air . . .

120

Where is thy tongue, great spectre? Hast thou not
Answered to others that with hearts like ours
Followed thee, poets, speakers in the earth?
Didst thou not show them? For they were as sure,
Returning, as those men whom the great sea
Chooses for danger that do no more fear
But inward certain leave the ill within
And laugh for trivial bawdy cause and watch the
New good living mellow earth and love it.
Didst thou not tell them? . . . and to us alone
Art always secret, always the void sign,
Always the still averted face whose unseen
Shape makes sick men of us, haunted fools,
Hag-ridden, blinking starers at the dark:
Always this blank of silence like a dial
That counts but will not keep our journey hours?
Didst thou not tell these others? And why art thou
Dumb but to us — or only mole-numb speech
That though we move from it, still under, still uneased,
Repeats the indecipherable will
And swears us to it? — though we know not what.

Where wilt thou lead us? Speak . . .
                                        and suddenly the grey
Light and the wind in the branches
                                and the dawn
                                        and all
Vanished, all at the scent of morning gone,
And leaves now, and the green again, and where
Our strained eyes started at the shape of fear
Only the foolish stones
                        and yet
                                to hear

The voice still under in the changing air
Cry "Swear!" —

    to see the measuring shadow on the wall

6

                whether before have been
Men in these valleys . . .
Whether, beneath the sand here, beneath the shallow
Earth are ashes, are fragments of jars, are the snow-worn
Limbs of goddesses . . .

              whether these now
I see in the dim air are men as I am
Wandering in this land
              how shall I know?
How shall we speak together of this saying
You . . . You too . . . You too have felt . . . You also
At night waking . . . Oh at night! . . . And walking
Under the trees at evening . . . the trees! . . . You too! . . .

Whether these man faces
             Come! Be honest!
Why will you not reply to me? Why do you always
Not understand what I say? I know your faces. *To him Ro-*
I know your names too. Nevertheless   *sencrantz and*
                                    Guildenstern
You are not friendly to me; you are not   *as friends.*
    of my people.

As for the place I go to —
              we seek water.
The water here is salt. We have seen neither
Birds nor green leaves since we found this country.

Why will you never listen? Why do you always
Turn your eyes away when I speak to you? Tell me,
Do none of you fear this place as I fear it?
Who has sent you to me? You have been sent
As spies. You are not friendly.

                              It may be
They are not there! . . .

                    or whether alone I
Of all men I only have passed these mountains.

7

Let there be shelters built in the wild fern
For girls at their first sickness; also hovels
Of green thorn on the hills for the times of women:
Let there be laws inscribed for the keeping of chastity
And knots made to number the days of the moon:
Otherwise harm will come of it!

                         Why should we be
Ashamed if it were not so? Why should we sleep
At noon with our knees bent in the darkness of plantains?
Why have we not uncovered ourselves in the sight
Of grown girls or gone by day through the paths
To the named place in the straw under the fruit trees?

Let them be crushed with stones who are found together.
Let their sex be consumed with lime and their bodies
Burned on the roots of trees slabbered by cattle. *Ophelia is put*
I tell you evil will come of it. Young girls   *to trap him:*
                                                      Polonius and the
Will draw us at dawn to the doors giving on   *uncle-father*
     silence   *behind.*

123

And women with loosened garments will bring us in
To the long room where the sun stands among columns:
We shall be overheard: we shall speak aloud
Telling them all! all! . . . and the vacant light, *Polonius,*
The bright void, the listening, idiot silence . . . *Claudius*
within.

Love, I said, O my love! and I leaned upon her.
I told her my heart in the soft fall of the plum blossoms.
Suddenly there were leaves stirred in the wind,
The sun was there! The sky stood there behind me!
"Ha," I said, "Are you fair?" Look! "Are you honest?"
I was betrayed. I rose from her.
                              No, not I;
        I never gave you aught.

I tell you we must be dumb in the earth, else
Evil will come of it: we shall be understood.
The thing will be known before time and prevented.
Those who can speak with foolishness, let them be heard:
The rest shall be still, the rest shall watch and keep silence.

And the bodies of those that die of love upon childbed,
Let them be buried in sand in a strange place.
Let them be put away far from their people.
It is a shameful thing. It has been forbidden.

8

                              Ay, sure, this is most brave;
That I . . .
        the live son of a dead father
Doomed by my living breath itself to die

Must, like a whore, unpack my heart with words

124

Why must I speak of it? Why must I always
Stoop from this decent silence to this phrase
That makes a posture of my hurt? Why must I
Say I suffer? . . . or write out these words
For eyes to stare at that shall soon as mine
Or little after me go thick and lose
The light too, or for solemn fettered fools
To judge if I said neatly what I said? —
Make verses! . . . ease myself at the soiled stool   *Hamlet . . .*
That's common to so swollen many! . . . shout   *sole.*
For hearing in the world's thick dirty ear! . . .
Expose my scabs! . . . crowd forward among those
That beg for fame, that for so little praise
As pays a dog off will go stiff and tell
Their loss, lust, sorrow, anguish! . . . match
My grief with theirs! . . . compel the public prize
For deepest feeling and put on the bays! . . .
Oh shame, for shame to suffer it, to make
A skill of harm, a business of despair,
And like a barking ape betray us all
For itch of notice.
                    Oh be still, be still,
Be dumb, be silent only. Seal your mouth.
Take place upon this edge of shadow where
The stale scene's acted to the empty skies.
Observe the constellations. Watch the face
Of heaven if it change to what it sees.
Spy on the moon. Be cunning.
                              And be still.
We have that duty to each other here
To fear in secret. For it is not known.
The dreams that trouble us may be the shape
Of ill within that by a faulted eye
Abuses us to damn us.

I'll have grounds
More relative than this . . .

9

The Play.

Bearing the long lance, their banners before them
Frayed to the painted pole, the reins slung
Loose at the neck, knees guiding at withers,
The Men, the Cloth-Clad Race, the People of Horses,
Move out of the East with the turning of seasons.
Westward they move with the sun. Their smoke hangs
Under the unknown skies at evening. The stars
Go down before them into the new lands.
Behind them the dust falls, the streams flow clear again,
Vultures rise from the stripped bones in the sand.
Slowly they move. The moons change. The sun changes.
The mares foal at their times. Girls are delivered
Screaming at dark in the skin tents. The harvests
Of dry seed fall in the grass by the horse way.
Westward they move. They come at last to the passes
Down to the hot lands. One after one they
Go by the stones: the scared horses, the women
Wearing the hammered stuff at their brown throats,
The babes slung at the left breast, the little ones
Riding the stumbling rumps, beating the flies off.
They march on the bare stones. They come to the rivers.
Before them cities stand in the cool of the date palms.
The walls go down. There is smoke. They wait for the sum-
    mer
Watching the streams fail. They cross by the sand bar.
Their horses drown in the slime. The bodies of children
Float in the slow suck of the ooze. They go on.
They follow the desert quail, they perish for water.

The Crime
enacted:
the guilt
shows . . .

"The dumb
show
enters."

Years pass. They come to the mountains. Beyond are
Rich plains, the grasses blowing in sunlight.
They march through green. They go on, thousands and thou-
sands,
Taking the lands, killing the male, consuming
The fat earth. They live in the land. They are lords there.
They know the sun on their heads, the salt taste
Of the rain drip on their faces. They know the smell
Of their own flesh. They know with their heels what the earth
is.
They know how the earth was made and who has the law of it.
They remember many things among them in common.
They please each other with words: they touch with their
fingers.
They have their homes in the earth. They have named the
mountains.
They kiss their hands to the sun and the moon. They know,
When the leaves fall, the coming again of the summer.
Nevertheless they cannot be still. They go onward.
They come to the land's end. The sea is before them.
They watch the sun go down in the infinite waters.
Still they go on. They push to the surf fall. They build of
Trees ships. They sail to the scattering islands.
They dwell at the last shores. Years pass.   *"He poisons him i'*
    They vanish.   *the garden for's*
                                              estate. His
They disappear from the light leaving   *name's*
    behind them   *Gonzago . . . "*
Names in the earth, names of trees and of boulders,
Words for the planting of corn, leaving their tombs to
Fall in the thickets of alders, leaving their fear
Of the howling of dogs and the new moon at the shoulder,
Leaving the shape of the bird god who delivered
Men from the ancient ill, and under the loam their
Bronze blades, the broken shafts of their javelins.

They vanish. They disappear from the earth.

And the sea falls.

Loud on the empty beaches

and above . . .

The King rises. . . . Lights, lights, lights!

Lights! Lights! The same stars! The same moon
Still over the earth!

I say there were millions
Died like that and the usual constellations.

10

MacLeish goes up the
Stair built by the ancestors.

Night.

Sea-suck under in the well of stone.
Rat-smell. Silence.

to the door
Where all

O my prophetic soul
Shall be revenged, where I shall speak.

*The uncle King at
prayers. To him
Hamlet sword in
hand: withdraws.*

The streak of light along the floor.
The shining on the promised sill.
Look now! I will! The door swings
Open.

And go in . . .

Now might I do it pat . . .

Silence.

The candle fat upon the chair.
The false equation on the obscene wall.

And look and there is no one there!

Giggle of the wind along
The empty gutters of the sky.
Snigger of the faint stars. Catcalls.

And look behind the broken chair.
And look along the shadow on the
Wall. Rat turds. Spiders.

There was no one ever there!
And hear within the hollow room
The clock tick Hurry. And behold
Our eyes grow older in the glass.

What is it that we have to do?

11

Or play the strong boy, spit in the world's face, shout
Whore! Ghoul! Harpy! at her. Call her
    Jakes.
Call her corpse-eating planet, worm's gut.
    Show
For once the true shape of her and say out
The thing she lives upon. Dig graves up.
    Pull
The half too rotten mummies from their
    earth
Like cyst from skin-crease. Crack the swollen tombs
And heave the dead up stinking. Oh be hard!
Show her your own dead darling whose young bones
Rot through the jelly of their flesh beneath
This simpering pink rose . . .

The Queen's closet.
He rebukes his
mother's lechery:
grows violent: kills
through the hanging
at the back the old
ridiculous innocent
vain man in the
King's stead.

129

> *Peace! sit you down*
> *And let me wring your heart . . .*

Oh play the strong boy with the rest of them!
Be hard-boiled! Be bitter! Face the brassy
Broad indecent fact and with ironical
Contemptuous understanding take the world's
Scut in your hands and name it! Name its name!
Stare at her dugs with undeceived wise eyes until
The hypocrite green smile fades over and
The guilt look shows! Be foul mouthed! Be blunt!
Tell her the thing she feeds on and the thing
That dandles with her in the sweaty dark
To breed these beauties. Tell her of what seed
She gets her womb up and what festering lust
Lies stewing with her in the adulterous spring.
Stare in her eyes! Sneer! Swagger! Oh be
Hard!

   and rise

      and through the arras at the back
Stab to the bloody braving hilt

         and hear
The rat squeak after

     hear the stuck dust fall!

12

Protect us help us forgive us help give
Oh have pity on us —
We that watch the lights of the other worlds,
Openers of curtains eastward when the room
 is dark
And alone in bed remembering our childhood:
We that have felt the light of the moon on our faces . . .
Have pity upon us!

*Ophelia, crazed
by the death of
Polonius, laments,
forgetting him,
her loss.*

How should I your true love know
From another one?
 By his silence in our hearts,
 By the empty room where he is gone.

Who will overhear our soliloquies?
We are alone in this place.
 He is dead and gone, lady,
 He is dead and gone;
  At his head the no-more-winged air,
  At his heels — the stone.

They must tell us if it means well . . .

We have learned the answers, all the answers:
It is the question that we do not know.
We are not wise. We have a way of saying,
What is the meaning of life? No one has answered us.
We have looked behind the leaves too, all the leaves.

 . . . we are alone too much . . .

We know what our fathers were but not who we are
For the names change and the thorns grow over the houses.
We recognize ourselves by a wrong laugh;
By a trick we have of resembling something. Otherwise
There are strange words and a face in the mirror.
          We know
Something we have forgotten too that comforts us.

 Yea-sayeth me this earth, this green
 Like music doth consent to me,
 The moon that standeth on the hill,
 The hollow sea.

How shall we learn what it is that our hearts believe in?
And they say we all die but death is a mystery.
Death is a gesture away from us. Death is a cry
And no sound. They have their backs to us going.
We do not know if earth stifles or infinite
Winds have blown the words of it all away.

Come down into the crumbling loam,
Come home into the curving wave,
The dark, dear heart, will fondle thee,
The earth will kiss thee in the grave.

I hope all will be well. We must be patient . . .

We must find a word for it men can say at night,
And a face for the dark brow.
We must find a thing we can know for the world changes.
We must believe, for it is not always sure.

Why then, let's take it. Look, let's all smile once,
All smile into each other's smiling, all
As men smile into mirrors slowly smile . . .
That's better. That's more comfortable.
    We aren't
Afraid now. Are we? Take it. There.
    Like
        that!

Oh! have pity upon us . . .

13

Why — what men were they that beneath the moon
Had mortal flagging hearts so passionate?
Who heaped these tombs? Who wept so?
   Who piled up
These brags of marble anguish, these bronze
   groans,
These cromlech sorrows? Who had griefs so vast
That only mountains evened them, felt so
Deep pain, so suffered, with such iron tongue
Cried Wo that time still hears it? Why, what proud
What desperate nations were they that would leave
No legend after but the unwrit stones
That say they wept here? Or who painted then
These mutilated violent hands that still
Thrust back oblivion from the sad grave door?

Ophelia's burial.
He quarrels with
Laertes in the
grave: protests
his passion . . .

What men were they that did protest so loud,
What broken, salty blooded, aching hearts
That could not cease in silence, what hoarse grief
That must be shouted at the narrow stars?
What dying men were they . . .

        Nay, an thou'lt mouth
  I'll rant as well as thou . . .

          I'll swell my gullet,
Leap in the common grave and like a cock
Crow from the carrion. I'll tell the world.

I'll make a book of it. I'll leave my rare
Original uncopied dark heart pain
To choke up volumes and among the rocks

Cry I! I! I! forever. Look,
My face here. I have suffered. I have lost
A child, a brother, friends. And do foreknow
My own corruption. There are also stars
But not to listen to. And the autumn trees
That have the habit of the sun and die
Beforetimes often. And at night. And skies.
And seas. And evening. I can read in print
But not these letters. And I was not born
Without a death pain either but that's known,
That's equal and we all go back. I had
No friends but day times. No one called me. There was
No one always underneath the bed.
I'll tell you how I loved too, all my loves,
My bed quilts, bolsters, blankets, my hot hands,
My limbs, my rumps; my wretchedness: my lust,
My weakness later and lascivious dreams.
I'll tell you. Oh, I'll tell you. Lean your ear.
By God, I'll match them at it. I'll be stripped
Naked as eels are, gutted, laid on salt,
Sold in the fish stalls. I'll be ox-chine nude,
Quartered to cold bare bone. Look, behold me
Bearing my dead son's body to the grave.
See how I weep. How many of them all
Have lost a son as I have? Or see here:
The Marne side. Raining. I am cold with fear.
My bowels tremble. I go on. McHenry
Hands me his overcoat and dies. We dig the
Guns out sweating. I am very brave:
Magnificent. I vomit in my mask.
Or here. In Belgium. Spreading on my young,
My three times buried brother's stony grave
The bone-pale scented violets and feeling
Yield at my knees the earth: and crying out

134

Two words. In agony . . .
                              I'll tell it. Oh
I'll tell it. Louder! Shriek!
                              The sky's there!

14

It is time we should accept,
Taught by these wordy fools, the staged
Encounter and the game-pit rules.
Whilst we have slept we have grown old.   *To whom the eloquent*
Age is a coldness leaching through.   *Osrick: communicates*
We must consent now as all men   *the invitation of*
Whose rage is out of them must do,   *Laertes to the Play-*
Cancel this bloody feud, revoke   *ful Bout . . .*
All tears, all pain, and to the drum,
Trump, cannon and the general cheer
Fight with a shining foil the feigned
Antagonist for stoops of beer.
Why should we want revenge of harms
Not suffered in the public street,
Or risk with sharp and hurting arms
The real encounter kept at night
Alone where none will praise our art?

It is time we should accept . . .

Thou wouldst not think
How ill all's here about my heart!

EINSTEIN (1929)

Standing between the sun and moon preserves
A certain secrecy. Or seems to keep
Something inviolate if only that
His father was an ape.
                         Sweet music makes
All of his walls sound hollow and he hears
Sighs in the paneling and underfoot
Melancholy voices. So there is a door
Behind the seamless arras and within
A living something: — but no door that will
Admit the sunlight nor no windows where
The mirror moon can penetrate his bones
With cold deflection. He is small and tight
And solidly contracted into space
Opaque and perpendicular which blots
Earth with its shadow. And he terminates
In shoes which bearing up against the sphere   *Einstein*
Attract his concentration,   *upon a public*
                               bench Wednesday the
                               ninth contemplates
              for he ends   *finity*

If there why then no farther, as, beyond
Extensively the universe itself,
Or chronologically the two dates
Original and ultimate of time,

Nor could Jehovah and the million stars
Staring within their solitudes of light,
Nor all night's constellations be contained
Between his boundaries,
                              nor could the sun
Receive him nor his groping roots run down
Into the loam and steaming sink of time
Where coils the middle serpent and the ooze
Breeds maggots.
                    But it seems assured he ends
Precisely at his shoes in proof whereof
He can revolve in orbits opposite
The orbit of the earth and so refuse
All planetary converse. And he wears
Cloths that distinguish him from what is not
His own circumference, as first a coat
Shaped to his back or modeled in reverse
Of the surrounding cosmos and below
Trousers preserving his detachment from
The revolutions of the stars.

Einstein descends the
Hartmannsweilerstrasse

His hands
And face go naked and alone converse
With what encloses him, as rough and smooth
And sound and silence and the intervals
Of rippling ether and the swarming motes
Clouding a privy: move to them and make
Shadows that mirror them within his skull

138

In perpendiculars and curves and planes
And bodiless significances blurred
As figures undersea and images
Patterned from eddies of the air.
                              Which are
Perhaps not shadows but the thing itself
And may be understood.   *Einstein provisionally*
                                before a mirror accepts
                                the hypothesis of
                    Decorticate *subjective reality*
The petals of the enfolding world and leave
A world in reason which is in himself
And has his own dimensions. Here do trees
Adorn the hillside and hillsides enrich
The hazy marches of the sky and skies
Kindle and char to ashes in the wind,
And winds blow toward him from the verge, and suns
Rise on his dawn and on his dusk go down
And moons prolong his shadow. And he moves
Here as within a garden in a close
And where he moves the bubble of the world
Takes center and there circle round his head
Like golden flies in summer the gold stars.

                                        . . . rejects it

Disintegrates.

                    For suddenly he feels
The planet plunge beneath him, and a flare
Falls from the upper darkness to the dark
And awful shadows loom across the sky
That have no life from him and suns go out
And livid as a drowned man's face the moon
Floats to the lapsing surface of the night
And sinks discolored under.

                              So he knows
Less than a world and must communicate
Beyond his knowledge.   *Einstein unsuccessfully*
                                  after lunch attempts to
                                  enter, essaying synthesis
                                  with what's not he, the
            Outstretched on the earth   *Bernese Oberland*
He plunges both his arms into the swirl
Of what surrounds him but the yielding grass
Excludes his finger tips and the soft soil
Will not endure confusion with his hands
Nor will the air receive him nor the light
Dissolve their difference but recoiling turns
Back from his touch. By which denial he can
Crawl on the earth and sense the opposing sun
But not make answer to them.
                              Put out leaves
And let the old remembering wind think through
A green intelligence or under sea
Float out long filaments of amber in
The numb and wordless revery of tides.

In autumn the black branches dripping rain
Bruise his uncovered bones and in the spring
His swollen tips are gorged with aching blood
That bursts the laurel.
                              But although they seize
His sense he has no name for them, no word
To give them meaning and no utterance
For what they say. Feel the new summer's sun
Crawl up the warmed relaxing hide of earth
And weep for his lost youth, his childhood home
And a wide water on an inland shore!
Or to the night's mute asking in the blood
Give back a girl's name and three notes together!

                              140

He cannot think the smell of after rain
Nor close his thought around the long smooth lag
And falter of a wind, nor bring to mind
Dusk and the whippoorwill.

*Einstein dissolved in
violins invades the
molecular structure of
F. P. Paepke's Sommer-
garten. Is repulsed*

But violins
Split out of trees and strung to tone can sing
Strange nameless words that image to the ear
What has no waiting image in the brain.

She plays in darkness and the droning wood
Dissolves to reverberations of a world
Beating in waves against him till his sense
Trembles to rhythm and his naked brain
Feels without utterance in form the flesh
Of dumb and incommunicable earth,
And knows at once, and without knowledge how,
The stroke of the blunt rain, and blind receives
The sun.
                When he a moment occupies
The hollow of himself and like an air
Pervades all other.
                But the violin
Presses its dry insistence through the dream
That swims above it, shivering its speech
Back to a rhythm that becomes again
Music and vaguely ravels into sound.

*To Einstein asking at the
gate of stone none opens*

So then there is no speech that can resolve
Their texture to clear thought and enter them.

The Virgin of Chartres whose bleaching bones still wear
The sapphires of her glory knew a word —

141

That now is three round letters like the three
Round empty staring punctures in a skull.
And there were words in Rome once and one time
Words at Eleusis.

                    Now there are no words
Nor names to name them and they will not speak
But grope against his groping touch and throw
The long unmeaning shadows of themselves
Across his shadow and resist his sense.

*Einstein hearing behind
the wall of the Grand
Hôtel du Nord the stars
discovers the Back Stair*

Why then if they resist destroy them. Dumb,
Yet speak them in their elements. Whole,
Break them to reason.

                  He lies upon his bed
Exerting on Arcturus and the moon
Forces proportional inversely to
The squares of their remoteness and conceives
The universe.

        Atomic.

              He can count
Ocean in atoms and weigh out the air
In multiples of one and subdivide
Light to its numbers.

            If they will not speak
Let them be silent in their particles.
Let them be dead and he will lie among
Their dust and cipher them — undo the signs
Of their unreal identities and free
The pure and single factor of all sums —
Solve them to unity.

          Democritus
Scooped handfuls out of stones and like the sea
Let earth run through his fingers. Well, he too,

He can achieve obliquity and learn
The cold distortion of the winter's sun
That breaks the surfaces of summer.

*Einstein on the
terrasse of The
Acacias forces the
secret door*

                        Stands
Facing the world upon a windy slope
And with his mind relaxes the stiff forms
Of all he sees until the heavy hills
Impend like rushing water and the earth
Hangs on the steep and momentary crest
Of overflowing rain.
                        Overflow!
Sweep over into movement and dissolve
All differences in the indifferent flux!
Crumble to eddyings of dust and drown
In change the thing that changes!
                        There begins
A vague unquiet in the fallow ground,
A seething in the grass, a bubbling swirl
Over the surface of the fields that spreads
Around him gathering until the green
Boils and under frothy loam the rocks
Ferment and simmer and like thinning smoke
The trees melt into nothing.
                        Still he stands
Watching the vortex widen and involve
In swirling dissolution the whole earth
And circle through the skies till swaying time
Collapses, crumpling into dark the stars,
And motion ceases and the sifting world
Opens beneath.
                        When he shall feel infuse
His flesh with the rent body of all else

143

And spin within his opening brain the motes
Of suns and worlds and spaces.

Einstein enters

                        Like a foam
His flesh is withered and his shriveling
And ashy bones are scattered on the dark.
But still the dark denies him. Still withstands
The dust his penetration and flings back
Himself to answer him.
                  Which seems to keep
Something inviolate. A living something.

CINEMA OF A MAN

The earth is bright though the boughs of the moon like a
    dead planet
It is silent it has no sound the sun is on it
It shines in the dark like a white stone in a deep meadow
It is round above it is flattened under with shadow

* * * *

He sits in the rue St. Jacques at the iron table
It is dusk it is growing cold the roof stone glitters on the gable
The taxis turn in the rue du Pot de Fer
The gas jets brighten one by one behind the windows of the
    stair

* * * *

This is his face the chin long the eyes looking

* * * *

Now he sits on the porch of the Villa Serbelloni
He is eating white bread and brown honey

The sun is hot on the lake there are boats rowing
It is spring the rhododendrons are out the wind is blowing

* * * *

Above Bordeaux by the canal
His shadow passes on the evening wall
His legs are crooked at the knee he has one shoulder
His arms are long he vanishes among the shadows of the alder.

* * * *

He wakes in the Grand Hotel Vierjahreszeiten
It is dawn the carts go by the curtains whiten
He sees her yellow hair she has neither father nor mother
Her name is Ann she has had him now and before another

* * * *

This is his face in the light of the full moon
His skin is white and grey like the skin of a quadroon
His head is raised to the sky he stands staring
His mouth is still his face is still his eyes are staring

* * * *

He walks with Ernest in the streets in Saragossa
They are drunk their mouths are hard they say qué cosa
They say the cruel words they hurt each other
Their elbows touch their shoulders touch their feet go on and
    on together

* * * *

Now he is by the sea at St.-Tropez
The pines roar in the wind it is hot it is noonday
He is naked he swims in the blue under the sea water
His limbs are drowned in the dapple of sun like the limbs of
    the sea's daughter

* * * *

146

Now he is in Chicago he is sleeping
The footstep passes on the stone the roofs are dripping
The door is closed the walls are dark the shadows deepen
His head is motionless upon his arm his hand is open

* * * *

Those are the cranes above the Karun River
They fly across the night their wings go over
They cross Orion and the south star of the Wain
A wave has broken in the sea beyond the coast of Spain

MEMORY GREEN

Yes and when the warm unseasonable weather
Comes at the year's end of the next late year
And the southwest wind that smells of rain and summer
Strips the huge branches of their dying leaves,

And you at dusk along the Friedrichstrasse
Or you in Paris on the windy quay
Shuffle the shallow fallen leaves before you
Thinking the thoughts that like the grey clouds change,

You will not understand why suddenly sweetness
Fills in your heart nor the tears come to your eyes:
You will stand in the June-warm wind and the leaves falling:
When was it so before, you will say, With whom?

You will not remember this at all: you will stand there
Feeling the wind on your throat, the wind in your sleeves,
You will smell the dead leaves in the grass of a garden:
You will close your eyes: With whom, you will say,

Ah where?

"NOT MARBLE NOR THE GILDED MONUMENTS"

for Adele

The praisers of women in their proud and beautiful poems,
Naming the grave mouth and the hair and the eyes,
Boasted those they loved should be forever remembered:
These were lies.

The words sound but the face in the Istrian sun is forgotten.
The poet speaks but to her dead ears no more.
The sleek throat is gone — and the breast that was troubled to
    listen:
Shadow from door.

Therefore I will not praise your knees nor your fine walking
Telling you men shall remember your name as long
As lips move or breath is spent or the iron of English
Rings from a tongue.

I shall say you were young, and your arms straight, and your
    mouth scarlet:
I shall say you will die and none will remember you:
Your arms change, and none remember the swish of your
    garments,
Nor the click of your shoe.

Not with my hand's strength, not with difficult labor
Springing the obstinate words to the bones of your breast
And the stubborn line to your young stride and the breath to
    your breathing
And the beat to your haste
Shall I prevail on the hearts of unborn men to remember.

(What is a dead girl but a shadowy ghost
Or a dead man's voice but a distant and vain affirmation
Like dream words most)

Therefore I will not speak of the undying glory of women.
I will say you were young and straight and your skin fair
And you stood in the door and the sun was a shadow of leaves
    on your shoulders
And a leaf on your hair —

I will not speak of the famous beauty of dead women:
I will say the shape of a leaf lay once on your hair.
Till the world ends and the eyes are out and the mouths
    broken
Look! It is there!

RETURN

When shall I behold again the cold limbed bare breasted
Daughters of the ocean I have not seen so long

Then it was always in sunshine
                         then they were running

There was this thunder of surf then to the left of us
Pines to the right
            cicadas
               We came alone
We left our people over the hill in the vineyard
There were sea birds here when we came . . .

149

                    But I remember
Sand there where the stones are and isles to seaward

It may be this was all in another land

Or it may be I have forgotten now how the sea was

YOU, ANDREW MARVELL

            And here face down beneath the sun
            And here upon earth's noonward height
            To feel the always coming on
            The always rising of the night:

            To feel creep up the curving east
            The earthy chill of dusk and slow
            Upon those under lands the vast
            And ever climbing shadow grow

            And strange at Ecbatan the trees
            Take leaf by leaf the evening strange
            The flooding dark about their knees
            The mountains over Persia change

            And now at Kermanshah the gate
            Dark empty and the withered grass
            And through the twilight now the late
            Few travelers in the westward pass

And Baghdad darken and the bridge
Across the silent river gone
And through Arabia the edge
Of evening widen and steal on

And deepen on Palmyra's street
The wheel rut in the ruined stone
And Lebanon fade out and Crete
High through the clouds and overblown

And over Sicily the air
Still flashing with the landward gulls
And loom and slowly disappear
The sails above the shadowy hulls

And Spain go under and the shore
Of Africa the gilded sand
And evening vanish and no more
The low pale light across that land

Nor now the long light on the sea:

And here face downward in the sun
To feel how swift how secretly
The shadow of the night comes on . . .

SALUTE

O Sun! Instigator of cocks!
                    Thou . . .

Quickener! Maker of sound in the leaves,
                              and of running
Stir over the curve of the earth like the ripple of
Scarlet under the skin of the lizard,
                    Hunter!
Starter of westward birds!

                    Be heard
Sun on our mountains! Oh be now
Loud with us! Wakener, let the wings
Descend of dawn on our roof-trees! Bring
Bees now! Let the cicadas sing
In the heat on the gummed trunks of the pine!
Make now the winds! Take thou the orchards!

    (We that have heard the beat of our hearts in the silence
    And the count of the clock all night at our listening ears)
                    Be near!
    Shake the branches of day on our roofs!
                              Oh

Be over us!

IMMORTAL AUTUMN

I speak this poem now with grave and level voice
In praise of autumn, of the far-horn-winding fall.

I praise the flower-barren fields, the clouds, the tall
Unanswering branches where the wind makes sullen noise.

I praise the fall: it is the human season.
                                Now
No more the foreign sun does meddle at our earth,
Enforce the green and bring the fallow land to birth,
Nor winter yet weigh all with silence the pine bough,

But now in autumn with the black and outcast crows
Share we the spacious world: the whispering year is gone:
There is more room to live now: the once secret dawn
Comes late by daylight and the dark unguarded goes.

Between the mutinous brave burning of the leaves
And winter's covering of our hearts with his deep snow
We are alone: there are no evening birds: we know
The naked moon: the tame stars circle at our eaves.

It is the human season. On this sterile air
Do words outcarry breath: the sound goes on and on.
I hear a dead man's cry from autumn long since gone.

I cry to you beyond upon this bitter air.

TOURIST DEATH

for Sylvia Beach

I promise you these days and an understanding
Of light in the twigs after sunfall.

                        Do you ask to descend
At dawn in a new world with wet on the pavements
And a yawning cat and the fresh odor of dew
And red geraniums under the station windows
And doors wide and brooms and sheets on the railing
And a whistling boy and the sun like shellac on the street?

Do you ask to embark at night at the third hour
Sliding away in the dark and the sails of the fishermen
Slack in the light of the lanterns and black seas
And the tide going down and the splash and drip of the
    hawser?

Do you ask something to happen as spring does
In a night in a small time and nothing the same again?
Life is neither a prize box nor a terminus.
Life is a haft that has fitted the palms of many,
Dark as the helved oak,
                  with sweat bitter,
Browned by numerous hands:
                        Death is the rest of it.
Death is the same bones and the trees nearer.
Death is a serious thing like the loam smell
Of the plowed earth in the fall.
                      Death is here:
Not in another place, not among strangers.
Death is under the moon here and the rain.

I promise you old signs and a recognition
Of sun in the seething grass and the wind's rising.

Do you ask more?
                Do you ask to travel for ever?

LAND'S END

for Adrienne Monnier

I
GEOGRAPHY OF THIS TIME

The peninsulas are held by an ancient people
And races skillful in iron, makers of amulets
Keep the sea isles.

These are they who interpret the flight of birds,
Who foretell the dawn from the light in the west at sunset.
These have been long in the earth, they know the seasons,
They know by the stinging of flies when the rains come,
They smell the snow on a dry wind, they are wise
In the changing of gales when the shape of the moon changes,
They stir in their sleep at night when the tide turns:

Only they speak in the tongue of another country.
There are names in their speech of fruits unknown in these
    valleys.
Also their gods are carved with the muzzles of jackals,
And their proverbs are proverbs made in a dry place:
Their festivals do not keep the days of the sea.
Their word for the sea is a word meaning the sorrow.

Only their songs are of high lands beyond mountains:
Their songs are of horses grazing a wide land,
Of stars through the roofs of tents woven of horsehair.
Theirs they say were the wars fought by the heroes:
Theirs were the battles the shouting of which comes over us
Like a sound of sleet in the dead grass in the marshes.

At the time of the floods in spring they have seen on the rivers
Branches bearing a round leaf and bridles
Knotted of straw and the wooden bow of a saddle.
They have seen the bodies of birds of a white plumage.
They have smelled the reek of the pastures in stale pools.
(The sea smells in spring of the thaw water . . .)
They draw their nets in spring by the brown streams.

II
EXHORTATION TO THE LIVING

                    that here by this unremembering
Sea O my people
                    and we have not known
Always the sea sound nor the taste of salt
Always
            rebuild these roofs of stone
                                    can we
O winter starved
                    eaters of fish guts
                                    blind
With reeking sod fires in the windy room
Can we return no more
                    take ship and call
The long rope over
                    ride the landward surge
High on the sea bar and where first the blue

Streaks with the dribble of the brown fresh foam
Drive up the channel with all oars
                              can we
No more return
                    that on these beaches O
Sea scalded eyes
                    salt broken nails
                                    rebuild
O Miserable the loose stones that were
Houses before us of forgotten men
On these last shores
                    can we no more
                                    no more
Return again to our own lands

III
RESPONSE OF THE ANCESTORS

These men do not speak, they sit
Right and left of the coals slicing
Thongs from seal leather, cleaning their long
Knives; they listen as men to bat talk,
Men to the whimper of dead old ones.
Ho! they are free, they can sleep where they will,
They are not afraid as we are here
For they know what the world is: they have seen
Actual shapes, things solid,
Not visions, not fog shapes only, not
Glister under the stone of fish gill
Nor images hanging in pools among
The sea anemones deeper than clouds are
Down or the underneath wings of the gulls go.

157

Sounds they have heard too, not the wave sound:
Not the no sound of the wind
Nor tide moan under drowned ledges —
Cry of gulls, gulls crying from
Water . . . No! but real things:
Riders, running of dogs, deer-fall.
Weight they have had in their hands of dead
Birds, of the breasts softly of women —
No! and love, the weed smell of it:
Front against front, not hair blown
Dark over eyes in a dream and the mouth gone.

These men do not speak; we have told them
Tales we know of the last seas,
Tales of the great waves and the wind there:
They listen, they do not speak, they have come
From the old lands of our people:
Hunters they are from father to son,
Herdsmen, drivers of plowshares.
These are men without names; they are called
After their lands, after their handwork.
Men will remember the smell of their garments,
Not as of us the sound only
Of words over earth door; not as the unborn
Dead shall remember the sounds we were called by.

These men do not speak: they have seen
Shapes solid and real, live things.

REPROACH TO DEAD POETS

You who have spoken words in the earth,
You who have broken the silence,
                              utterers,
Sayers in all lands to all peoples,
Writers in candle soot on the skins
Of rams for those who come after you,
                              voices
Echoed at night in the arched doors,
And at noon in the shadow of fig trees,
Hear me!
                    Were there not
Words?
Were there not words to tell with?
Were there not leaf sounds in the mouths
Of women from over-sea, and a call
Of birds on the lips of the children of strangers?
Were there not words in all languages —
In many tongues the same thing differently,
The name cried out, Thalassa! the sea!
The Sea!
The sun and moon character representing
Brightness, the night sound of the wind for
Always, for ever and ever, the verb
Created after the speech of crickets —
          Were there not words to tell with?
                              — to tell
What lands these are:
                    What are these
Lights through the night leaves and these voices
Crying among us as winds rise,

Or whence, of what race we are that dwell with them?

Were there not words to tell with,
                                    you that have told
The kings' names and the hills remembered for battles?

MEN

(on a phrase of Apollinaire)

Our history is grave noble and tragic.
We trusted the look of the sun on the green leaves.
We built our towns of stone with enduring ornaments.
We worked the hard flint for basins of water.

We believed in the feel of the earth under us.
We planted corn grapes apple-trees rhubarb.
Nevertheless we knew others had died.
Everything we have done has been faithful and dangerous.

We believed in the promises made by the brows of women.
We begot children at night in the warm wool.
We comforted those who wept in fear on our shoulders.
Those who comforted us had themselves vanished.

We fought at the dikes in the bright sun for the pride of it.
We beat drums and marched with music and laughter.
We were drunk and lay with our fine dreams in the straw.
We saw the stars through the hair of lewd women.

Our history is grave noble and tragic.
Many of us have died and are not remembered.
Many cities are gone and their channels broken.
We have lived a long time in this land and with honor.

EPISTLE TO BE LEFT IN THE EARTH

. . . It is colder now,
                 there are many stars,
                             we are drifting
North by the Great Bear,
                 the leaves are falling,
The water is stone in the scooped rocks,
                         to southward
Red sun grey air:
             the crows are
Slow on their crooked wings,
                 the jays have left us:
Long since we passed the flares of Orion.
Each man believes in his heart he will die.
Many have written last thoughts and last letters.
None know if our deaths are now or forever:
None know if this wandering earth will be found.

We lie down and the snow covers our garments.
I pray you,
         you (if any open this writing)
Make in your mouths the words that were our names.
I will tell you all we have learned,
                     I will tell you everything:
The earth is round,
            there are springs under the orchards,
The loam cuts with a blunt knife,
                 beware of
Elms in thunder,
           the lights in the sky are stars —
We think they do not see,
               we think also
The trees do not know nor the leaves of the grasses hear us:

The birds too are ignorant.
                              Do not listen.
Do not stand at dark in the open windows.
We before you have heard this:
                              they are voices:
They are not words at all but the wind rising.
Also none among us has seen God.
(. . . We have thought often
The flaws of sun in the late and driving weather
Pointed to one tree but it was not so.)
As for the nights I warn you the nights are dangerous:
The wind changes at night and the dreams come.

It is very cold,
                    there are strange stars near Arcturus,

Voices are crying an unknown name in the sky

AMERICAN LETTER
   for Gerald Murphy

The wind is east but the hot weather continues,
Blue and no clouds, the sound of the leaves thin,
Dry like the rustling of paper, scored across
With the slate-shrill screech of the locusts.
                              The tossing of
Pines is the low sound. In the wind's running
The wild carrots smell of the burning sun.
Why should I think of the dolphins at Capo di Mele?
Why should I see in my mind the taut sail
And the hill over St.-Tropez and your hand on the tiller?

162

Why should my heart be troubled with palms still?
I am neither a sold boy nor a Chinese official
Sent to sicken in Pa for some Lo-Yang dish.
This is my own land, my sky, my mountain:
This — not the humming pines and the surf and the sound
At the Ferme Blanche, nor Port Cros in the dusk and the har-
    bor
Floating the motionless ship and the sea-drowned star.
I am neither Po Chü-i nor another after
Far from home, in a strange land, daft
For the talk of his own sort and the taste of his lettuces.
This land is my native land. And yet
I am sick for home for the red roofs and the olives,
And the foreign words and the smell of the sea fall.
How can a wise man have two countries?
How can a man have the earth and the wind and want
A land far off, alien, smelling of palm-trees
And the yellow gorse at noon in the long calms?

It is a strange thing — to be an American.
Neither an old house it is with the air
Tasting of hung herbs and the sun returning
Year after year to the same door and the churn
Making the same sound in the cool of the kitchen
Mother to son's wife, and the place to sit
Marked in the dusk by the worn stone at the wellhead —
That — nor the eyes like each other's eyes and the skull
Shaped to the same fault and the hands' sameness.
Neither a place it is nor a blood name.
America is West and the wind blowing.
America is a great word and the snow,
A way, a white bird, the rain falling,
A shining thing in the mind and the gulls' call.
America is neither a land nor a people,

A word's shape it is, a wind's sweep —
America is alone: many together,
Many of one mouth, of one breath,
Dressed as one — and none brothers among them:
Only the taught speech and the aped tongue.
America is alone and the gulls calling.

It is a strange thing to be an American.
It is strange to live on the high world in the stare
Of the naked sun and the stars as our bones live.
Men in the old lands housed by their rivers.
They built their towns in the vales in the earth's shelter.
We first inhabit the world. We dwell
On the half earth, on the open curve of a continent.
Sea is divided from sea by the day-fall. The dawn
Rides the low east with us many hours;
First are the capes, then are the shorelands, now
The blue Appalachians faint at the day rise;
The willows shudder with light on the long Ohio:
The Lakes scatter the low sun: the prairies
Slide out of dark: in the eddy of clean air
The smoke goes up from the high plains of Wyoming:
The steep Sierras arise: the struck foam
Flames at the wind's heel on the far Pacific.
Already the noon leans to the eastern cliff:
The elms darken the door and the dust-heavy lilacs.

It is strange to sleep in the bare stars and to die
On an open land where few bury before us:
(From the new earth the dead return no more.)
It is strange to be born of no race and no people.
In the old lands they are many together. They keep
The wise past and the words spoken in common.
They remember the dead with their hands, their mouths dumb

They answer each other with two words in their meeting.
They live together in small things. They eat
The same dish, their drink is the same and their proverbs.
Their youth is like. They are like in their ways of love.
They are many men. There are always others beside them.
Here it is one man and another and wide
On the darkening hills the faint smoke of the houses.
Here it is one man and the wind in the boughs.

Therefore our hearts are sick for the south water.
The smell of the gorse comes back to our night thought.
We are sick at heart for the red roofs and the olives;
We are sick at heart for the voice and the foot fall . . .

Therefore we will not go though the sea call us.

This, this is our land, this is our people,
This that is neither a land nor a race. We must reap
The wind here in the grass for our soul's harvest:
Here we must eat our salt or our bones starve.
Here we must live or live only as shadows.
This is our race, we that have none, that have had
Neither the old walls nor the voices around us,
This is our land, this is our ancient ground —
The raw earth, the mixed bloods and the strangers,
The different eyes, the wind, and the heart's change.
These we will not leave though the old call us.
This is our country-earth, our blood, our kind.
Here we will live our years till the earth blind us —

The wind blows from the east. The leaves fall.
Far off in the pines a jay rises.
The wind smells of haze and the wild ripe apples.

I think of the masts at Cette and the sweet rain.

Be proud New-York of your prize domes
And your docks & the size of your doors & your dancing
Elegant clean big girls & your
Niggers with narrow heels & the blue on their
Bad mouths & your bars & your automo-
biles in the struck steel light & your
Bright Jews & your sorrow-sweet singing
Tunes & your signs wincing out in the wet
Cool shine & the twinges of
Green against evening . . .

When the towns go down there are stains of
Rust on the stone shores and illegible
Coins and a rhyme remembered of
                                    swans, say,
Or birds or leaves or a horse or fabulous
Bull forms or a falling of gold upon
Softness.

Be proud City of Glass of your
Brass roofs & the bright peaks of your
Houses!
        Town that stood to your knees in the
Sea water be proud, be proud,
Of your high gleam on the sea!

                        Do they think,
                                Town,
They must rhyme your name with the name of a
Talking beast that the place of your walls be remembered?

166

Conquistador (1932)

DEDICATION

"O frati," dissi, "che per cento milia
Perigli siete giunti all' occidente"

The Divine Comedy
Inferno, Canto xxvi, lines 112, 113

PROLOGUE

And the way goes on in the worn earth:

and we (others) —

What are the dead to us in our better fortune?
They have left us the roads made and the walls standing:
They have left us the chairs in the rooms:

what is there more of them —

Either their words in the stone or their graves in the land
Or the rusted tang in the turf-root where they fought —
Has truth against us?
                    (And another man

Where the wild geese rise from Michigan the water
Veering the clay bluff: in another wind. . . .)

Surely the will of God in the earth alters:

Time done is dark as are sleep's thickets:
Dark is the past: none waking walk there:
Neither may live men of those waters drink:

And their speech they have left upon the coins to mock
    us:
And the weight of their skulls at our touch is a shuck's
    weight:
And their rains are dry and the sound of their leaves
    fallen:

(We that have still the sun and the green places)
And they care nothing for living men: and the honey of
Sun is slight in their teeth as a seed's taste —

What are the dead to us in the world's wonder?
Why (and again now) on their shadowy beaches
Pouring before them the slow painful blood

Do we return to force the truthful speech of them
Shrieking like snipe along their gusty sand
And stand: and as the dark ditch fills beseech them

(Reaching across the surf their fragile hands) to
Speak to us?
                 as by that other ocean
The elder shadows to the sea-borne man

Guarding the ram's flesh and the bloody dole. . . .
Speak to me Conquerors!
                       But not as they!
Bring not those others with you whose new-closed

(O Brothers! Bones now in the witless rain!)
And weeping eyes remember living men:
(Not Anticlea! Not Elpenor's face!)

Bring not among you hither the new dead —
Lest they should wake and the unwilling lids
Open and know me — and the not-known end! . . . .

And Sándoval comes first and the Pálos wind
Stirs in the young hair: and the smoky candle
Shudders the sick face and the fevered skin:

And still the dead feet come: and Alvarádo
Clear in that shadow as a faggot kindled:
The brave one: stupid: and the face he had

Shining with good looks: his skin pink:
His legs warped at the knee like the excellent horseman:
And gentleman's ways and the tail of the sword swinging:

And Olíd the good fighter: his face coarse:
His teeth clean as a dog's: the lip wrinkled:
Oléa — so do the winds follow unfortune —

Oléa with the blade drawn and the clinging
Weeds about him and the broken hands:
And still they come: and from the shadow **fixes**

Eyes against me a mute armored man
Staring as wakened sleeper into embers:
This is Cortés that took the famous land:

The eye-holes narrow to the long night's ebbing:
The grey skin crawls beneath the scanty beard:
Neither the eyes nor the sad mouth remember:

Other and nameless are there shadows here
Cold in the little light as winter crickets:
Torpid with old death: under sullen years

Numb as pale spiders in the blind leaves hidden:
These to the crying voices do not stir:
So still are trees the climbing stars relinquish:

And last and through the weak dead comes — the uncer-
    tain
Fingers before him on the sightless air —
An old man speaking: and the wind-blown words

Blur and the mouth moves and before the staring
Eyes go shadows of that ancient time:
So does a man speak from the dream that bears his

Sleeping body with it and the cry
Comes from a great way off as over water —
As the sea-bell's that the veering wind divides:

(And the sound runs on the valleys of the water:)

And the light returns as in past time
                              as in evenings
Distant with yellow summer on the straw —

As the light in America comes: without leaves. . . .

BERNÁL DÍAZ' PREFACE TO HIS BOOK

"That which I have myself seen and the fighting". . . .

And I am an ignorant man: and this priest this
Gómara with the school-taught skip to his writing

The pompous Latin the appropriate feasts
The big names the imperial decorations
The beautiful battles and the brave deceased

The onward marches the wild Indian nations
The conquests sieges sorties wars campaigns
(And one eye always on the live relations) —

He with his famous history of New Spain —
This priest is a learned man: is not ignorant:
And I am poor: without gold: gainless:

173

My lands deserts in Guatemala: my fig-tree the
Spiked bush: my grapes thorns: my children
Half-grown: sons with beards: the big one

Breaking the small of his back in the brothel thills
And a girl to be married and all of them snarling at home
With the Indian look in their eyes like a cat killing:

And this Professor Francisco López de Gómara
Childless; not poor: and I am old: over eighty:
Stupid with sleepless nights: unused to the combing of

Words clean of the wool while the tale waits:
And he is a youthful man: a sound one: lightened with
Good sleep: skilled in the pen's plaiting —

I am an ignorant old sick man: blind with the
Shadow of death on my face and my hands to lead me:
And he not ignorant: not sick —
                                                but I

Fought in those battles! These were my own deeds!
These names he writes of mouthing them out as a man
        would
Names in Herodotus — dead and their wars to read —

These were my friends: these dead my companions:
I: Bernál Díaz: called del Castíllo:
Called in the time of my first fights El Galán:

I here in the turn of the day in the feel of
Darkness to come now: moving my chair with the change:
Thinking too much these times how the doves would
        wheel at

174

Evening over my youth and the air's strangeness:
Thinking too much of my old town of Medina
And the Spanish dust and the smell of the true rain:

I: poor: blind in the sun: I have seen
With these eyes those battles: I saw Montezúma:
I saw the armies of Mexico marching the leaning

Wind in their garments: the painted faces: the plumes
Blown on the light air: I saw that city:
I walked at night on those stones: in the shadowy rooms

I have heard the chink of my heel and the bats twittering:
I: poor as I am: I was young in that country:
These words were my life: these letters written

Cold on the page with the split ink and the shunt of the
Stubborn thumb: these marks at my fingers:
These are the shape of my own life. . . .

                            and I hunted the

Unknown birds in the west with their beautiful wings!

Old men should die with their time's span:
The sad thing is not death: the sad thing

Is the life's loss out of earth when the living vanish:
All that was good in the throat: the hard going:
The marching singing in sunshine: the showery land:

The quick loves: the sleep: the waking: the blowing of
Winds over us: all this that we knew:
All this goes out at the end as the flowing of

Water carries the leaves down: and the few —
Three or four there are of us still that remember it —
Perish: and that time's stopt like a stale tune:

And the bright young masters with their bitter treble
Understanding it all like an old game!
And the pucker of art on their lips like the pip of a
    lemon! —

"The tedious veteran jealous of his fame!"
What is my fame or the fame of these my companions?
Their tombs are the bellies of Indians: theirs are the
    shameful

Graves in the wild earth: in the Godless sand:
None know the place of their bones: as for mine
Strangers will dig my grave in a stony land:

Even my sons have the strangeness of dark kind in them:
Indian dogs will bark at dusk by my sepulchre:
What is my fame! But those days: the shine of the

Sun in that time: the wind then: the step
Of the moon over those leaf-fallen nights: the sleet in the
Dry grass: the smell of the dust where we slept —

These things were real: these suns had heat in them:
This was brine in the mouth: bitterest foam:
Earth: water to drink: bread to be eaten —

Not the sound of a word like the writing of Gómara:
Not a past time: a year: the name of a
Battle lost — "and the Emperor Charles came home

"That year: and that was the year the same
"They fought in Flanders and the Duke was hung — "
The dates of empire: the dry skull of fame!

No but our lives: the days of our lives: we were young
      then:
The strong sun was standing in deep trees:
We drank at the springs: the thongs of our swords un-
      slung to it:

We saw that city on the inland sea:
Towers between: and the green-crowned Montezúma
Walking the gardens of shade: and the staggering bees:

And the girls bearing the woven baskets of bloom on their
Black hair: their breasts alive: and the hunters
Shouldering dangling herons with their ruffled plumes:

We were the first that found that famous country:
We marched by a king's name: we crossed the sierras:
Unknown hardships we suffered: hunger:

Death by the stone knife: thirst: we fared by the
Bitter streams: we came at last to that water:
Towers were steep upon the fluttering air:

We were the lords of it all. . . .
                              Now time has taught us:
Death has mastered us most: sorrow and pain
Sickness and evil days are our lives' lot:

Now even the time of our youth has been taken:
Now are our deeds words: our lives chronicles:
Afterwards none will think of the night rain. . . .

177

How shall a man endure the will of God and the
Days and the silence!
                        In the world before us
Neither in Cuba nor the isles beyond —

Not Fonséca himself the sagging whore —
Not the Council the Audience even the Indians —
Knew of a land to the west: they skirted the Floridas:

They ran the islands on the bare-pole winds:
They touched the Old Main and the midland shores:
They saw the sun go down at the gulf's beginning:

None had sailed to the west and returned till Córdova:
I went in that ship: Alvarez handled her:
Trusting to luck: keeping the evening before him:

Sighting after the third week land
And no report of a land there in that ocean:
The Indians clean: wearing the delicate bands:

Cape Catoche we called it: conës catoche —
So they cried to us over the sea flood:
Many idols they had for their devotion

Some of women: some coupled in sodomy
So we sailed on: we came to Campéchë:
There by the sweet pool they kindled the wood-fire:

Words they were saying like Castilán in their speech:
They warned us by signs to be gone when the logs
      charred:
So we turned from them down to the smooth beaches:

The boats followed us close in: we departed:
Afterwards there was a *nortë* with fine haze:
We stood for Pontonchán through the boil of the nar-
   rows:

There they attacked us crossing the green of the maize
   fields:
Me they struck thrice and they killed fifty
And all were hurt and two taken crazy with

Much pain and it blew and the dust lifted
And the thirst cracked the tongues in our mouths and
   before us the
Sea-corrupted pools where the river drifts:

And we turned back and the wind drove us to Florida:
There in the scooped sand in the withered bed —
There by the sea they encountered us threatening war:

So we returned to the islands half dead:
And Córdova did die: and we wrote to Velásquez —
Diégo the Governor — writing it out: and we said —

"Excellence: there are lands in the west: the pass is
"Clean sailing: the scuts of the men are covered:
"The houses are masonry: gold they have: baskets

"Painted with herbs: the women are chaste in love" —
Much else of the kind I cannot remember:
And Velásquez took the credit for this discovery:

And all we had was our wounds: and enough of them:
And Fonséca Bishop of Búrgos (for so he was called)
President of the Council: he write to the Emperor

179

Telling the wonderful news in a mule's volley
And not a word of our deeds or our pains or our battles:
And Charles gone: and Joanna the poor queen stalled

In Tordesíllas shaking the peas in a rattle:
And Barbarossa licking his chin in Algiers:
And trouble enough in Spain with all that

And the Cardinal dying and Sicily over the ears —
Trouble enough without new lands to be conquered and
Naked Indians taken and wild sheep sheared:

But as for us that returned from that westward country —
We could not lie in our towns for the sound of the sea:
We could not rest at all in our thoughts: we were young
    then:

We looked to the west: we remembered the foreign trees
Borne out on the tide from the unknown rivers
And the clouds like hills in the air our eyes had seen:

And Grijálva sailed next and we that were living —
We that had gear to our flesh and the gold to find
And an old pike in the stall with the haft to it slivered —

We signed on and we sailed by the first tide:
And we fought at Potonchán that voyage: I remember
The locusts covered the earth like a false shine to it:

They flew with a shrill sound like the arrow stem:
Often we took the whir of the darts for the locusts:
Often we left our shields from our mouths as they came:

I remember our fighting was much marred by the locusts:
And that voyage we came to the river Tabasco:
We saw the nets as we came in and the smoke of the

Sea over the bar: and we filled the casks there:
There first we heard of the farther land —
"Colúa" they said "Méjico" — we that were asking the

Gold there on that shore on the evening sand —
"Colúa" they said: pointing on toward the sunset:
They made a sign on the air with their solemn hands:

Afterward: north: on the sea: and the ships running
We saw the steep snow mountain on the sky:
We stared as dream-awakened men in wonder:

And that voyage it was we came to the island:
Well I remember the shore and the sound of that place
And the smoke smell on the dunes and the wind dying:

Well I remember the walls and the rusty taste of the
New-spilled blood in the air: many among us
Seeing the priests with their small and arrogant faces:

Seeing the dead boys' breasts and the idols hung with the
Dried shells of the hearts like the husks of cicadas
And their human eyeballs and their painted tongues

Cried out to the Holy Mother of God for it:
And some that stood there bore themselves the stone:
And some were eaten of wild beasts of their bodies:

And none of us all but had his heart foreknown the
Evil to come would have turned from the land then:
But the lives of men are covered and not shown —

181

Only late to the old at their time's ending
The land shows backward and the way is there:
And the next day we sailed and the sea was against us

And our bread was dirty with weevils and grown scarce
    and the
Rains began and the beans stank in the ovens
And we soldiers were thoroughly tired of sea-faring:

So we returned from that voyage with God's love:
And they talked about nothing else in the whole of Cuba:
And gentlemen sold their farms to go on discoveries:

And we that had fought in the marshes with no food —
We sat by the palms in the square in the green gloaming
With the delicate girls on our knees and the night to lose:

We that had fought in those lands. . . .
                        and the eloquent Gómara:
The quilled professors: the taught tongues of fame:
What have they written of us: the poor soldiers:

We that were wounded often for no pay:
We that died and were dumped cold in the bread sacks:
Bellies up: the birds at us: floating for days

And none remembering which it was that was dead there
Whether of Búrgos or Yúste or Villalár:
Where have they written our names? What have they
    said of us?

They call the towns for the kings that bear no scars:
They keep the names of the great for time to stare at —
The bishops rich-men generals cocks-at-arms:

Those with the glaze in their eyes and the fine bearing:
The born leaders of men: the resonant voices:

They give them the lands for their tombs: they call it
    America!

(And who has heard of Vespucci in this soil
Or down by the lee of the coast or toward the Havana?)
And we that fought here: that with heavy toil

Earthed up the powerful cities of this land —
What are we? When will our fame come?
An old man in a hill town
                              a handful of

Dust under the dry grass at Otúmba

Unknown names
                hands vanished
                                    faces

Many gone from the day
                        unspeakable numbers

Lives forgotten
                deeds honored in strangers

"That which I have myself seen and the fighting" . . .

THE TRUE HISTORY OF BERNÁL DÍAZ

THE ARGUMENT

Of that world's conquest and the fortunate wars:
Of the great report and expectation of honor:
How in their youth they stretched sail: how fared they

Westward under the wind: by wave wandered:
Shoaled ship at the last at the ends of ocean:
How they were marching in the lands beyond:

Of the difficult ways there were and the winter's snow:
Of the city they found in the good lands: how they lay in it:
How there were always the leaves and the days going:

Of the fear they had in their hearts for their lives' sake:
How there was neither the night nor the day sure: and the
Gage they took for their guard: and how evil came of it:

How they were dead and driven and endured:
How they returned with arms in the wet month:
How they destroyed that city: and the gourds were

Bitter with blood: and they made their roofs with the gun
   stocks:

Of that world's conquest and the fortunate wars. . . .

THE FIRST BOOK

So does a man's voice speak from the dream that bears his

Sleeping body with it and the cry
Comes from a great way off as over water —
As the sea-bell's that the veering wind divides. . . .

Now is it Díaz in the Book —

              . . . . where

                  lost in the. . . .

Santiágo de Cuba it was: I remember. . . .

Hoisted over the. . . .

              king's arms and a cross on it. . . .

Cortés I mean and the pleat of his purse empty:
And they made him captain: Duéro did: and the split-up
Three ways and as for the Governor. . . .

                 slept. . . .

November and warm in. . . .

        surf. . . .

            the dry winter:

Palms ragged with sea-gust. . . .

           all careened with the

Weed in the rusty chains and the keelsons splintered. . . .

Bleaching with sun and the. . . .

          nights in. . . .

             elegant knees like the

Girls in Spain and the sand still hot from the sun and the
Surf slow. . . .

      wind over. . . .

          palm-trees sweeping the

Stars into darkness. . . .
               weeks. . . .
                     waited. . . .
                             the guns
Brassy in. . . .
               loading the cobbed maize and the pigs and
Powder enough for a . . .
                    ropes on the. . . .
                            eight tons:

And we launched the last of them well out and the brigan-
    tine
Cocked in the poop like a Genoa. . . .
                       sixteen horses:
Alvarádo's the mare the sorrel the big one:

Montéjo's the galled gelding: his rump sore with it:
Puertocarréro's grey that the captain bought him:
A fast dark chestnut horse of de Mórla's:

Ortíz the musician's stallion: well taught:
Clever under the bit: the mare La Rabóna:
The captain's hack that died of the foul water:

Láres the excellent horseman a strong roan:
Gonzálo de Sandovál's La Motílla: the best of them:
A chestnut bearing a white star: and the loan of a. . . .

And we lay by for the beans and they told Cortés. . . .
Governor knew of the. . . .
                    wild and the writ signed
And the sergeants out in the King's square to arrest him:

And the captain heard it at dusk and the wind rising
And he ordered the lot of us down to the ships by dark
And the chains short. . . .

              bucking the. . . .

                        all that night. . . .

Sentries at. . . .

        waked and beachward and still stars and the
Governor riding his white horse on the fish nets
Big in the fault of the light and his men armed

And the palms back of him black and the leaves threshing:
We cold on the dew-wet decks: yawning: our
Mouths sour with sleep: the pimpling flesh

Crawling under the thin cloths: and at dawn the
Captain out in the oared boat: and we hoisted the
Jibs on the rest of them: getting the low airs: yawing

Wide to the ruffle of squalls and we cleared the buoys
And we luffed up by the quay with the gear rolling
And Velásquez cried to him there in his bull's voice —

"How is it O my Compadre I see you go?
"Is this the right way to take leave of the Governor?"
Hollow it was on the gale as a conch blowing:

And Cortés below there and the quay above:
And he stood to the swing of the sea in the boat's stern
Baring his head and the tune of his voice like a lover's —

"Señor! there are some things in this sinful world
"Best done before they're thought of! At your orders!"
And they stared across the water with no words:

187

So did we sail dragging the boat aboard:
And we bought supplies at Trinidad and Havana:
And Velásquez wrote to the said towns and he warned them

Blaming us all: and as for that shameless man
Let them arrest the son-of-a-bitch for a traitor
Shipping him down with the oats or. . . .

      "given my hand this

"Tenth day of December Fifteen Eighteen":
And they came with the writ in their belts and their mouths
 dumb:
And Cortés was an eloquent man: skilled in orations:

And even the Governor's messenger signed up:
And the town clerk had a quill in the ink for Velásquez —
"That the hare was still as the tuft of a turf till you jumped
 him:

"And the boar a suckling till you bruised his back:
"And as for the Captain Cortés — Your Honor's obedient
"True man and a loyal tongue and irascible:

"And better armed than the Constable's guard or the Veedor
"And peaceful at heart: and they feared he would burn the
 town!"
And they sent that off by a nigger for God speed:

And Cortés had a service of sound plate and a gown and a
Gilded knot to his shirt and his chain gold
And a smile for the troops with the orders. . . .

     month. . . .

      bound for the. . . .

Burden of pork and we borrowed her rope and we towed
 her. . . .

THE SECOND BOOK

(10 Feb.
1519)

             . . . .So
Sailed we out from the Island to Cozumél:
Winter it was and a wind and a swell rolling

And the stain of the foam on the long flank of the swells:
And they gave us the signals for night with the swung lan-
    terns
And the chains came in: foul with the tatters of kelp:

And the bow fell off from the wind and the sails slatted:
Shaking aloft: filling the bunt: the sea furrow
Following under the drawn keel: land

High on the northward and the windy birds:
And they told the pilot: the old man: the Comácho
(Showing him wax on the seal and the ink words)

He should lie-to off the capes and Cortés would catch us:
And he was a sea-going man: a native of Pálos:
One that would trust God — but he'd try the hatches!

He said: "I'll lie-to when I can't sail!"
And the capes went down and we took the sun for a bearing
Keeping the breeze on her beam: and the windward stays

Stiff in the smoking chocks: in the chains: and the airs
Swung east and the swells came in on the quarter
Kicking her off: and he held her down as he dared:

So it went: and the fourth day and to starboard
A low line like the blur of the wind on the sea
And we worked her in with the oared boats to that harbor:

189

Shoals there were and the blue channels between them
And the herons rising to the rake of oars
And the wash under the dark banks in the tree roots:

We lay to leeward of that silent shore
And the drip of the dew came down from the slack sails
And the stir of mangroves when the wind was toward us:

All night were the stars above our faces
And the smell blown seaward of that unknown earth:
(The air of the unknown lands has a strange taste to it):

And the next day we. . . .
                         gone and the coals burning
And corn enough in the crocks and the thread to weave
And neither a man nor a dog nor a hen nor the skirt of a

Running girl in the town: and he came that evening
Feeling his way like the blind-man's boy with the cook:
Ten ships on the oars and the anchors reeved:

The leads going like carpenters' hammers: the look-outs
Thick on the chains and the ropes and the spars and the
      decks like a
Sick flock waiting for sun in a rookery:

And he ordered us out of the bags of our beds and he lec-
      tured us —
"Did we think it was fox and geese we were there playing?
"Did you pacify people taking their gold and their chickens?

"And these were nothing: a poor folk: and our way was
"Far on to the west: and the gold was piled in the
"Open fields in that land: and to learn patience":

And he sent word to the chiefs it was their island:
And the girls ran in the village like tame boys:
And their breasts were bare and their brown throats and they
    smiled at us:

And the orders of Captain Cortés were not to annoy them
   . . . .

Trees toss in the. . . .
                   dunes: how the surf was dumb the
Inaudible thunder. . . .
             for a Cuban coin

Or a new skirt or a cake. . . .
                  how the gulls would come
Drifting to windward: how the wiry turf would
Smell of a strange herb and a strong summer:

I remember the dry leaf shook in the shudder of surf:
I remember the gulls would veer where we were hidden
Wheeling to leeward and the wing-tips curved. . . .

Girl's comb or a. . . .
             sea far out with the tinned
Hazy glitter of gales on it. . . .
                 so was. . . .
                    days:
And the anchors up and they told Cortés there were Indians

Come from the mainland — how they stood amazed:
How they would thumb at a man's beard: and the signs as of
Heavy toil and of bowed backs they had made: and their

Hands to their hearts: and their spittle to their eyes:
And he stared at the dazzle of sun where the day leaned and
 he
Spoke — "It may be in the lands behind are

"Men as we are: Spaniards: naked: gleaning the
"Garnered earth for a slave's grist . . ." and he pulled the
Lug of his lip as his way was — "for we needed an

"Ear to our skulls to sleep among these wolves:
"And the aid of a tongue to our teeth to drive these asses:
"And the slave will speak as his lord: and if God would
 there were

"Ways to be saved in that land": and he sent Ordás
And two boats and the guides and twenty men
And a cheap chain in a box and assorted brass goods:

And he bound him out for a week: and a letter — "Gentle-
 men:
"I am at Cozumél the island: if you that are
"Slaves there in that nation live I send to you:

"My ships will stand to the shore till the eighth noon:
"The price of your hides herewith: God aiding I
"Sail for the land beyond as the sea proves it":

And six days were gone and the next and they waited
And neither an Indian's boy nor a dog but the shore and the
Bird's wing and the pelican's cry and they sailed and

Crossed and returned: and the wind fair: and we boarded
And broke sail: and the tide was in: and we ran for it
South by the shoals with the wind on the port quarter:

And but for God we had gone: but de Escalánte
Hove to and his ship down and the bread was
Banked all in that ship and her masts canted:

So we returned: God's mercy defended us:
There it was as they watched from the low land
Looking to northward where the shallows ended

An Indian boat came south by the sea channel
Riding the roil of the surf: the stem down:
Standing the stern-lift an old naked man:

Lean he was of his great age and bowed with it:
His hair white on his eyes: his breech clouted:
And he leapt in the suck of the wave where the ship
    grounded:

Wet with the sea: the weed on him: crying out —
And the sound over the surf — "Diós y Santa . . ."
And lost as the wave came down: and our men shouted:

And the officers came to the shore: and we all ran:
And they told Cortés and he came and stood and he saw the
Brown skin and he cried — "Where is this Spaniard?" —

Yes! and the old man on his naked haunches
Crouching as Indians by the surfy shore
Wearing the yellow rag: the lean jaw of him

Grey with the hair-lock: and the sand before:
The sea past: answering — "I am he!"
He spoke slowly saying the words like a foreigner —

"When I was come to the long sands to the sea
"No sails were riding: the heart failed in me then:
"I said: thinking it: God has forsaken me:

"Now I perceive that God will be my friend:
"I am Jeronimo de Aguilár:
"Priest I was in the time: from Darién we

"Sailed: striking on stones the beams started:
"The wind drove hither: we were seventeen:
"Now in the ending there are two to part:

"Long have I dwelt in the land where your fortune leads
    you:
"I have interpreted many tongues: I have read the
"Painted rock by the roads where the dead are eaten:

"My two hands I have laid in the springs in the beds of
"Water: my tongue in the bitter rinds: I have broken the
"Sweet bones of the hare and she has fed me:

"I dwelt before you in those lands": and he spoke:
And Cortés was dumb and we brought salt for we feared him
And shoes to his feet and an oil and he was clothed:

And we caulked the ship in the one night. . . .
                                    steering by
East and north: and the 4 March: and at midnight

Gale from the. . . .
                wash. . . .
                        the boat gone. . . .
                                    morning veered

194

South and the swell on it. . . .
                    cape called *of the Women.* . . .
Hove to in a bight with an iron aft. . . .

Bellies of stone and stone breasts and their limbs like. . . .

And standing away out: for the shoals are flat
And the coast a lee coast if you catch a norther
And sand bottom and no stub for the gaff: and the

Smudge of the land up wind: and to west before us
Nothing: the sea-glare and the sunward glass:
And we stood west on the wind and the seventh morning

Wore ship to a shuffle of air and she slacked and the
Sea was brown and the bog-root on the water:
And we of Grijálva remembered the empty casks

And the corn and the river Tabasco and how they had
      brought us the
Roast fish on that shore: and we talked of trade:
And of gold from the god-trees — and instead they fought!

We poled in by the palms and the swamp brayed with them:
And Aguilár in that ship: and he told the mangroves —
Grinding it out — how we meant well and to pay

And to tell them the truth of God to their own advantage:
And they made a noise with their mouths as a mule's let:
And they rattled the rig of their bows: and that was their
      answer:

And the King's notary writing it down: and they sent us
Words enough with the arrows: and we to the waist
Fought in the sea-flow. . . .
                    of defenceless men. . . .

195

Fled and the naked fallen. . . .

                      by that gate
Taking the city: and at dusk Cortés:
And he read the oath by a lamp and a proclamation

Saying the town was the king's town to defend and
Die if we must: and the bats went up from the nettles:
Nevertheless there was more done in the end of it. . . .

And the night was in that city: and we slept:
And the doors were stone to the streets; and I was wounded:
I woke with the smart of my throat at the guard's step:

The shadow of roofs lay strong along the moonlight:
The surf was faint far off on the sea front:
And my head was clear with the fighting and no food:

And I watched the moths in the moon at their silent hunt-
    ing:
I thought then — with the pain of my throat and the win-
    ter of
Moon over it — fear was in that country. . . .

THE THIRD BOOK

So came we again to the sea water:

And our wounds we laid in the ravel of torn sleeves
Larded — so did we lack all things — from dead men:
And they sent to us over the marshes to make peace:

They were sick of the battles of horses! and that war ended:
And the chiefs came down with a golden dog and some
    lizards
And five ducks and of gold and the masks of men

(And the gold in that province is poor and the work
    flimsy:)
And cloth ("for the common troops: for their excellent
    services":)
And one score very superior women

("Not for the troops!" — and the town was skinned like a
    turbot!)
Young girls they were and well mannered:
All of them clean: some said to be virgins:

And one was that Malinál of Painalla we Spaniards
Called Marina and loved well: of women
None had more honor ever at men's hands:

A tall girl she was and a straight-limbed:
Her face smooth and pleasant to see for an Indian:
Not embarrassed but frank-seeming and simple:

And Puertocarréro had her: and after him
The Captain Cortés: and her own people obeyed her:
And she knew the tongues of Tenochtitlán and of Cintla
    . . . .

197

So did we sail on and the noon shade lay
Sharp to starboard: standing to the equal winds:
Water under the bow-wash green: the wading

Keel clean in the eddyless swirl of it: rinse of the
Salt wake slaking the sea: and we came to the
Outmost ocean: and the light was thin

And we saw the mountains beyond in the faint day:
And they sang to him — "Cata Francía Montesinos!
"Cata París la Ciudad!" as to say

Those were the lands beyond where he should lead us:
Those were the waters — "Do van a dar en la mar!"
And the odor of shallow surf was on the sea:

And the wind swung with the light: and we heard the yard-
    arms
Back to a breaking wind and the sails flatten:
And the air came cold against the creaking spars:

Sea ruffled with squalls: ships scattering:
And we held her northward as the weather wore:
Heeling the gusts: her head down: the hoists slatting:

Standing with morning to an island shore:
And the wind was toward us and we knew that place:
We few — Grijálva's soldiers that before

Sailed in those waters where the low sun paces —
We did remember: and with sideways eyes
Sought and yet looked not in each other's faces:

(So do those men upon whose sky arises
Signalled by solemn bells the ominous star
Turn to each other with the same surmise!)

And we stood: and they saw us how our eyes were darkened:
And a voice cried out from the ship — "Men of Grijálva!
"Veterans! You of the fights! Look to your hearts!"

And we heard them laugh in their hands: and the voice of
    de Ávila
Filling the slack of the surf like a boy's bugle —
"Did they eat the tongues from the root of your throats like
    calves?

"Have they taken the words from your mouths Veterans?"
    — screwing the
Sneer in the twist of his teeth: and the wind suddenly
Fresh out of that shore and the smoke moving:

And the smell under the smoke of the burning blood:
And the bitter odor of death: and Alvarádo —
"Why are you silent Ávila? What have we done to you"
  . . . .

And we worked in to a. . . .
              fathoms of. . . .
                         shelving bottom
And no hang for the hooks and a leeward shoal:
And he beached us under the banks in the breaking water:

And we built oasts of the wilting weed to our shoulders:
And the heat was great on the dunes: it was Good Friday:
The heat of the sand was strong where the sun rode:

And they brought us bread and the sweet plums were ripen-
    ing:
There we slept: and at dawn on the second day
When the mist rose from the smother of surf and the light
    came

199

Men were among us of other dress and of faces
Proud and with blunt brows: of great stature:
Their garments woven of thread: and they moved gracefully:

And they carried staves in their hands of a green plant:
And they smelled a rose as they came: their Indian servants
Driving the flies from them: lifting the silver fans:

And they turned their faces among us with no word:
And we saw the look in their eyes that they smiled together:
And they bowed and laid their fingers to the earth:

And they brought us gifts as a burden for many men —
A wheel like a sun and of gold and great as a cart-wheel:
And one as a moon in silver: and a helmet

Spilling with. . . .
                    shaped like lions and their parts. . . .
And golden monkeys and a golden. . . .
                                        scornful and
Natural looking with stone eyes and the carving. . . .

And all of it worth by weight in the. . . .
                            pesos de oro:
And we could not speak for the wonder of these things:
And he that was first and of fine dress and the lord of them

He stood alone on that shore on the steep shingle
Facing the sea: and he spoke: and the sound was harsh and
    was
Dry like the cackle of quick flame with the wind in it:

And the girl Marína spoke it to Aguilár:
And Aguilár interpreted — "Montezúma
"Emperor over the earth and of those stars:

"The sun is toward him and the altering moon:
"He has beheld your shadows in his houses:
"His are the lands: the glass of the sea knew you:

"Now does he send you from his endless thousands
"These and this treasure: in Tenochtitlán
"Armies are harvested like summer's flowers":

So did he speak and he pointed with raised hand
Westward out of the sun: and Cortés was silent
And he looked long at his feet at the furrowed sand:

And his voice when he spoke was a grave voice without guile
    in it —
"Say that we thank him well: say also
"We would behold this Emperor": and he smiled:

And the voice of Marína cried in the sea fall
And they stood on the dunes and were still and the sky back
    of them:
And their plumes moved in the wind as the tree tosses:

And he that had spoken — "Proud and ignorant man!
"Hardly now is your heel's mark on these grasses:
"The grooves of your ships go down to the sea bank:

"Already you name that king! West of the passes:
"Westward of Xícho and of Ixuacán
"And the salt plains and the corn plains and the pastures:

"West of the city where the earth-mound stands:
"West of the burning and the woman mountain:
"There is his town: there is Tenochtitlán:

"The clean wave runs among the island flowers:
"Ancient is all that earth: a long-used dwelling:
"The dead are silent in that ashy ground:

"Old are the gods there: — in the stone-made shelters
"Utter the dry bones their unspoken names:
"The locusts answer in the summer nettles:

"None have conquered that land . . ."
                          and they: as they came to us. . . .

"That he had no writ nor right to lie in that country:
"That His Honor's commission was well-known — to trade
"And return with it (viz. return with the cash money):

"That His Honor and all their gentlemen's honors had made
"And won and secured (with share for share to Velásquez)
"Adequate quotes and were quit and were well paid for it:

"That their farms were unmanned and their wives as they
        hoped (but the backs of the
"Cuban boys were quick at a man's toil
"And a straw will do to stopple an empty flask:)

"That many were dead of them even now with their loins
        and the
"Stones and the sticks and the arrows and such tools:
"And they had no ease at all in that war and no joy of it:

"That he ought to return forthwith to the island of Cuba:
"That he (Cortés) was the governor's man to obey him:
"That he had no title to rest as he well knew":

And more of the like sort: and the Captain played at it
Pursing the nib of a No on his lip: and he started and
Let pass: and he paused as a man persuaded:

And that was the sign: and we of his own party
Pushing the governor's men with our knees — we shouted
And raised banners in air and our naked arms and we

Cried out we were cogged of the dice and were down
And had lost the blood of our lives in a Jew's venture
Trading for gold: and here was an unknown ground

And a land to be taken: and as for the sums spent —
What were they to a new land? and we cursed at him
Asking him what we were: what men —

"Did we come to the gate of a ground like this to return
    from it?
"If he had no writ of Velásquez's hand let him find one!
"Let him establish a king's town for the birds

"Taking his writ from the Emperor Charles and the spiders
"And damned to Velásquez's deed!"
                    And our speech prevailed with him!
And he founded the town of the True Cross with a sign-
    post:

And he made a gallows of wood and a good jail
And the rest in ink with an eloquent text for the mortar:
And the jail he gave to the Governor's men: and they lay
    there

Two nights: and their gall turned gilt like a story:
(Ah what a salve is gold to console the mind!)
And the City making him General-in-Chief for Wars with a

Fifth (and the lick of the public dish on the side)
Of any and all or gold or goods or discoveries:
He to precede: and so done: and we signed and

Sealed and delivered and gave: and we gave enough!
And even so there was more: for he besought us
Seeing the state of grace he had in the Governor

We should enlarge the Emperor's ear with our thoughts:
    and
Offer our loves: and lay our lives to his measure —
And speak of the Captain Cortés as our hearts taught us:

And so we did as he said: for the wind threshes
And the thrush must dance to the wind: and we drew stems
And it fell to the Captain himself to write: to Cortés:

And he lined the ink on the page: and he cried — "Remem-
    ber your
"Deeds Castilians!"
                    and the sand was strewn —

"Holy Cæsarean and Catholic Emperor!

"We the least of Your Majesty's subjects: used
"Long to the wave-lift: wind-led: sea-suffered:
"Beached now on this last land: we salute you!

"We sailed to westward from the Island Gulfs:
"Bore three days outward on unmeasured ocean:
"Came to the shores before-seen: saw thereof

"Certain and good towns: forests: the land low:
"And we fought them off by day in the tramped straw:
"Thence we sailed westward as the water showed:

"And there came to us down to the grounding sea in the
    dawn
"Those that uttered a new name! (And our mouths are
"Sick of the standing meats and the stale water —

"For the springs in Your Majesty's lands are a dry drouth
"And the food is an eaten food and still they devour it
"And they drink the drench of their fathers' loins and their
    houses are

205

"Limed with the dottle of dead bones and are sour
"And their speech is fallen to women and old men
"And cheapened and base in the coin and the gilt scoured

"And the shape of a pound will pass at a few pence:
"And our backs are turned from these lands and from these
    waters:)
"And now is the new world toward us in the west!

"We are as men and without food and the daws are
"Feeding before them in the orchards! Now have we
"Found how the way goes up: and the roads lawfully:

"North by the rock have we chosen a ships' town:
"With our heels we have quartered the earth for a church
    and an arsenal:
"We have staked the sunrise on the eastern ground:

"Latrines are ditched in the dry shale and a market:
"The house of the judge is squared on the left hand:
"Everything stands as a town should: and the carpenters

"Pencil the oak: the lime burns in the sand-pits:
"Water is channeled with good joints and the vents made:
"Here shall the ships lie in: and we by the lands: by the

"Sun: to westward: marching: . . . and already
"Mallets have started the loud beams: therefore we
"Pray your aid and arms to our hearts' strength —

"We that to west now: weirdless: by fates faring
"Follow on star-track: trust have we neither now:
"Traceless this ground: by the grazing deer by the hare
    crossed:

"A king's name to our road: and the beckoning boughs
"Lead but with onward arms to the wind's ending:
"False-followed is moon-path also: the mountains

"Stand long on the stone of the sky like illegible
"Last inscriptions of departed kings:
"The sun misleads us into night: men

"Nameless: secret: of unknown hearts: drink at the
"Streams before us: and abandoned fires
"Flush on our roadways with the morning wind:

"Few we are to march in the great sky
"And the wild swing of the moon and the wandering nations
"Silence before us and the sea behind:

"The sun stands to our west at the endless shades:
"Only the great hope we have of that country
"Heartens our ominous thoughts now: therefore we pray you

"Stay our hands with the arm of your strength: be unto us:
"Take you these lands! — lest the lean swine devour them
"And our deeds be lost in the earth and our times
    done. . . ."

And he named Velásquez in two words: "how had
"Fonséca Bishop of Búrgos by God's Grace and
"Inscrutable Providence President of the Council

"Pledged to the said Diégo Velásquez his (say)
"Niece and the deal was for loot in the new countries:
"And we that should win them to walk the ruts for our pay!

"And rot in the bleeding fields and die with our guts out!
"The old inherit the earth and the young fatten it!
"After the wounds: after the war's done

"The old ones sit with the itch of their stones and the rattle
    of
"Age in the rake of their throats like the sleet in the stubble
"Bounding the new-won lands by the bones of the battle-
    fields!

"They weep for the dead with their mouths and the wet
    comes!"
And we proffered the Captain Hernán Cortés to his love:
"How he was a right man and His Majesty's humble and

"True servant in God and he ought to be governor
"Guarding the new-saved souls and the coast and the
    profits": and
Praising his good looks: and we wrote enough:

And we signed in the run of our rank and we sent it off:
And the sons of scorpions ran her in to Havana:
And the Island knew in a night: and Diégo coughed like a

Hooked horse when he heard of the heft of the platters
(For all that treasure was borne in the one ship
And little there was with us but the cut and the cantles:)

And he sent with troops and with smooth talk but they
    slipped him
Running it north and east in a good blow
And they sailed the Bahamas Pass by the Pole and the Dip-
    per:

So they came to Tercéra and Cádiz Roads:

And the King was gone and they fell to the Bishop of Búr-
gos!

But time and our deeds and his debts and the weight of the
gold

And the cold and the late spring and the French all worked
for us:

And His Majesty came to a Just Conceit of the Truth:

And he talked of nothing for several days but our Services:

And Gentlemen praised the cloth: and the silver moon:

And the gold sun: and the monkeys in gold: and the In-
dians:

And as for the Bishop of Búrgos — at la Coruña

The roofs are green with the rain and the sea wind!

As for ourselves — the ship went out with the evening:
All we knew was the last sun on the sail-cloth:
We stood a long time watching on that beach:

And the low night came in from the sea: and we lay by the
Ashes of grass and the journey of stars went over us:
Slow too from our sleep went out that sail:

And some dreamed of the ship: — and some woke to it!
I was the watch that night: I heard the water
Swirl as an oar would or a great fish roll:

And afterward there was the creak of a rope pulled taut:
And I called: and we beat on the constable's drum: and they
    ran:
And their heels scattered the quick coals and we caught
    them —

The bread aboard and the oil and the fish and the lanterns
And water enough for a long voyage in the tubs:
And he judged them there by the flare of their wicks and
    the fat of their

Own oil — "that the Pilot Gonzálo de Umbria
His feet be struck from his flanks": and the thing was done:
And they bungled the blow in the bad light and the drum-
    beats

And Juan Cerméño and Escudéro were hung:
And Cerméño fell and they choked his chaps in the halter
His face in the sand like a drowned dog's like a drunkard:

And Cortés was sick of the night's work: and he called
And he ordered us out and to take arms and the horses and
March — "and as for the damned town let it fall to the

"Hurt and the halt and the traitors at heart and their
    corpses!
"Let flies inhabit it! Why should we breed worms
"With the clean towns to be won and the west before us?"

And more of the like: and we marched by the night surf
Keeping the sand dunes and the water's sound. . . .

And he was a subtle and secret man of his purposes:

We lay at Cempoála the soft town:
And messengers came from the fleet by night and the word
    was
Four of the brigs were full and the best foundered —

"And what with the rotten pitch and the rust and the worms
"And the wood cracked as it was and the wear of the rigging
"Feared much for the look of the lot but deferred. . . ."

And Cortés was astonished and stared like a dumb nigger
And the next day there were more: and the next: and the
    end of it
Nine gone and the tenth a launch and the pick of the

Bleeding fleet for a duck-pond: and he — Cortés —
Still amazed and still talking of Providence!
And that was the break of the back for the Governor's
    gentlemen!

They stood in the streets at night like a French mob
Scaring the Indian girls with their words and their strut-
      ting —
"Did he think he was Jesus Christ? Did he think by God

"He could bring them out like a levy of goats to be gutted
"And fed to the idols and burn their ships and their steel was
"Yellow with rain and their guns worse and the country

"Undiscovered and not known and between them
"All the waters of earth and the westward heaven
"Near over the hills and it might be

"The last wall of the world: and they few left and to
"Follow the plunging sun in the uttermost oceans
"And die and be drowned and their souls lost and bereft of
      the

"Sweet air and the Spanish earth and their ghosts
"Wander forever the waters of no sail
"And no shore but a wind and a wave's motion!"

That was the weight of their wild breath: and they railed at
      him
Cursing the bed that bore the bum of his mother
And damning his father's fork for an ape's tail

And himself for the two-figged get of a goat and the brother
      of
Whores and a hare's scut and a bull's gear
And a gull and a kite: one first and another:

And he there in the dark of the huts hearing it:
And all at once was their breath gone: and he spoke:
They turned as at the stick crack the scared deer —

"Your Honors are eloquent men but your good-will chokes
        you:
"The husk of your love is brittle to your teeth:
"You will eat more softly when the shell is broken:

"As for your words — they are true: there is no fleet:
"And you say the land is a dangerous land: it is dangerous!
"That this is the world's end westward: it may be

"This is the world's end and the serpent rages:
"That our steel rots in the rain: Aye! and our skins do:
"That the place of our death is not known: it is strange

"But men die and unknown and the crows think of them!
"That this is an undiscovered and dark land:
"Of doubtful and ignorant gods: peopled by Indians —

"This is an undiscovered and dark land:
"All this that you say is true: but the words of your
"Fear are not true: there is one ship: man her!

"Take what you will of the store: a keel's burden:
"Spain is east of the seas and the peaceful countries:
"The old tongues: the ancient towns: return to them!

"Why should you waste your souls in the west! You are
        young:
"Tell them you left us here by the last water
"Going up through the pass of the hills with the sun:

"Tell them that in the tight towns when you talk of us!
"The west is dangerous for thoughtful men:
"Eastward is all sure: all as it ought to be:

213

"A man may know the will of God by the fences:
"Get yourselves to the ship and the stale shore
"And the smell of your father's dung in the earth: at the
    end of it

"There where the hills look over and before us
"Lies in the west that city that new world
"We that are left will envy your good fortune!"

And he walked between them and went and no man stirred;
And none spoke of the ships again in that army:
And they chewed their tongues in their mouths like shamed
    girls:

THE SIXTH BOOK

So did we pray: and took arms: and we marched: and
We left that sea-remembering land and last known
Ocean: bore bones' weight each one and his arms:

Meagerest burden of beggars our backs had:
And we ate of the grain of the grass for our mouths' meat:
Water we found: our bread also was fasting:

Ever before us lay vast earth secret with
Sun with the green sound with the singing of grasshoppers:
The earth was still against our living feet:

No man of us all that knew that land nor the
Way of the trees in it: neither were waters known:
Neither the customs of the wind: our shadows

Entered the silent shadows of the stones:
And the mouse cried in his tongue: the cricket answered:

Ah but the mark of a man's heel is alone in the

Dust under the whistling of hawks!
                              Companion of
Constellations the trace of his track lies!
Endless is unknown earth before a man. . . .

And we marched in the great plain under the sky-star:
Close footing in steep sun: narrowly
Laid we our feet along the wheeling light:

And the plain went up: rock-colored: barren:
Roses and wild plums over the waters:
Far south of us much snow: as in Aragon

215

Over the level winter: and we caught
Evening in that place: the smoke standing
West with the wind: with few stars: and we saw the

Knees of mountain on the naked land:
Great wall it was on the west: and at daybreak
Climbing: and had the rain up the barrancas:

And had a pass and a town and the troops lay there
Stewing the thin drizzle on green wood:
(And the smell of the smoke is sour in such places)

And we ate nothing or ill: and we ate roots: and our
Bellies were bitter for bread among those mountains:
So did we follow the waters: and we stood

The third day clear of the unequal ground:
Rocks over: snow hard in the crevices:
And the hawks were under us turning and far down:

A man could look for a great space under heaven
Standing above there: he beheld sea water:
He beheld the sun on countries he had left:

That way do they stand on the ships at Sáltes:
The sea opens before and the tide takes them:
They watch the Spanish land and the fields falling:

They watch the ship-road and the drifting wake. . . .

Then came snow from the pass and the wind under it —
The southwest smoking over ragged acre:

The sun like a stale moon with the stringy scud:
We could not see for the swarming cold: and our thigh-
        bones
Bitten with steel: our beards rimed: stung with the

Strong sleet: weak in the blood from the islands:
And the cloth we had to our ribs was the raw steel:
We coughed in the wind all night by the flat fires:

(This mountain has no descent but to eastward:
The west is level country: as from ocean
Climbing the shadow of the crag the eagles

Wheel into sun and inland and are low
To shallow gorse: their vans run over flowers:
Darkening leaves: the bees start from them: so

Was land to westward level from that mountain —
A withered earth and an unwatered meadow:
The winter's ashes were scattered on cold ground:

This was the wind's dryness: the north that bends the
Boughs up elsewhere with its rain here wandered
In shapes of dust as a ghost and the drought was shed from
        it:

I say that the whole country moved as on the
Cloudy steel the image of hands passes over:
So on the plain the image of wind wandered:

Neither were wells nor streams but the salt only:
The roads were as tracks: a goat's rut: *despoplado*:
Even the soil had a bitter taste and the stones of it:)

And we came by day among the desert gods:
And we came to the towns at dusk and the dogs yelping
And the smoke of the corn on the coals and the parched
    pods and the

Old men waiting by the shadowy dwellings
Turning the reeds of their necks as they stared among us:
Talking as crows do — "Look now!"

                                "At a step . . ."

"And a great battle of men indeed in their hunger!"

"Bearing these arms they march to the King Montezúma!"

"Or are they as gods — each man as a hundred?"

"Nevertheless in Tenochtitlán there is room for them":

"Ho! Aye! there is room within on the altars
"And without in the ditches of water is much room!"

And they sniggered as children with shut eyes: and they
    called to the
Indian bearers bending their brittle nails
And they made the obscene sign with their mouths mocking
    them:

And Cortés — shouting it — "Whose is this mountain pale?"
And the old men: changing their voices: shielding their
Lids from the faint light and their fingers shaking —

"Montezúma the king's land! Of our people
"Clear to the sea's edge was the river corn:
"And they came from the west with their hard eyes and
    their eagles:

"Once we were short of spears: once were the fords deep:
"Now they take what they will in the whole land:
"They rut in our daughters' beds: it is evil fortune:

"We have no name of a man now: our ancestors —
"They that planted the orchards: they were Totónacs:
"I that speak this was a free-born man:

"Beware of the land Colúa you that go to it!"

To the place called of the Red Land. . . .

and between the
Fields valleys of great depth: and went down and
Marched in the valleys:

and the pools were green a

Copper water: and stank: the earth powder:
No stalk of a leaf in all those valleys:
We alone there and the whispering ground:

The great heat of the sun on us: neither shadow:
Neither shade of the cracked rock in that cañon:
The tree of the sun on our necks: the burning saddle:

So came we to strath's end: lanterns:
Cricked walls: heaped plaster: smell of the
Old men: of the straw: the dogs scattering.

The dusk under that street: the moon withheld:
A thin smoke of the moon on the high barranca:
Mountains after those mountains: and tongues telling us —

Old men's voices — "There are the Tlaxcaláns!
"There does the way go in by the earth openly:
"And these are a violent and harsh race: and a man may

"March by the sword in their lands: and they fear no one —
"Only they hate the Colúans and wage war:
"And they wear at their wrists the skull-bone of the crow:

"And a man may enter in violence by that door
"And go as he can and march by the strong places
"And pass them by in the sun and with blows and with
    swords —

"Not by night nor by doubt nor the dark sayings":

And we slept and woke with the stars above the cañon:
And the moon fumbled the blurred helms: the braziers

Burned in the black of the wind to a man's hand:
And we marched: and the night was westward: and we fol-
    lowed:
And the sky returned to us covering stars:

                                        we had the

Light first in the leaves: we saw Tlaxcála
Under the shallows of the sun: we saw the
Grass-fires floating in the windless hollows. . . .

So stood to the mountains for that dawn:
And the trees came out of the night and the light under
    them:
And he marched us down by the brook by the bracken
    shaws:

And we chewed the slip of the alder for dry cud:
Dragging the guns: whispering: foot-sound: creak of the
Cracked spoke in the rut: hearing among the

Waters voices as a man were speaking:
Night-smell under the smell of the fern: the light
Rigid with silence in the net of trees:

And a wind touching our mouths: and the grass whiter:
And our hands were stiff with the taut ropes and the lag of
    the
Oaken fellies and the stubborn withes:

So we came by day to that savanna:
Vast meadow it was: with rush rooted:
Rank with the dock-weed: there the cricket sang:

Wold was that country under heaven: woodless:
A crow's pasture and a bitter ground:
Téhua they called it: stones of that city stood:

There: covering earth: countless: we found them:
And we lay in the scald of the creek and the cane between
Waiting for sunlight: and we heard the sound

As a surf far off in the fog (and the wind weakens
And falls and silence and the slack sail shakes:)
And our ears were deaf with our blood and we could not
    speak:

And we made signs with the swing of our pikes we should
    break them and
Head them off by the pools and to stand west:
And they came like dogs with their arms down: and their
    faces

Painted and black and with death's eyes and their breasts
Quilted with cotton and their naked arms:
And the hard hammer of sun on the gold: and their crests
    like a

Squall of rain across the whitening barley —
We that were mortal and feared death — and the roll of the
Drums like the thud in the ear of a man's heart and the

Arrows raking us: rattle of metal: the goad
Stuck in the fat of the hand: and we standing there
Taking the sting of it. . . .

                      No! we were good soldiers —

Nevertheless it was ill weird for a man
One against many on those dangerous plains
And the sea behind and the hills: and we chocked the can·
    non

Ramming the stone to the stock and the stiff blaze of it
Flat to the grass: burning the gorse with the powder:
Taking them clean in the bellies with link chain:

And they near in the sun: and they took it shouting:
They threw dust in the air: when the smoke lifted
The dead were vanished from the bloody ground. . . .

Then indeed did our hearts fail us to give
All force and the Indians still in their numbers:
The dead gone: the plain dark with the living:

And still Cortés and the horsemen had not come:
And we must have died by the day's end in that meadow:
And our throats were thick with the dust and our mouths
    dumb:

And even as we were overcome they fled!
They ran in the rut of the field as the flush and the scatter of
Quail out of corn: and we stood and were near death

And we hoped nothing of these things: and the battle
Wheeling to westward: and the fighting ceased
And the swords fell: and suddenly there were the galloping

223

Horsemen before us the thud and the shuddering beat and
the
Shod feet on the turf and the shout and the quickening
Kick of the calk on the clay and the sound of it easing and

Gone by and beyond. . . .
                              that was a victory!
That was a sight to have seen in a man's time!
Domínguez driving the mad horse with the stick of his

Lance straight in the air and his mouth wide:
Alvarádo behind him: the horse of Cortés —
The flea-bitten rump that he had and the froth on the
bridle —

On straight legs: scuffing the dust up: crazed with the
Smell of the spatter of blood: his neck twisted —
That was a sight to have seen in a man's days!

And we lay in the dust where we stood: in the bloody litter:
And we had the words in our dry mouths and the wine in us:
And our hearts were big as a bird in a girl's fist:

And we would have slept where we lay. . . .
                              and they came behind us
Bearing us other war!
                    And we were one
And they were ten to the one of us: and they died:

They fell by scores and they came again by their hundreds:
And the blood of our veins was run in the earth with our
victories:
Day after day we fought and we always won!

And we sent them word they were well wealed: and to think
    of it:
And they came again with their crow's cry and their
    feathers:
And they fought us back in the brake: and our bellies sick-
    ened:

And we saw soon how our bodies were near death
And how we should take that battle with our lives
And pass them by with our bare bones into Mexico —

And nevertheless we fought them lest we die:
And they came at last in the mid-watch: the Modórra:
And we saw the maize-field moving in the night:

And we rode them down in the furrows of plowed corn
And the tuft was over a man's knees when he mounted
And the leaves like a lash on his wrists: and we reined the
    horses

Driving the stiff of the steel to the squealing clouts:
And that was the ending of one war: and they made the
Peace with their backs: and the old men came out to us. . . .

Never were any in all lands that laid their
Loins to the quilt with more comfort than we had
Wounded and sick as we were and our blood faint:

And that was a good and a loyal and true peace:
And they brought us in by their town and their hempen gar-
    ments
Painted and red: and we came by the water trees

And the green look of the land and the girls their arms like
Harvest withes about the shocks of flowers:
And all laughing with words: and they brought us garlands:

It smelled of the sun and of dust in that town:
They sprinkled the dry earth with the odor of water:
The shape of the shadows faded from morning ground:

And we laid us down in the doors where the moon haunted:
The broom-water smelled on the streets of the heat to come:
We woke with our knees across the stones of dawn
there. . . .

So was it those days: dead summer:
The rains off for the year: and clear: and nights like
Nights north in Navarre: no drums to it:

Sun enough and a floor and the rushes dry:
The rattle of wind in the leaves: the sun's shadow
Cool in the corner of noon as a dog would lie:

The long talk in the dusk — "of us Spaniards:
"Since to believe we were not gods would degrade them. . . ."
Of Montezúma — how were our weapons sand

And our wars were lost in the wind if we sought that nation:
And none had conquered that city with man's arms:
And they themselves in their time had thought to take it:

And they took dust: and the drought to their mouths: and
the smart of the
Smoke in their gullets for all good:
                                        of Cholúla —
How was it treacherous thin earth and artful

And false and with gods unsure: the dead ruled it:
And nevertheless there was way west by that city:
But as for themselves the wells of their eyes were fooled with
    the

Shadows of sorrow in that place: and the spittle of
Dreams in their eyes as a sleight: and their fathers knew this:

And we marched by day to the south and we saw the hill
And the god's flame on the hill and the town Cholúla. . . .

The falsifiers of things seen!
                                the defamers of
Sunlight under the name of our sky!
                                and we slew them:

And who are ye to be judge of us? Ye that say. . . .

And their treasons were open and shameless and many knew
    them:
And they thrust their hands through the guises of this world
    as a
Negro's hand in a girl's breast: and they drew the   *The Mas-*
                                                        sacre at
                                                        Cholúla
Truth as a bee's-comb from a wall to serve them:
And the world they said was a dream and a stale:
    and they offered us
Sadness to suck for our thirst — as a maker of words to an

Idle woman at dusk that her heart be softened:
And they would have destroyed us in that place: the de-
    basers of
Leaves! of the shape of the wild geese on the waters!

Calumniators of evening! priests! betrayers of
Light in the hood of our eyelids! they that discredit the
Silence of death on the dry mouths — and they trace the

Sign between the eyebrows of the dead:
Maligners of evil they were: of the pure ill
Like a crystal of quartz in the heel where the flesh will tread
    it!

228

And they told us Tenochtitlán was a whitened filth and a
Great guilt in the air: and deception: and falseness:
And filled with the salt of the dead as a reed with pith:

And they themselves had beheld it —

                         and we saw their
Eyes like sorcerers and the uncertain
Shadows behind them on the height of walls:

And they said to us — "Have you not known? Have you not
    heard?"
And they said — "Has it not been told you from the begin-
    ning?"
"Has it not been said from the founding of the earth?"

And they said we should enter and come and lie within
And dwell in trust and with faith sure —

                         and we knew the
Odor of death on their tongues as a thawing wind!

And we caught them under the cleanness of dawn:
                         and we slew them!

And who are ye to be judge of a man's fault?
They stood about us in the town Cholúla

And the sun was under the sill of the east and he called to
    them
Shouting the words out: (and the stones were wet —
I see the young-leaved morning on that wall)

"Was it the loyal love of their hearts that sent them
"With such smiling and glad mouths? Or perhaps the
"Poles they had cut for our necks and the withy pens!

"Did they come to deliver our feet from the falls and the
    traps
"And the barricadoes of stone they had built? In what god
    did they
"Trust for reason? Let them trust the grass!

"For indeed he had read in their hearts as a split cod
"And he knew their souls by their slime as a snail his
    journey —
"How they had salt for our flesh and a boiling pot:

"But that which our hands should pay them they had
    earned!"

And they cried as sheep to be sheared and some confessed it:
And the fault was their lord the great king's: and to turn our

Wrath upon Mexico: there was the string stretched:
And Cortés on the stone and the sword drawn — "Now had
    they
"Done with words? For the tongues in their mouths were
    of dead men!"

And even then they would smile for their hearts could doubt
    him:
They stood as deer in thicket and the sun
Puzzled their eyes with the blink and their heads were
    down. . . .

Afterward they were blind with the raw blood:
They died slowly with much pain like serpents:
Our hands were lame with the sword when the thing was
    done. . . .
And who are ye to be judge of us . . . ?

"The road back has been covered with many winds:
"The pinch of the five toes in the dust is illegible:
"Before us are other lands and a new winter:

"(Already on rusty quills are the crows threshing:)
"Nevertheless we go on: we are not returning:
"Strange as it is that men: wanderers: wretched:

"Deceived often: misled: their way lost: thirsting:
"March on in the sun! But so the desire has
"Strength over us . . . and the love the love of this earth
    . . . .

"(All the crows of the sky have crossed our fires:
"It is a bad sign: a chill winter: dangerous:
"At this season they fly high-up and in silence:

"Their shadows vanish like years on the flat plain:)
"And we that are strong: we march on descending the
"West with evening: and the leaves of sage

"Taste in our mouths of the labor of living men:
"We have bitten the acid oak and the harsh holly:
"We have said — 'This is a good land! we will dwell in it!'

"(But who has trodden the way the crows follow?)
"Like the nail of a woman in love is the twig's smart
"Stinging the lips!"
                        And we came by the land and the col:

And we took the willows for night once and the farms:
(The stars over stubble) and we took the snow:
We took the cold for the one night and the larches:

231

When we were come to the pass and the down-going
That land was under us! There were the longed-for skies!
We stared as drunken men in dusk: as those

That watch for Teneriffe: and the sun rising
Raises that mountain and they stand amazed
Seeing the mark so near them and so high:

To speak clearly with right words I say the
Land lay at our feet as a close or orchard
That keeps within walls and is green and the plow labors:

Not with another ruggedness nor more the
Rock encircles as they say that water
Where the chafing Rhone lies silent on his shores

Than there those mountains: and we saw the straw
Cut in the swaths and gilt and the valley still as
Meadows in July sun where the bees throng them:

(O living-kindness of God's love that permitted our
Sinful eyes to behold these sights and wonders!
How have we thanked thee with words even! how little!)

And we marched down by the hoed fields in the sunlight:
We had forgotten the hunger and hard days:
The town lay on the lake like sleeping gulls:

The stone dyke divided the water: tasting the
Liquor of melons we marched by the lake road:
The king sat on his gold chair awaiting us:

They bore the sun at his forehead on willow poles:
Nobles and lords of that rich land supported him:
Even the straps of the shoes of his feet were golden:

So we were brought between the posts of morning:
And he turned and he stood in the gates and he said smil-
    ing —
"Malinchi! these are your houses: these your doors:

"Yours and your brethren's: you may rest awhile":

THE TENTH BOOK

O halcyon! O sea-conceiving bird!
The bright surf breaking on thy silver beaches

And the life goes out of us leaving the chucked sherds!

Leaving an old man's memories to leach
Like a cock's jewels of gravel and worn thin
With the sleepless caul of the heart and hard and clean:

Leaving within the eyes behind the fingers
Back of the soft lid and the scarlet vein
The harsh flash of the steel where the light lingers! . . .

Leaving the slag in us. . . .
                                   leaving us those days. . . .

And I see well as from dark into light lying here:
The lint of the broom-straw turns in the sun's ray:

The cocks sing in the heat: there are cakes frying:
The drinking water drops from the hung gourd:
The rafters circle with the dozing flies:
The dogs rise and cross to the cool of the urine:

I see well in the dark of the room — as through shutters the
Sun is white on a street and the shadows sure —

As men move under tree-boughs and the sunlight
Leaps like a cat on their gilt capes and clings
And is swept off by the next branch: shunted. . . .

So I remember it: yes: and the evening bringing the
Doves down from the air: their wings steep to it!
And thou Colúa! and the paddles rinsed in the

Clear pools of thy sun! I cannot sleep for the
Light under my lids of thy bitter water:
I cannot sleep for thy cries and the walls keeping the

Leaning weight of thy sun by night and the autumn
Smelling of flowers as spring does: (wearing the
Cotton sleeves we were drunk and the wind caught in
    them):

And the girls they gave us for love with the scented hair:
The green light through the leaves: the slow awakening:
How there were many and small birds in the air then. . . .

We were like those that in their lands they say
The steers of the sun went up through the wave-lit orchards
Shaking the water drops and those gold naked

Girls before them at their dripping horns!
And they ate the sea-doused figs with the salt taste:
And all their time was of kine and of sea and of morning:

So did we lie in that land in the long days:
And they gave us a king's house to our heads and we dwelt
    in it:
And the house was smooth and of clean walls and so spa-
    cious

And well made and with lime and the stone set there was
Place for us all and the guns and our goods and our Indians:
Each man his mat under him smelling of

235

Lake grass and of leeks and an ell in width
And his painted cloth with the corn and the cones and the
     aloes
(For in that land there were men skilled in these images —

Such as sit with a day's sun in their laps
And they stare in the eyes of the trapped hare in the
     stubble:)
And the rooms smelled of the sweet wood like a chapel:

And all were of plank and were ceiled and of pinned lumber
And painted with scarlet beams and their out-walls bur-
     nished
And made to shine as a good coin: and some were

Built to the water and the light returned
And spilled up from the float of the ripples and ran on the
Wall's glare as a flame where the sunlight blurs it:

And some were shadowed to the cool canals:
And they poled in with their slow skiffs and their melons
Leaning against the gaff's end and the slash and

Drip of the stroke came back: and the cries sending the
Sun-bright birds up — and the beat of sound
Would pass and float on the stream and the wings settle:

(For all the isle was channeled as that ground
That takes its stars from Istria and their eyes
See first the new moon toward the Tuscan Mountain:)

And the town rang with the clang of oars and the cries:
And they brought the corn through the water-streets and the
     faggots:
They poled in with the heaped fish: the hides

Smelling of oak: the bowls slobbered with maguey:
They stood in the cool of the dark arcades in the market:
Many there were of them: tall men with the hank of the

Coarse skein on their wrists and their thumbs parting it:
Sellers of split fruits: of blue stones:
Of brass: of the nubile slaves — their hands bargaining:

Stroking the breasts up: and the thing was shown:
Merchants of sweet nuts and of chives and of honey:
Of leaves of dock for the eyes: of a calf's bone for the

Gloss of the hair as the hand draws it: of dung
For salt for the tanning of leather: sellers of yarn:
Old men with the sun-bleached hair and the bunches of

Herbs: of lettuces washed cool: of garlic
Dried brown on a withy of plaited grass:
Sellers of cooked dough by the coal-fires larding the

Stained skirt with the spittle of burning fat:
Those the makers of ropes: those that shredded the
Silken down of a seed and their fingers fastened the

Stone to the twist of it turning the scarlet thread:
Sellers of good dreams: of blue clay for the
Baking of gods: of quills of the gold: of henequen:

Sellers of beetles for red dyes: makers of
Stone masks of the dead and of stone mirrors:
Makers of fortunate knots: magistrates in the

Swept porch — and they kept the names of the year:
They took the tax on the red stones and the herons:
They judged of the levies of salt: venders of syrups:

Of harsh drugs for the old from the coupling of hares:
Of dry seeds: of sweet straws . . . many and
Strange cries that they had . . . and they stood wearing the

Knotted and white cloths like capes and they went with
Strong knees through the heat of the sun and their thighs
were
Straight and their bellies like knuckles of bronze: and they
set their

Heels in the sand of the earth as a man riding a
Wave's back in the sea and their sex was naked
And stained with the salt of the sun like a golden hide:

And the tall girls there were in the wind and the way of the
Sun was under their knees and the way of the wind
Like a hand over them: smoothing the scarves out: shaking
an

Odor of noon from their skirts like the odor at midday of
Clean cloths to bleach on the water stones
(And the butterfly opens his slow wings:) and their skin
like the

Rain's fragrance of water: (one alone
Returns from a shadow of plantains and her mouth
Secret with lust as the honey of black combs):

And their loins were heavy with love and they laid them
down
Under the lids of their eyes as under a garment:
They gave themselves in the green herb and the flowers:

Ah how the throat of a girl and a girl's arms are
Bright in the riding sun and the young sky
And the green year of our lives where the willows are!

How they were slender with strong breasts and the light of
    the
Leaves over them! How there were tall men
And the wading lake to their wrists and their wet thighs

Dabbled with sunlight: and they drew the nets
In the green sedge of the shore and they came singing:
The sea-film silvered in the lifting web:

Ah how the land was a good land! and the king of it
Rich and with young wives and with gold and his gardens
Sounding with water: and he went to drink

At noon at the grooved stone by the sheds and the jars were
Choked with the float of the sun: and he ate simnel
And sweet cakes he ate and a kind of partridges:

And none knew his ways or his times with women:
Silent he was and not seen and he came by
Dark: and his desire was in their limbs as an

Odor of plums in the night air and they wakened
Stretching their arms out and between their knees
Delight like the sun's mouth and the water's weight:

And all his house was sounding as of trees
And the leaves of the trees were dark and a dew came down
    from them:
Even at noon the dew fell like an ease of

Dusk to comfort a man's eyes: and the ground was
Trodden with naked heels: and he kept beasts:
And birds he kept in a grove and the green loud with the

Locusts and golden and shrill wrens and the bees
In the split hive of the wall and the names of serpents
Curled in the painted vessels at his feet:

And he kept marks on a stone for the sky's turning —
For the way of stars in the trees and the moon's toil:
Niter and salt he ate from the quick earth:

They brought baskets of sweetened seeds and of oil to him:
They cried to him Lord! my Lord! my great Lord!
They came with naked feet and the small voices:

Ah how the land was a good land! and the doors with
Morning with many leaves with the clean odor of
Water sluiced on the night stones: (and the core of the

Broken melon smelled of a girl's robe:)
We woke scenting the slot of the heat on the air:
We rinsed our mouths in the sun: by the listed boats

Purging ourselves to the coarse sand the glare of the
Sun was a cleanness of pebbles: far out
The fisherman leaned to his line and the silent herons:

And we lay under a lift of the green and their gowns were of
Spun twist in our hands: the hollow groin
Beat with a small heart: we heard the trowels

Strike on the brick of the roofs like silver coins:
We heard the whistle of tamed birds: to our tongues
Our mouths were sweetened with the scented ointment:

And we drank of the milk of the aloe and were drunk:
And the words hived in the heap of our bones and we praised
 the
Taste of a bitter leaf: we praised the sun

And the earth for the odor of men in its hot days —
For a woman's color of pink shell or the pock of the
Purple vein at her breast as a bruise made in it:

We praised the trampling of sun as a gilt cock:
Our hearts were singing as hammered bronze and our mouths
 with
Sound as the corn is where the wind goes: and we mocked
 the

Shape of love with our thumbs: we cried aloud of the
Great sky: of the salt rock: of the land. . . .

And nevertheless it was not so: for the ground was

Silent against us: on our foreign hands
The dust was a solemn and red stain: our tongues were
Unskilled to the pulp of their fruits as a language of

Sullen stones in our mouths: we heard the sun in the
Crackle of live trees with the ears of strangers. . . .

And they passed with their cries at dawn and their deep
 drums:

And we saw them go by the stone courts and the cages:
And all clean and with coarse lime and the temple
Steep in the reach of the sky . . .

                              and the boy was slain!

The belly arched to the stone knife: I remember
They sang and were glad as a small child in the sunlight
And they ate the limbs for a feast and the flesh trembled

    . . . .

THE ELEVENTH BOOK

The smoke for a sign my people as the churn of
Crows above death's burning on the beach. . . .

And the shadow of terror arises on this world as a
Cloud out of the northeast: and death is
Everywhere like a resemblance. . . .

                                  sleeping we heard the

Sound of the lake in the water streets that weather:
Waking we thought of the narrow dyke and the bridges!

Ever behind us by night was the water's breath:

Before us: uncovered in the windy ditch: their
Teeth uttering slow sand the slain
Unnumbered dead were dumb and their eyes hidden:

Hearing the ceaseless waves we were afraid!
We rose in the dark of the mid night with no stars:
We cried to the walls of the town we were there waiting!

The lake-sound answered us! fools — we wished in our
        hearts to
Live in the land and the town safe and secure in it:
We thought in our fear their king should be our guard —

"Why should we suffer the dark chance or endure the
"Skill of the moon on our dreams or the fortune's changing?
"Seizing this king the silences were sure!"

And we marched down by the torches in dark way:
And we found him under the garden trees and his shoulders
Shone in the torchlight in the leafy rain:

He stood there: answering —

"..... gladly if to go
"Now were our ordinance: for we were men
"Sent from before-time: and the thing was known

"Long since in his land and his doors were ready:
"We were those men they knew of that should come:
"And therefore our terror was ill-taught to defend our

"Bodies and fear death: for death was dumb
"And mute and of lawful life as an herb or as beasts or
"Rain is: and savage as stones: and humble:

"And death also was ours and our bread and to eat as
"One out of many corns: and as one among them
"Tasting of silence and of smoke and peace:

"Seeing the bones of a man have many hungers
"And need death as the doe salt: and fear is
"Witless among us and its cricket tongue

"Thin as the whistle of dry straw and as tears of
"Salt dried on a stone for bitterness: let us be
"Warned and taught of the true word and to hear the

"Birds of death in our trees as the god sent them:
"Neither to stand in violence and with force:
"For we came to his house with loud cries and as enemies!

"How should it serve our fortune to make war
"Or to bind his limbs with our steel? Though our metal
     held him
"How should we hold death? There were many doors:

"And a man spills from the cup of his bones as spelt —
"From the shape of stone on his wrist as running water:

"Nevertheless he would follow as we led":

And Cortés was wild with the night's work —
                                        "Had we brought the
"Whore of death to our beds and our house to serve us?
"How should we profit by these deeds? And we thought our

"Ills were done! And the wheel of our luck turned!
"And the toss was tamed to our hands! But it was not so
"But evil fortune and the last and worst and

"Great fault of those wars!"
                              and so as he spoke the
Die fell: and we lost our lives: and we lost the
Land for it after: and the town was sown as

Dry salt with the bitter seed: and with slaughters
And much death in that house: the thousands slain. . . .
Sleeping among those walls we heard the water

Treading behind us with its ceaseless waves.

THE TWELFTH BOOK

When have the old forgiven us these things
Or the new lands or the sun on them?

. . . . we being lords in that town and our hearts insolent!
And the word came up there were ships hove-to in the
   offing:
And we knew well the Governor's men had the wind of us:

And we knew Fonséca was rooting in that trough —
The fat brach that he was: the breeding monk's-head:
And Velásquez was in it with two tongues and the soft of
   the

Fry in his bib like a glibbed boar in a bucket:
And their writ came up by the road with the ink sanded —
How we were traitors before God and His Son and the

King Charles and the Holy Church and the Spaniards and
Him Bishop of Búrgos and him Velásquez
And one thousand four hundred they had of the

Brave Biscayans and horses and all that brass
And the new bows and the iron balls and the powder:
How we had entered without law nor with act nor

Writing nor good writ nor with warrant: how we had
Crossed seas to that land and had made discoveries:
How we had marched to the new west and had found a

New nation of new tongues and had suffered a
Strange land and ways and wars and had dwelt with them:
How we were traitors and lacking in right love

And right care of our own kind and begetters of
New sorts as we were and inventors of wind
And our souls guilty as his was that in Hell

The horned flame muffled and his voice within —
"And as for our pride in our great deeds we should swallow
    it:
"Nevertheless they accepted our lands for the widows!"

And he called us out on the Square — such as would follow
    him:
And Alvarádo he left in the armed town:
And we marched east by the hills to Cempoála: . . .

The Biscayans they were but we — we brought them down!
And they fought us the one night in a wet rain:
And we were the fewer of men's names but they counted the

Sparks of the flies for our gun-matches: and they were
Ten to the one of us: and as for matches —
As for powder we used pikes: and lame with the

March down: and we set the flame to the thatch and they
Fell like the burning bees where the winds toss them:
And Narváez (he was my Lord's man of Velásquez

And Captain-General of that lot and he lost an
Eye by a light spear and he lay fettered)
He cried to Cortés in his vault's voice — "to have fought

"And won with unequal numbers — he must send it a
"Great feat of his arms!" and Cortés answered him —
"As for winning he thanked God and these gentlemen:

"But as for the taking of him (Narváez) that was the
"Least thing he had labored in New Spain":
And he made them a speech from the drums and they
     changed masters:

And the field was ours and the land and our lives safe in it!
And we lay in the meadows with no watch: and our pride
     was
Ripe as wine in our hearts: and we slept —
                              and the day was

Not yet dark on the hills when the luck denied us!
For the news came down of a great war on the causeway —
How they had opened the dry ditch and had prised the

North door by the gelding's stall and the hause was
Heaped full of their dead and of ours seven:
And Alvarádo had written it —
                         "As for cause there was

"No cause but a trap and the fools had set it:
"And they came in on a clear day to dance:
"And he gave them the usual king's writ to assemble:

"And they left their arms in a priest's house in the passages:
"And he saw they were many and great chiefs and he knew
     the
"Plumes they had were of war: and he saw their plan:

"And he locked the gates: and the guns and the corporals
     slew them:
"And nevertheless they were made mad by that slaughter:
"And they came like wasps in swarms as the wind blew:

248

"And the ways were full of their slit mouths and they fought
    like
"Wild dogs: we should ride well if our tongues would
"Talk to his living ears for he lacked water":

And Cortés was dumb with his rage and he walked among
    us
Praying to God to punish a violent fool!
And Alvarádo should bleed and burn and be hung for it:

And he swung heel to the mare and marched and at noon
    it was
No stay but to stand nor at dusk neither
Nor rest by road-side: and the time was June

And late light in the loft air: and the evening
Smelling of sad leaves and we marched casting a
Thin shadow as glass: and the road beneath us

Leading as last year's road by last year's passes:
But the look of the land was changed from the last year:
And the towns empty and changed and the cook-wood scat-
    tered:

The kettles blackened with the charring ears:
And we saw their smokes on the near hills for our coming:
And our way went up with the smokes: and our bellies
    feared it

Hearing the Spanish metal and the drums
And the dry bleat of the wheels and the silent mountains!
And nine days out of ten the nags stumbled:

And the tenth Colúa: and we saw that ground:
And there where the throngs were once along the gardens
Now did the bird rise from the shaken bough:

249

And void wave where the boats were then: and dark: the
Sea-slap only and the late bird's wing:
The night: the windless water bearing stars:

And we marched in by the hard road: and the ring of
Stone to hoof-shoe was the iron sound:
And we saw walls in the bat's light and a blink of

Lamps and entered and our own were round us
Whispering words: their mouths white by the lanterns:
The swung light upward on the jut of brows:

Meager they were in the small light: a man could
Taste the salt of their tears on their silent tongues:
Their eyeballs glittered to the gunner's matches:

And the place smelled of the doused ash and of hunger and
Sick men's nights and of death: and the dead were slack in
     the
Bloody straw of the earth as a coat is slung: and he

Said (Alvarádo) "The Captain's back!
"It's a quiet city Captain!" and he: hoarse —
"And a green grove for apes and a jakes for jackals!

"And not so did I leave this town!" and he bore the
Mare round on the short rein and he left him:
And we weary with long way and the swords like

Scalds across us and the heavy metal:
We were the sleepers leaning where we could:
And we lay down as the dead do under heaven:

And the walls above us: and the watchmen stood:
And nevertheless there was no sound in that city —
Only the roaches in the blistered wood:

Only the she-mouse hunting in the thistle:
We laid us down as dead men and we slept:

. . . eyelids covering many stars. . . .

THE THIRTEENTH BOOK

                                    . . . And this was

Late watch of that sky and the Ram was set and
Night lay westward with her stars:
                                    and waked
Foolish with sleep with a man's cry and the step of

Steel on cope-stay: and the day was breaking
Bringing the water smell along the stones:
The Pole Star faded from the fading Wain:

And we woke in the straw in the half light: and León was
There above us on the brink of wall:
And Sandovál: and the silence. . . .
                                    and we rose

And we went on the wall by the three rungs and we saw it!

Mother of Heaven there were many men!
Even in Spain at Sevílla when at dawn they

Pray and the bread is broken and the tens and
Thousands stand there in the narrow streets
And they kneel down to the bells are not so many —

Neither so silent! and our eyes could see them
East and south by the great square and their crests were
Floated in lake-fog: and their naked feet

Hushing the earth: and stood: and when the west was
Light the faint stir. . . .
                                    and they saw the sun!

Mother of God! in age now: forgetting the

Wars in Mexico and all men's tongues and
Cries and shouting and the clamorous words I
Hear those voices shouting and those tongues!

And they came like wolves in the streets: and the water
      birds
Rose with the shouting: and we heard the wind in the
Shrill nipple of stone as a wasp: and we heard the

Slings as scythes and the deep drums and they kindled the
Cook-room walls to the up-wind and the court was
Strawed with their throws as a threshing floor: and we killed
      them

Hacking their hands from the scarp: and there came more:
And they tore their hands on the slash of the steel but they
      reached us —
We that were lame with the weight of our own swords:

And only night was our aid then: and for sleep we
Pleached roofs with the rack of the spears: and we knew
      there was
No help but the king's help or to flee for it:

And our mouths were bitter with the bloody rheum:
And we stood by the kettles and many were near death
And our wounds cold and we talked of Montezúma:

And we called his name from the burned sheds:
                           and Cortés was
There among us eating and he spoke —
"That we save our throats for sucking up our breath!

"That we keep our mouths for the meat seeing there go to
"Death journeys of such haste! that our fault was
"Then when we took this God's-butt for our hold and

"Pledge and hostage: that our fears had brought our
"Fears upon us: and had lost the town:
"And our lives were to lose if they circled the west wall:

"That the laws of this land were foreign and not ours
"And they laid death as a wafer on their tongues
"And he had no hope of the harvest of that ground:

"That men were fools to take the god among them:
"For a man's part is to labor and fear death
"And die in pain as he must and in his hunger:

"And the gods were of other lands: nevertheless
"As our will was: and our wisdom: let us do. . . ."

And the smoke coiled on the cold stones: and we went by

Dawn on the wall-head there: and Montezúma
Clad in the gold cloth: gilded: and he smiled:
He climbed by the stair and smiling and they slew him:

He stood on the stone in the gold in the first light
And the war below: and they fought like dogs in the ditches
Whistling and shrieking: and we heard a sigh as the

Sound in leaves when the storm ends and the pitch of
Rain runs over and far on and the wind is
Gone from the willows and the still leaf drips:

254

And all at once there were stones and the sky hidden:
And he stood in gold not falling: and he fell:
The lances blurred in the sun as a wheel spinning:

His eyes were lewd with the strange smile: and they yelled as
Fiends in Hell and as beasts: and when we thought it
Least for the bitter fighting he was dead:

All that day and into dark we fought:
And we lay in the straw in the rank blood and Cortés was
Hoarse with the shouting — ". . . for a man was wronged
    and a

"Fool to suffer the Sure Aid but to best it and
"Fight as he might: and he prayed all of us pardon
"And grace if he spoke our hurt: but we were men:

"And we saw well what weapon was our guard:
"And now there was none: only the night: and the ways
    were
"Barred before us and the ditches barred

"And the dykes down by the banks and the water-breaks
"Open and armored and they held the roads:

"And nevertheless we had the choice to take them! . . ."

By night: by darkness: turning from the sun. . . .

And he ordered us out by the south wall and the horse-
    men —
"And none were to follow him grudging by that road:
"And no man's name was needful to those wars

"For the women in Spain have borne and still bear sol-
    diers. . . ."
And de Ávila answered him — "Soldiers and captains too:
"And we well deserved that he should tell us so!"

And he ordered the gold from the stone-room for the
    troops:
And Narváez's people were weighted as great lords:
And nevertheless there was metal enough to lose of it —

Seven hundreds of thousands of *pesos de oro*
And the pelts of birds and the jade and the painted cot-
    ton —
The rape of Mexico: the riches of that war —

And it lay in the sift of the ash and men's feet trod it:
And he ordered a bridge of planks for the broken causeways
And men to bear it: and they drew the lots

And we lined up in the dark court and the straws were
Drawn by candle: and we saw the rain for the
Flame spat to the wick: and León had lost and

Alvarádo: and they swung the gate
And we marched out by the still street and the smell of the
Rain was rank with the rotting blood with the taint of it:

We talked little in that time: ahead the
Walls came toward us with the marching feet:
And the street turned and the sound fell: we held the

Metal muffled: and a man could see to the
Man's shape before in the rain: and still there was
No sound but our own and the town was sleeping:

And we knew the causeway by the water silt:
We heard the rain in the reeds. . . .
                                    and the rear-guard halted
Sending the word up that the planks were split

And the bridge bogged at the last break — at the water —
And all that a man could do they. . . .
                                    and we heard the
Sedges sliding: and we heard a call.

And a call beyond and fainter as of birds
Waked in the rushes: and again the rain and
Silence and the water sedge: and the word was

Wild among us and the bridge still stayed:
And one Botéllo: a bowman: a maker of charms —
And they found in his boxes after as a shape of

Hide and of flock-wool: stuffed: as a man's parts:
And a book with signs and written — "Shall I die?"
And afterward — "Thou shalt not die!" and farther —

"Shall I be slain alas in the sad fighting?"
And under it — "Thou shalt not!" and again
"So shall my horse die also?" and the sign —

"Yes they will kill it!" — and this fool Botéllo
Crying beyond in the night and his voice hoarse —
"Sorrow I see like smoke of rain descending!

"Death's seal is made in the flesh of your foreheads:
"Your limbs Oléa lie in a shallow sod:
"I too. . . ."
                    and we heard de Mórla's horn

And the rear-guard answering and Alvarádo:
And all at once there was some word they were shouting:
And the ranks were broken: and we cried to God

Driving the fore-guard on: and the bridge was out: and the
Stones were shrill in the thick air and the arrows:
We saw the water where the dykes went down:

We drove as cattle drive against the barriers
Bearing before us: and the plunging horse
High on the heap: and the wheels: and the dyke narrow:

Blinded with darkness: and the ditch before. . . .
(They fell in the road and were not raised: their cloaks
Muffled the stone: in their hands were their broken swords:

In the ditches of water they drowned and the sand choked
    them:)
We struck their arms from our knees in the blind fighting:
By the dead we came over: and the dead were most:

And the morning light was rising on that sky:
And we came to the land there: and we saw the lake
Silent and under mist and the city lying

258

Lost and behind us as a man should waken. . . .

And we were but few men standing and the rest to come:
And we saw where five came toward us: their heads naked:

Running: bloody with many wounds: and one was
Alvarádo with the stumbling step:
And after these was the road: and no man other:

And the morning rose and the low sun: and we wept
Seeing so few alive that left so many:
Seeing that once-loved city. . . .
                            Yes!
                                    and we set our

Eyes to northward: and León was dead
And Láres and de Mórla and there died of
All eight hundred and the powder spent:

The guns gone: the gun-men gone: to ride the
Wounded horses: to eat earth: drums in the
Ear of the night in the yellow lands beside us:

And the whistling and jeering: and they held the scrub.
And they drove us up in the dust with the jack spears:
And they herded round us in the field Otúmba:

And the plumes sawed in the sun like maize: and we feared
      them and
Fought blind and with God's grace we came out of it:
And we lay beyond the mountains for that year. . . .

Conquistador. . . .

And we marched against them there in the next spring:

And we did the thing that time by the books and the sci-
ence:
And we burned the back towns and we cut the mulberries:
And their dykes were down and the pipes of their fountains
dry:

And we laid them a Christian siege with the sun and the
vultures:
And they kept us ninety and three days till they died of it:
And the whole action well conceived and conducted:

And they cared nothing for sieges on their side:
And the place stank to God and their dung was such as
Thin swine will pass for the winter flies and the

Whole city was grubbed for the roots and their guts were
Swollen with tree-bark: and we let them go:
And they crawled out by the soiled walls and the rubbish —

Three days they were there on the dykes going —
And the captains ill of the bad smell of that city
And the town gone — no stone to a stone of it —

And the whole thing was a very beautiful victory:
And we squared the streets like a city in old Spain
And we built barracks and shops: and the church con-
spicuous:

And those that had jeered at our youth (but the fashion
    changes:)
They came like nettles in dry slash: like beetles:
They ran on the new land like lice staining it:

They parcelled the bloody meadows: their late feet
Stood in the passes of harsh pain and of winter:
In the stale of the campments they culled herbs: they
    peeled the

Twigs of the birch and they stood at the hill-fights thinking:
They brought carts with their oak beds and their boards and
    the
Pots they had and the stale clothes and the stink of

Stewed grease in the gear and their wives before them
Sour and smelling of spent milk and their children:
They built their barns like the old cotes under Córdova:

They raised the Spanish cities: the new hills
Showed as the old with the old walls and the tether of
Galled goats in the dung and the rock hidden. . . .

Old . . . an old man sickened and near death:
And the west is gone now: the west is the ocean sky. . . .
O day that brings the earth back bring again

That well-swept town those towers and that island. . . .

NOTE: Where I have followed the historical chronicles
of the Conquest of Mexico I have, in general, followed
the account given by Bernál Díaz del Castillo, one of the
Conquerors, in his *True History of the Conquest of New
Spain*. I have however altered and transposed and in-

261

vented incidents. I am indebted to the excellent notes of Mr. Alfred Percival Maudsley in his (Hakluyt Society) edition of the *True History*. My account of the topography of the march from the seacoast to the Valley of Mexico is based upon my own experience of the route and the country by foot and mule-back in the winter of 1929 and differs from that of the historians. Indian names have been given their Spanish pronunciation for obvious reasons. (Professor John Hubert Cornyn's *Song of Quetzalcoatl* has a note on Aztec pronunciation for those who are interested.) Proper names have been accented for the reader's convenience even when no accent would be required in Spanish. I hope that the strength of my attachment to the country of Mexico may, to some degree, atone for my presumption, as an American, in writing of it.

from FRESCOES FOR
MR. ROCKEFELLER'S CITY (1933)

LANDSCAPE AS A NUDE

She lies on her left side her flank golden:
Her hair is burned black with the strong sun.
The scent of her hair is of rain in the dust on her shoulders:
She has brown breasts and the mouth of no other country.

Ah she is beautiful here in the sun where she lies:
She is not like the soft girls naked in vineyards
Nor the soft naked girls of the English islands
Where the rain comes in with the surf on an east wind:

Hers is the west wind and the sunlight: the west
Wind is the long clean wind of the continents —
The wind turning with earth, the wind descending
Steadily out of the evening and following on.

The wind here where she lies is west: the trees
Oak ironwood cottonwood hickory: standing in
Great groves they roll on the wind as the sea would.
The grasses of Iowa Illinois Indiana

Run with the plunge of the wind as a wave tumbling.

Under her knees there is no green lawn of the Florentines:
Under her dusty knees is the corn stubble:
Her belly is flecked with the flickering light of the corn.

She lies on her left side her flank golden:
Her hair is burned black with the strong sun.
The scent of her hair is of dust and of smoke on her shoulders:
She has brown breasts and the mouth of no other country.

WILDWEST*

There were none of my blood in this battle:
There were Minneconjous, Sans Arcs, Brules,
Many nations of Sioux: they were few men galloping.

This would have been in the long days in June:
They were galloping well deployed under the plum-trees:
They were driving riderless horses: themselves they were few.

Crazy Horse had done it with few numbers.
Crazy Horse was small for a Lakota.
He was riding always alone thinking of something:

* Black Elk's memories of Crazy Horse recorded by Neihardt.

He was standing alone by the picket lines by the ropes:
He was young then, he was thirty when he died:
Unless there were children to talk he took no notice.

When the soldiers came for him there on the other side
On the Greasy Grass in the villages we were shouting
"Hoka Hey! Crazy Horse will be riding!"

They fought in the water: horses and men were drowning:
They rode on the butte: dust settled in sunlight:
Hoka Hey! they lay on the bloody ground.

No one could tell of the dead which man was Custer . . .
That was the end of his luck: by that river.
The soldiers beat him at Slim Buttes once:

They beat him at Willow Creek when the snow lifted:
The last time they beat him was the Tongue.
He had only the meat he had made and of that little.

Do you ask why he should fight? It was his country:
My God should he not fight? It was his.
But after the Tongue there were no herds to be hunting:

He cut the knots of the tails and he led them in:
He cried out "I am Crazy Horse! Do not touch me!"
There were many soldiers between and the gun glinting . . .

And a Mister Josiah Perham of Maine had much of the
land Mister Perham was building the Northern Pacific
railroad that is Mister Perham was saying at lunch that

forty say fifty millions of acres in gift and
government grant outright ought to be worth a
wide price on the Board at two-fifty and

later a Mister Cooke had relieved Mister Perham and
later a Mister Morgan relieved Mister Cooke:
Mister Morgan converted at prices current:

It was all prices to them: they never looked at it:
why should they look at the land? they were Empire Builders:
it was all in the bid and the asked and the ink on their
    books . . .

When Crazy Horse was there by the Black Hills
His heart would be big with the love he had for that country
And all the game he had seen and the mares he had ridden

And how it went out from you wide and clean in the sunlight

BURYING GROUND BY THE TIES

Ayee! Ai! This is heavy earth on our shoulders:
There were none of us born to be buried in this earth:
Niggers we were, Portuguese, Magyars, Polacks:

We were born to another look of the sky certainly.
Now we lie here in the river pastures:
We lie in the mowings under the thick turf:

We hear the earth and the all-day rasp of the grasshoppers.
It was we laid the steel to this land from ocean to ocean:
It was we (if you know) put the U. P. through the passes

Bringing her down into Laramie full load,
Eighteen mile on the granite anticlinal,
Forty-three foot to the mile and the grade holding:

It was we did it: hunkies of our kind.
It was we dug the caved-in holes for the cold water:
It was we built the gully spurs and the freight sidings:

Who would do it but we and the Irishmen bossing us?
It was all foreign-born men there were in this country:
It was Scotsmen, Englishmen, Chinese, Squareheads, Aus
      trians . . .

Ayee! but there's weight to the earth under it.
Not for this did we come out — to be lying here
Nameless under the ties in the clay cuts:

There's nothing good in the world but the rich will buy it:
Everything sticks to the grease of a gold note —
Even a continent — even a new sky!

Do not pity us much for the strange grass over us:
We laid the steel to the stone stock of these mountains:
The place of our graves is marked by the telegraph poles!

It was not to lie in the bottoms we came out
And the trains going over us here in the dry hollows . . .

OIL PAINTING OF THE ARTIST
AS THE ARTIST

The plump Mr. Pl'f is washing his hands of America:
The plump Mr. Pl'f is in ochre with such hair:

America is in blue-black-grey-green-sandcolor.
America is a continent — many lands:

267

The plump Mr. Pl'f is washing his hands of America.
He is pictured at Pau on the place and his eyes glaring:

He thinks of himself as an exile from all this,
As an émigré from his own time into history

(History being an empty house without owners
A practical man may get in by the privy stones:

The dead are excellent hosts, they have no objections,
And once in he can nail the knob on the next one

Living the life of a classic in bad air
With himself for the Past and his face in the glass for Pos-
    terity).

The Cinquecento is nothing at all like Nome
Or Natchez or Wounded Knee or the Shenandoah.

Your vulgarity, Tennessee: your violence, Texas:
The rocks under your fields Ohio, Connecticut:

Your clay Missouri your clay: you have driven him out.
You have shadowed his life Appalachians, purple mountains.

There is much too much of your flowing, Mississippi:
He prefers a tidier stream with a terrace for trippers and

Cypresses mentioned in Horace or Henry James:
He prefers a country where everything carries the name of a

Countess or real king or an actual palace or
Something in Prose and the stock prices all in Italian.

There is more shade for an artist under a fig
Than under the whole rock range (he finds) of the Big Horns.

EMPIRE BUILDERS

THE MUSEUM ATTENDANT:

This is *The Making of America in Five Panels:*

This is Mister Harriman making America:
Mister-Harriman-is-buying-the-Union-Pacific-at-Seventy:
The Santa Fe is shining on his hair.

This is Commodore Vanderbilt making America:
Mister-Vanderbilt-is-eliminating-the short-interest-in-Hudson:
Observe the carving on the rocking chair.

This is J. P. Morgan making America:
(The Tennessee Coal is behind to the left of the Steel Com-
    pany.)
Those in mauve are braces he is wearing.

This is Mister Mellon making America:
Mister-Mellon-is-represented-as-a-symbolical-figure-in-alumi-
    num-
Strewing-bank-stocks-on-a-burnished-stair.

This is the Bruce is the Barton making America:
Mister-Barton-is-selling-us-Doctor's-Deliciousest-Dentifrice.
This is he in beige with the canary.

You have just beheld the Makers making America:
This is The Making of America in Five Panels:
America lies to the west-southwest of the switch-tower:
There is nothing to see of America but land.

"To Thos. Jefferson Esq. his obd't serv't
M. Lewis: captain: detached:
                    Sir:

Having in mind your repeated commands in this matter,
And the worst half of it done and the streams mapped,

And we here on the back of this beach beholding the
Other ocean — two years gone and the cold

Breaking with rain for the third spring since St. Louis,
The crows at the fishbones on the frozen dunes,

The first cranes going over from south north,
And the river down by a mark of the pole since the morn-
    ing,

And time near to return, and a ship (Spanish)
Lying in for the salmon: and fearing chance or the

Drought or the Sioux should deprive you of these dis-
    coveries —
Therefore we send by sea in this writing.

                              Above the
Platte there were long plains and a clay country:
Rim of the sky far off, grass under it,

Dung for the cook fires by the sulphur licks.
After that there were low hills and the sycamores,

And we poled up by the Great Bend in the skiffs:
The honey bees left us after the Osage River:

270

The wind was west in the evenings, and no dew and the
Morning Star larger and whiter than usual —

The winter rattling in the brittle haws.
The second year there was sage and the quail calling.

All that valley is good land by the river:
Three thousand miles and the clay cliffs and

Rue and beargrass by the water banks
And many birds and the brant going over and tracks of

Bear, elk, wolves, marten: the buffalo
Numberless so that the cloud of their dust covers them:

The antelope fording the fall creeks, and the mountains and
Grazing lands and the meadow lands and the ground

Sweet and open and well-drained.
                                    We advise you to
Settle troops at the forks and to issue licenses:

Many men will have living on these lands.
There is wealth in the earth for them all and the wood
    standing

And wild birds on the water where they sleep.
There is stone in the hills for the towns of a great
    people . . ."

You have just beheld the Makers Making America:

They screwed her scrawny and gaunt with their seven-year
    panics:
They bought her back on their mortgages old-whore-cheap:

271

They fattened their bonds at her breasts till the thin blood
    ran from them.
Men have forgotten how full clear and deep
The Yellowstone moved on the gravel and the grass grew
When the land lay waiting for her westward people!

BACKGROUND WITH REVOLUTIONARIES

And the corn singing Millennium!
Lenin! Millennium! Lennium!

When they're shunting the cars on the Katy a mile off
When they're shunting the cars when they're shunting the cars
   on the Katy
You can hear the clank of the couplings riding away.

Also Comrade Devine who writes of America
Most instructively having in 'Seventy-four
Crossed to the Hoboken side on the Barclay Street Ferry.

She sits on a settle in the State of North Dakota,
O she sits on a settle in the State of North Dakota,
She can hear the engines whistle over Iowa and Idaho.

Also Comrade Edward Remington Ridge
Who has prayed God since the April of 'Seventeen
To replace in his life his lost (M.E.) religion.

And The New York Daily Worker *goes a'blowing over Arkansas,*
The New York Daily Worker *goes a'blowing over Arkansas,*
The grasses let it go along the Ozarks over Arkansas.

Even Comrade Grenadine Grilt who has tried since
August tenth for something to feel about strongly in
Verses — his personal passions having tired.

I can tell my land by the jays in the apple-trees,
Tell my land by the jays in the apple-trees,
I can tell my people by the blue-jays in the apple-trees.

Aindt you read in d' books you are all brudders?
D' glassic historic objective broves you are brudders!
You and d' Wops and d' Chinks you are all brudders!
Havend't you got it d' same ideology? Havend't you?

When it's yesterday in Oregon it's one A M in Maine
And she slides: and the day slides: and it runs: runs over us:
And the bells strike twelve strike twelve strike twelve
In Marblehead in Buffalo in Cheyenne in Cherokee:
Yesterday runs on the states like a crow's shadow.

For Marx has said to us, Workers what do you need?
And Stalin has said to us, Starvers what do you need?
You need the Dialectical Materialism!

She's a tough land under the corn, mister:
She has changed the bone in the cheeks of many races:
She has winced the eyes of the soft Slavs with her sun on them:
She has tried the fat from the round rumps of Italians:
Even the voice of the English has gone dry
And hard on the tongue and alive in the throat speaking.

She's a tough land under the oak-trees, mister:
It may be she can change the word in the book
As she changes the bone of a man's head in his children:
It may be that the earth and the men remain . . .

There is too much sun on the lids of my eyes to be listening.

"The first I knew was the spirit of my fellow, Elpenor, whose body was not yet interred under the ample ground. We had left him unwept and unburied in the halls of Circe, for that these other labors came upon us urgently. When I saw him I had compassion and sharply cried across to him: 'Elpenor, how come you here into the gloomy shades? Your feet have been quicker than my ship.' He ... answered me":

From Book xi of *The Odyssey*
(Lawrence's translation)

It is I, Odysseus —Elpenor —
Oarsman: death is between us.

Three days I have waited you,
Coming my own way,
Not your way,

(The oar-handle hard to the nipple):
Not being come in the ship,

Neither by dry earth,
There being no dry earth,

But roundabout by an art:
By the deft-in-air-darting

Way of an art severing
Earth or air or whatever.

And the place I believe to be Hell from the
Many dead and the pelts of

Great captains, emperors,
Princes, leaders-of-men,

Their rumps turned round to the wind,
And the rich with their eyes hidden,

And the redblooded, twofisted, gogetting,
He-ghosts froghonking wretchedly,

And from cairns and from creeks and from rock piles,
And out of the holes of foxes,

Fools booming like oracles,
Philosophers promising more

And worse to come of it yet
And proving it out of the textbooks.

Also the young men
Their rears strung out on the fences

Watching for shifts in the breeze:
And beyond under the lee the

Actual dead: the millions
Only a god could have killed.

The place I believe to be Hell from the
Cold and the cries and the welter of

Kings, dukes, dictators,
Heroes, headmen of cities,

Ranting orations from balconies,
Boasting to lead us back to the

Other days: to the odor of
Cooked leeks in the cold and our

Wives and the well-known landmarks —
To the normal life of a man as in

Old time and in sun,
The noon's work done

And the butterflies in their pairs
Under the beams of the areas.

*

Is it to these shores,
Odysseus, contriver of horses,
You, of all men born,

Come, and alive, demanding
The way back to your land? —
The way back to the sands and the

Boat-grooved beaches of years
Before the war and the spear-handling?

Wishful still to return
Do you ask way by the earth

Or by dark sea to a country
Known under *other* suns?

Roads on the sea fade,
And only the old ladies

Remembering scarlet coats
Hope to return to the lotuses.

Let tit-formed Tiresias tell you,
Tasting the bloody helm,
The way back by the bell or the

Book or the wars or the envy of
Men aroused against men
With a Heaven-on-earth at the end of it!

For myself — if you ask me —
There's no way back over sea water,

Nor by earth's oaks, nor beyond them:
There is only the way on.

You had best, trusting neither to
Charts nor to prophets but seamanship,
Take to the open sea,

Till you come to a clean place
With the smell of the pine in your faces and

Broom and a bitter turf
And the larks blown over the surf and the

Rocks red to the wave-height:
No sound but the wave's:

No call of a cock from the
Windward shore nor of oxen —

Gull's shadow for hawk's,
Gull's cry for the hawk's cry —

Take to the open sea
And head for the star at evening,

For an unplowed country,
Pure under cleansing sun,

With the dung burned dry on the gravel
And only the sand to have,

And begin it again: start over,
Forgetting the raised loaves and the

Home cows and the larders of
Sweating stone — the arms of the

Girl you left under lamb-skins: —
Begin it again with the hammer of

Hard rain on your heads and the
Raw fern for your bedding and

Thirst and the sea-cow's cough,
Lifting your smoke aloft
In spite of gods and the prophecy!

You have only to cross this place
And launch ship and get way on her

Working her out with the oars to the
Full wind and go forward and

Bring yourselves to a home:
To a new land: to an ocean

Never sailed. Not to Ithaca,
Not to your beds — but the withering

Seaweed under the thorn and the
Gulls and another morning . . .

*

As long as you bury me there on the beach
With my own oar stuck in the sand
So that ships standing along in
May see the stick of it straighter (though grey) than the
Olives, and ease all, and say —
"There is some man dead there that once pulled
"Water as we do with these and the thing is his
"Oarsweep" . . .
        As long as you bury me there
What will it matter to me if my name
Lacks, and the fat-leaved beach-plants cover my
Mound, and the wood of the oars goes silver as
Drift sea wood goes silver. . . .

PONY ROCK

for the memory of H.T.C.

One who has loved the hills and died, a man
Intimate with them — how their profiles fade
Large out of evening or through veils of rain
Vanish and reappear or how the sad
Long look of moonlight troubles their blind stones —
One who has loved them does not utterly,
Letting his fingers loosen and the green
Ebb from his eyeballs, close his eyes and go:

But other men, long after he is dead,
Seeing those hills will catch their breath and stare
As one who reading in a book some word
That calls joy back but can recall not where —
Only the crazy sweetness in the head —
Will stare at the black print till the page is blurred.

COOK COUNTY

The northeast wind was the wind off the lake
Blowing the oak-leaves pale side out like
Aspen: blowing the sound of the surf far
Inland over the fences: blowing for
Miles over smell of the earth the lake smell in.

The southwest wind was thunder in afternoon.
You saw the wind first in the trumpet vine
And the green went white with the sky and the weather-vane
Whirled on the barn and the doors slammed all together.
After the rain in the grass we used to gather
Wind-fallen cold white apples.

                        The west
Wind was the August wind, the wind over waste
Valleys, over the waterless plains where still
Were skulls of the buffalo, where in the sand stale
Dung lay of wild cattle. The west wind blew
Day after day as the winds on the plains blow
Burning the grass, turning the leaves brown, filling
Noon with the bronze of cicadas, far out falling
Dark on the colorless water, the lake where not
Waves were nor movement.

                  The north wind was at night
When no leaves and the husk on the oak stirs
Only nor birds then. The north wind was stars
Over the whole sky and snow in the ways
And snow on the sand where in summer the water was . . .

AETERNA POETAE MEMORIA

The concierge at the front gate where relatives
Half after two till four Mondays and Fridays
Do not turn always to look at the hospital,
Brown now and rusty with sunlight and bare
As the day you died in it, stump of the knee gangrenous,
"Le ciel dans les yeux" and the flea-bitten priest with the wafer
Forgiving you everything — You! — the concierge hadn't
Heard of you: Rimbaud? Comment s'écrit ça, Rimbaud?

But Sidis the, well, American dealer in manuscripts —
Sidis has sold the original ink decree:
Verlaine versus Verlaine [Divorce] with your name as
How do we say between gentlemen — anyway all
OK, the facts, the actual story . . .

Men remember you, dead boy — the lovers of verses!

MEN OF MY CENTURY
LOVED MOZART

Changed by this last enchantment of our kind
That still had power with our Protean souls —
This keeping charm that could constrain the mind
As nymphs in amber or in woody boles
Of oak, the live limbs by the spell confined —
Changed to ourselves by this enforcing hand
We lay like silver naked Proteus on the sand:

283

The pelt fell from us and the sea-cow's shape,
The fish's scarlet, the shark's wrinkled skin,
The seal's eyes and the brine encircled nape,
The foam's evasion the down-diving fin —
All cheats and falsehoods of our vain escape:
Changed to ourselves, sea-sleeked and dripping yet,
Our limbs lay caught and naked in the taking net.

The pure deliberate violence of the sun
Burned for an instant at our wincing eyes:
We gasped in air and struggled on the stone:
Our knees were twisted in the knotted plies:
Then suddenly to roping sand would run
The cord that bound us on that blazing shore:
We plunged in sea and breathed the grateful dark once more.

Never did we hear Mozart but the mind,
Fished from its feeding in some weedy deep,
And wound in web that must more closely bind
The more it altered from itself, would keep
One moment in that bond its perfect kind —

Never, when we would question it, but shone
Through breaking cordage silver and the god was gone.

CRITICAL OBSERVATIONS

Let us await the great American novel!

Black white yellow and red and the fawn-colored
Bastards of all of them, slick in the wrist, gone

Yank with a chewed cigar and a hat and a button,
Talking those Inglish Spich with the both ends cut:
And the New York Art and the real South African Music
(Written in Cincinnati by Irish Jews)
Dutchmen writing in English to harry the Puritans:

Puritans writing in Dutch to bate the Boor . . .

Let us await!   the great!   American novel!

And the elder ladies down on the Mediterranean,
And the younger ladies touring the towns of Spain,
And the local ladies Dakota and Pennsylvanian
Fringing like flowers the silvery flood of the Seine,

And the Young Men writing their autobiographies,
And the Old Men writing their names in the log —

Let us await the late American novel!

SENTIMENTS FOR A DEDICATION

Not to you,
Unborn generations,
Irrefutable judges of what must be true,
Infallible reviewers of neglected reputations,

("Posterity,"
The same critics,
Professor Phlip in Doctor Phlap's goatee,
The usual majority of female metics),

Not to you (though Christ
Is my sure witness,
The fame I've got has not in all respects sufficed
And rediscovery would have its fitness),

Not to you these books.
I choose the living.
I'll take (I've taken) the blank brutal looks:
You keep your sympathetic too late learned too generous for-
    giving.

I speak to my own time,
To no time after,
I say, Remember me, Remember this one rhyme
When first the dead come round me with their whispering
    laughter.

Those of one man's time
They shall be dead together:
Dos that saw the tyrants in the lime,
Ernest that saw the first snow in the fox's feather,

Stephen that saw his wife,
Cummings his quick fillies,
Eliot the caul between the ribs of life,
Pound — Pound cracking the eggs of a cock with the beautiful
    sword of Achilles.

I speak to those of my own time,
To none other,
I say, Remember me, Remember this one rhyme,
I say, Remember me among you in that land my brothers.

O living men, Remember me, Receive me among you.

THE REVENANT

O too dull brain, O unperceiving nerves
That cannot sense what so torments my soul,
But like torn trees, when deep Novembers roll
Tragic with mighty winds and vaulting curves
Of sorrowful vast sound and light that swerves
In blown and tossing eddies, branch and bole
Shudder and gesture with a grotesque dole,
A grief that misconceives the grief it serves.

O too dull brain — with some more subtle sense
I know him here within the lightless room
Reaching his hand to me, and my faint eyes
See only darkness and the night's expanse,
And horribly, within the listening gloom,
My voice comes back, still eager with surprise.

DE VOTRE BONHEUR IL NE RESTE
QUE VOS PHOTOS

Since . . .

And the rain since,
And I have not heard
Leaf at the pane all winter
Nor a bird's wing beating as that was.

I have not seen
All year your leaning face again:

Since I have never wakened but that smell
Of wet pine bark was in the room.

LINES FOR AN INTERMENT

Now it is fifteen years you have lain in the meadow:
The boards at your face have gone through: the earth is
Packed down and the sound of the rain is fainter:
The roots of the first grass are dead.

It's a long time to lie in the earth with your honor:
The world, Soldier, the world has been moving on.

The girls wouldn't look at you twice in the cloth cap:
Six years old they were when it happened:

It bores them even in books: "Soissons besieged!"
As for the gents they have joined the American Legion:

Belts and a brass band and the ladies' auxiliaries:
The Californians march in the OD silk.

We are all acting again like civilized beings:
People mention it at tea . . .

The Facts of Life we have learned are Economic:
You were deceived by the detonations of bombs:

You thought of courage and death when you thought of war-
    fare.
Hadn't they taught you the fine words were unfortunate?

Now that we understand we judge without bias:
We feel of course for those who had to die:

Women have written us novels of great passion
Proving the useless death of the dead was a tragedy.

Nevertheless it is foolish to chew gall:
The foremost writers on both sides have apologized:

The Germans are back in the Midi with cropped hair:
The English are drinking the better beer in Bavaria.

You can rest now in the rain in the Belgian meadow —
Now that it's all explained away and forgotten:
Now that the earth is hard and the wood rots:

Now you are dead . . .

SEAFARER

And learn O voyager to walk
The roll of earth, the pitch and fall
That swings across these trees those stars:
That swings the sunlight up the wall.

And learn upon these narrow beds
To sleep in spite of sea, in spite
Of sound the rushing planet makes:
And learn to sleep against this ground.

VOYAGE

for Ernest Hemingway

Heap we these coppered hulls
With headed poppies
And garlic longed-for by the eager dead

Keep we with sun-caught sails
The westward ocean
Raise we that island on the sea at last

Steep to the gull-less shore
Across the sea rush
Trade we our cargoes with the dead for sleep.

THE NIGHT DREAM

to R.L.

Neither her voice, her name,
Eyes, quietness neither,
That moved through the light, that came
Cold stalk in her teeth
Bitten of some blue flower
Knew I before nor saw.
This was a dream. Ah,
This was a dream. There was sun
Laid on the cloths of a table.
We drank together. Her mouth
Was a lion's mouth out of jade
Cold with a fable of water.

Faces I could not see
Watched me with gentleness. Grace
Folded my body with wings.
I cannot love you she said.
My head she laid on her breast.
As stillness with ringing of bees
I was filled with a singing of praise.
Knowledge filled me and peace.
We were silent and not ashamed.
Ah we were glad that day.
They asked me but it was one
Dead they meant and not I.
She was beside me she said.
We rode in a desert place.
We were always happy. Her sleeves
Jangled with jingling of gold.
They told me the wind from the south
Was the cold wind to be feared.
We were galloping under the leaves —

This was a dream, Ah
This was a dream.
                    And her mouth
Was not your mouth nor her eyes,
But the rivers were four and I knew
As a secret between us, the way
Hands touch, it was you.

UNFINISHED HISTORY

We have loved each other in this time twenty years
And with such love as few men have in them even for
One or for the marriage month or the hearing of

Three nights' carts in the street but it will leave them.
We have been lovers the twentieth year now:
Our bed has been made in many houses and evenings.

The apple-tree moves at the window in this house:
There were palms rattled the night through in one:
In one there were red tiles and the sea's hours.

We have made our bed in the changes of many months —
The light of the day is still overlong in the windows
Till night shall bring us the lamp and one another.

Those that have seen her have no thought what she is:
Her face is clear in the sun as a palmful of water:
Only by night and in love are the dark winds on it. . . .

I wrote this poem that day when I thought
Since we have loved we two so long together
Shall we have done together — all love gone?

Or how then will it change with us when the breath
Is no more able for such joy and the blood is
Thin in the throat and the time not come for death?

BEFORE MARCH

The gull's image and the gull
Meet upon the water.

All day I have thought of her:
There is nothing left of that year.

(There is sere-grass
Salt colored.)

We have annulled it with
Salt.

We have galled it clean to the clay with that one autumn:
The hedge-rows keep the rubbish and the leaves.

There is nothing left of that year in our lives but the leaves
    of it,
As though it had not been at all.

As though the love the love and the life altered.
Even ourselves are as strangers in these thoughts.

Why should I weep for this?

What have I brought her?
Of sorrow of sorrow of sorrow her heart full.

The gull
Meets with his image on the winter water.

BROKEN PROMISE

That was by the door.
Leafy evening in the apple trees.
And you would not forget this anymore
And even if you died there would be these

Touchings remembered.
                    And you would return
From any bourne from any shore
To find the evening in these leaves —
To find my arms beside this door . . .

I think, O, my not now Ophelia,
There are not always (like a moon)
Rememberings afterward:
                       (I think there are
Sometimes a few strange stars upon the sky.)

EPISTLE TO LÉON-PAUL FARGUE

I do not know what we say. I know that your poems
Move on my mind as the hand's shade of the fisherman
Blackens the brass shine out on the sea pool,
As the branch blows over the dazzle of sun on the window.
Do we call it remembering, Fargue, when the earth's shadow
Dissolves the prisms of air for us?
                       nigger leaning
At noon over the aft gunnel, sunglaze
Gone where the shade falls, where the ship's counter . . .

Reef far down and the wrecked hull . . .
Rocks shelve into blackness.
                                        Or the stars
Under the shadow of the earth like
Minnows under an old keel.

And where the elm blows over, the blind glare
Fading upon the window glass,
And they were there,
The pale forgotten faces,
They were always there:
We had not always seen them but they saw.

I do not know what we say. Your poems are not like
Names or an old scarf or the date on a photograph
Or somebody speaking Erse in the crowd at the corner
Or burned leaves — not as we say "Remember"!

INVOCATION TO THE SOCIAL MUSE

Señora, it is true the Greeks are dead.

It is true also that we here are Americans:
That we use the machines: that a sight of the god is unusual:
That more people have more thoughts: that there are

Progress and science and tractors and revolutions and
Marx and the wars more antiseptic and murderous
And music in every home: there is also Hoover.

Does the lady suggest we should write it out in The Word?
Does Madame recall our responsibilities? We are
Whores, Fräulein: poets, Fräulein, are persons of

Known vocation following troops: they must sleep with
Stragglers from either prince and of both views.
The rules permit them to further the business of neither.

It is also strictly forbidden to mix in maneuvers.
Those that infringe are inflated with praise on the plazas —
Their bones are resultantly afterwards found under newspapers.

Preferring life with the sons to death with the fathers,
We also doubt on the record whether the sons
Will still be shouting around with the same huzzas —

For we hope Lady to live to lie with the youngest.
There are only a handful of things a man likes,
Generation to generation, hungry or

Well fed: the earth's one: life's
One: Mister Morgan is not one.

There is nothing worse for our trade than to be in style.

He that goes naked goes further at last than another.
Wrap the bard in a flag or a school and they'll jimmy his
Door down and be thick in his bed — for a month:

(Who recalls the address now of the Imagists?)
But the naked man has always his own nakedness.
People remember forever his live limbs.

They may drive him out of the camps but one will take him.
They may stop his tongue on his teeth with a rope's argu-
    ment —
He will lie in a house and be warm when they are shaking.

Besides, Tovarishch, how to embrace an army?
How to take to one's chamber a million souls?
How to conceive in the name of a column of marchers?

The things of the poet are done to a man alone
As the things of love are done — or of death when he hears the
Step withdraw on the stair and the clock tick only.

Neither his class nor his kind nor his trade may come near him
There where he lies on his left arm and will die,
Nor his class nor his kind nor his trade when the blood is
    jeering

And his knee's in the soft of the bed where his love lies.

I remind you, Barinya, the life of the poet is hard —
A hardy life with a boot as quick as a fiver:

Is it just to demand of us also to bear arms?

NAT BACON'S BONES

    Nat Bacon's bones
    They never found,
    Nat Bacon's grave

297

Is wilderground:
Nat Bacon's tongue
Doth sound! Doth sound!

The rich and proud
Deny his name,
The rich and proud
Defile his fame:
The proud and free
Cry shame! Cry shame!

The planter's wife
She boasts so grand
Sir William's blood
Makes white her hand:
Nat Bacon's blood
Makes sweet this land.

GALÁN

They killed him on the gallows tree,
They tore his body part from part,
His head they took from his neck bone,
They burned before his face his heart.

They left him neither mound nor grave,
They left no tongues to speak him well,
They left no stones to mark his house,
No stone to mark: no tongue to tell.

On Guádas pole they put his head,
Socorro lifted his right hand,
San Gil his left hand lifted up,
In Charalá his foot did stand.

Socorro, when your sons forget,
San Gil, when you forget this man,
When you forget him, Charalá,
The stones — the stones — will cry Galán.

POLE STAR

Where the wheel of light is turned,
Where the axle of the night is
Turned, is motionless, where holds
And has held ancient sureness always:

Where of faring men the eyes
At oar bench at the rising bow
Have seen — torn shrouds between — the Wain
And that star's changelessness, not changing:

There upon that intent star,
Trust of wandering men, of truth
The most reminding witness, we
Fix our eyes also, waylost, the wanderers:

We too turn now to that star:
We too in whose trustless hearts

All truth alters and the lights
Of earth are out now turn to that star:

Liberty of man and mind
That once was mind's necessity
And made the West blaze up has burned
To bloody embers and the lamp's out:

Hope that was a noble flame
Has fanned to violence and feeds
On cities and the flesh of men
And chokes where unclean smoke defiles it:

Even the small spark of pride
That taught the tyrant once is dark
Where gunfire rules the starving street
And justice cheats the dead of honor:

Liberty and pride and hope —
Every guide-mark of the mind
That led our blindness once has vanished.
This star will not. Love's star will not.

Love that has beheld the face
A man has with a man's eyes in it
Bloody from the slugger's blows
Or heard the cold child cry for hunger —

Love that listens where the good,
The virtuous, the men of faith,
Proclaim the paradise on earth
And murder starve and burn to make it —

Love that cannot either sleep
Or keep rich music in the ear
Or lose itself for the wild beat
The anger in the blood makes raging —

Love that hardens into hate,
Love like hatred and as bright,
Love is that one waking light
That leads now when all others darken.

SPEECH TO THOSE WHO SAY COMRADE

The brotherhood is not by the blood certainly,
But neither are men brothers by speech — by saying so:
Men are brothers by life lived and are hurt for it.

Hunger and hurt are the great begetters of brotherhood:
Humiliation has gotten much love:
Danger I say is the nobler father and mother.

Those are as brothers whose bodies have shared fear
Or shared harm or shared hurt or indignity.
Why are the old soldiers brothers and nearest?

For this: with their minds they go over the sea a little
And find themselves in their youth again as they were in
Soissons and Meaux and at Ypres and those cities:

A French loaf and the girls with their eyelids painted
Bring back to aging and lonely men
Their twentieth year and the metal odor of danger.

It is this in life which of all things is tenderest —
To remember together with unknown men the days
Common also to them and perils ended:

It is this which makes of many a generation —
A wave of men who having the same years
Have in common the same dead and the changes.

The solitary and unshared experience
Dies of itself like the violations of love
Or lives on as the dead live eerily:

The unshared and single man must cover his
Loneliness as a girl her shame for the way of
Life is neither by one man nor by suffering.

Who are the born brothers in truth? The puddlers
Scorched by the same flame in the same foundries,
Those who have spit on the same boards with the blood in it,

Ridden the same rivers with green logs,
Fought the police in the parks of the same cities,
Grinned for the same blows, the same flogging,

Veterans out of the same ships, factories,
Expeditions for fame: the founders of continents:
Those that hid in Geneva a time back,

Those that have hidden and hunted and all such —
Fought together, labored together: they carry the
Common look like a card and they pass touching.

Brotherhood! No word said can make you brothers!
Brotherhood only the brave earn and by danger or
Harm or by bearing hurt and by no other.

Brotherhood here in the strange world is the rich and
Rarest giving of life and the most valued,
Not to be had for a word or a week's wishing.

SPEECH TO THE DETRACTORS

What should a man do but love excellence
Whether of earth or art,
Whether the hare's leap or the heart's recklessness?

What honor has any man but with eagerness,
Valuing wasteless things,
To praise the great and speak the unpraise meagerly?

Because the heroes with the swords have vanished
Leaving us nearer by
Actual life and the more human manhood —

Because the common face, the anonymous figure,
The nameless and mortal man,
Is our time's birth to bear and to be big with —

Because the captains and the kings are dust —
Need we deny our hearts
Their natural duty and the thing they must do?

Not to the wearers of wreaths but those who bring them,
Coming with heaped-up arms,
Is fame the noble and ennobling thing.

Bequeathers of praise, the unnamed numberless peoples
Leave on the lasting earth
Not fame but their hearts' love of fame for keeping.

They raise not alone memorial monuments:
Outlasting these
They raise their need to render greatness honor.

The ignorant and rabble rain erases
Dates and the dead man's kind.
It leaves the blindness of the stones that praised him.

Why then must this time of ours be envious?
Why must the great man now,
Sealed from the mouths of worms, be sucked by men's mouths?

Refusing ribbons that the rest have clowned for,
Dying and wishing peace,
The best are eaten by the envy round them.

When Lawrence died the hate was at his bier.
Fearing there might have lived
A man really noble, really superior,

Fearing that worth had lived and had been modest,
Men of envious minds
Ate with venom his new buried body.

We cheat ourselves in cheating worth of wonder.
Not the unwitting dead
But we who leave the praise unsaid are plundered.

SPEECH TO A CROWD

Tell me, my patient friends, awaiters of messages,
From what other shore, from what stranger,
Whence, was the word to come? Who was to lesson you?

Listeners under a child's crib in a manger,
Listeners once by the oracles, now by the transoms,
Whom are you waiting for? Who do you think will explain?

Listeners thousands of years and still no answer —
Writers at night to Miss Lonely-Hearts, awkward spellers,
Open your eyes! There is only earth and the man!

There is only you. There is no one else on the telephone:
No one else is on the air to whisper:
No one else but you will push the bell.

No one knows if you don't: neither ships
Nor landing-fields decode the dark between.
You have your eyes and what your eyes see, is.

The earth you see is really the earth you are seeing.
The sun is truly excellent, truly warm,
Women are beautiful as you have seen them —

Their breasts (believe it) like cooing of doves in a portico.
They bear at their breasts tenderness softly. Look at them!
Look at yourselves. You are strong. You are well formed.

Look at the world — the world you never took!
It is really true you may live in the world heedlessly.
Why do you wait to read it in a book then?

Write it yourselves! Write to yourselves if you need to!
Tell yourselves there is sun and the sun will rise.
Tell yourselves the earth has food to feed you.

Let the dead men say that men must die!
Who better than you can know what death is?
How can a bone or a broken body surmise it?

Let the dead shriek with their whispering breath.
Laugh at them! Say the murdered gods may wake
But we who work have end of work together.

Tell yourselves the earth is yours to take!

Waiting for messages out of the dark you were poor.
The world was always yours: you would not take it.

THE LOST SPEAKERS

Never do sea birds sing,

Never on earth's shingle
Any man — keeper of
Ocean-salted sheep —
Heard from the surge music.

Neither were seamen used,
Light aloft in the east
And the soft night wind increasing,
Wakening to have heard
Wild music of birds.

The sea makes all things silent:
Even these that in isles
And inland covert of thickets
Sing till the air is quick and the
Leaf stirs, creatures
Most formed for the sweet
Heartlessness of singing.

Wings — not even the wing,
Strongest of all things mortal,
Gives to the mind before
Unending rings of horizon
Desire to sing.

            Their eyes
Changed, their work broken,
Many of ours who spoke in the
Inland years are dumb now,
Seeing our march has come to the
Land's end and beyond is
Surf and the sea to wander.

Restless at dusk they turn from the
Beach and the sea's churning.
They do not look to the sea.
They are silent: their mouths move secretly.

POEM FOR THE TIME OF CHANGE

There were over me three hawks.

> This was the season when the flies will walk
> The chimney stones, the kitchen ceilings.

Three hawks wheeled in the
Ragged and rushing sky:
Head to the wind's violence.

> This was the season when the dopey flies
> In house-room groping where the vapor rises
> Cling and live a little till the wry
> Cold
> Kills them with their numb wings weakly folded.

Three hawks soared in the
Rushing sky: before them
Winter and its snow,
Sleet, the wind blowing.
Three hawks soared.

THE GERMAN GIRLS! THE GERMAN GIRLS!

*(They recall the promises in the books and the
uniforms of their childhood. They recall and compare)*

Are you familiar with the mounted men?

Who asked us this? The linden leaves? The pianos
Answering evening with yesterday — they or the leaves?

Who asked us this in the cat's hour when evening
Curls in the sitting-room listening under the lamps
To the linden leaves in the wind and the courtyard pianos?

Are you familiar with the mounted men —
The cavalry lot with the hot leap at the fences,
Smellers of horse-sweat, swingers of polished boots,
Leather crotch to the britches, brave looters,
Lope over flowerbeds, wheel on the well-kept lawn,
Force your knees in the negligée under the awning,
Bold boys with a blouse, insolent handlers,
Bring you the feel again, bring you the German man:
Bring you the blood to the breasts and the bride's look on you —
Laughter fumbling at the clumsy hooks.

Are you familiar with the mounted men?

Who asks us this? The broken doors? The dead boys
Answering morning with yesterday — they or the doors?
Who asks us now in the dog's hour when morning
Sniffs at the dead boys in the prison trench
And wakes the women whom no mouth will waken?

Are we familiar with the mounted men! —
The grocery lot with the loud talk in the restaurants,
Smellers of delicatessen, ex-cops,
Barbers, fruit-sellers, sewers of underwear, shop-keepers,
Those with the fat rumps foolish in uniforms,
Red in the face with the drums with the brass tunes,
Fingerers under a boy's frock, playfellows,
Tricksters with trousers, whip-swingers, eye-balls glazed:
Bring you the feel again — bring you the crawling skin!
Bring you the blood to your throat and the thighs wincing!

Are you familiar with the mounted men —

Who sold us so? Who told us this to tempt us?

There was a voice that asked us in those evenings
Peaceful with always when our muslin sleeves
Moved through the past like promises, and children
Played as forever and the silence filled:
There was a voice among the afternoons
That asked us this — the crowds? — the red balloons?
The July flowers in the public gardens?
There was a voice that asked us under stars too —

Are you familiar with the mounted men?

Who asked us this upon the Sunday benches?
What pimp procured us to leave loose our doors
And made us whores and wakened us with morning?
Only by us the men of blood came in!
Only by women's doors, by women's windows —
Only by us the flags, the flagrant brass,
The belts, the ribbons, the false manhood passes!
Only by women's tenderness can come
The midnight volley and the prison drum-beat!

Are you familiar with the mounted men?

Who asked us this?

THERE WAS A VOICE THAT ASKED US!

"DOVER BEACH" — A NOTE
TO THAT POEM

The wave withdrawing
Withers with seaward rustle of flimsy water
Sucking the sand down, dragging at empty shells.
The roil after it settling, too smooth, smothered . . .

After forty a man's a fool to wait in the
Sea's face for the full force and the roaring of
Surf to come over him: droves of careening water.
After forty the tug's out and the salt and the
Sea follow it: less sound and violence.
Nevertheless the ebb has its own beauty —
Shells sand and all and the whispering rustle.
There's earth in it then and the bubbles of foam gone.

Moreover — and this too has its lovely uses —
It's the outward wave that spills the inward forward
Tripping the proud piled mute virginal
Mountain of water in wallowing welter of light and
Sound enough — thunder for miles back. It's a fine and a
Wild smother to vanish in: pulling down —
Tripping with outward ebb the urgent inward.

Speaking alone for myself it's the steep hill and the
Toppling lift of the young men I am toward now,
Waiting for that as the wave for the next wave.
Let them go over us all I say with the thunder of
What's to be next in the world. It's we will be under it!

THE SUNSET PIECE

*for Phelps Putnam upon the completion
of our fortieth year in this place*

Christ but this earth goes over to the squall of time!
Hi but she heels to it — rail down, ribs down, rolling
Dakotas under her hull! And the night climbing
Sucking the green from the ferns by these Berkshire boulders!

She'll roll the two of us clean of her one day lifting —
Draining the dark from her gutters with slick slide,
The night running off from her — you and me like driftwood:
Men we've known like litter on a tide.

She'll roll us clear of her, drowned in a dragging wake,
Time going over us, touching us like a sea —
You and me that bragged our berths were taken
For death's eventual wharves and foreign quay:

You and me that bragged of an end to the journey —
The bow brought fast, the stern warped in, the screw
Dead in a dirty wash and the sea gulls turning:
Earnest faces and no face we knew.

You and me!
             And watch her! She's God's planet!
She luffs in the wind and she logs in the seaway rolling.

This earth's no ship to board for any land —
Even for death's.
                 The night among the boulders. . . .

WORDS TO BE SPOKEN

for Baoth Wiborg son of Gerald and Sara Murphy who died in New England in his sixteenth year and a tree was planted there

O shallow ground
That over ledges
Shoulders the gentle year,

Tender O shallow
Ground your grass is
Sisterly touching us:

Your trees are still:
They stand at our side in the
Night lantern.

Sister O shallow
Ground you inherit
Death as we do.

Your year also —
The young face,
The voice — vanishes.

Sister O shallow
Ground
       let the silence of
Green be between us
And the green sound.

THE WOMAN ON THE STAIR

THE WHITE POEM

With haste, with the haggard color,
With shad-blow, plum-blossoms (multitudes)
Came and again spring,
Sole on a bush, single in
Apple branches, tasteless,
Filling the low places as
Water in flood fills them:
Leaving blossomless hills.

Over were three gulls
And the oak making little cover,
And you were ashamed of love
Lacking the sheet, looking up
Mile after mile in the cup of the
Open sky and the birds in it —
Candle lacking and words.

Over were three gulls
And your mouth like salt and you hated me.
Why? For the winter's wait? —
For the haste? For the haggard color?

(ii)
THE ABSENCE

Hunger nor thirst nor any bodily famine
Failing bread to be eaten, meat consumed,
Is comparable or any way to be likened to

This, this lack, this absence, this not to be found
Of you whom neither may tongue take nor fingers
Break to be broken nor the mouth devour —

Only by hands arms starved be with
Momentarily taking nothing away
But the need to return to you taking nothing away.

No hunger was ever sharp as this hunger —
The absence of you on a plain bed in this city
Counting the night out by the iron tongues.

(iii)
THE TREACHERY

As a candle flame is straight within the curve of hands
So strictly stands

That moment in the violence of the snow.
Although the wind could blow,

Although the white unable wandering of the air
Whirled everywhere,

Although the storm drove wildly through the winter street,
The unnamed sudden doubt of her deceit

Stood in that violence like a breathless flame.
Where wildest winter came

There stood as still as candle to the palm
The desperate heart's inexplicable calm.

(iv)
The Quarrel

I never said that you were changed.
I said — and if I looked at you
With fear it was my natural heart —
I said dear love that you were true.

I said your body was still yours
And bore no bruise where he had been:
Your mouth was still the mouth I knew,
The hair was yours, the throat, the skin.

I said I could not see his eyes
In your eyes doubled: could not hear
The whisper of his actual breath
Beneath your hair, against your ear.

I never said that you were changed:
I said — in dread as though you came
Unaltered from the earth of death —
I said your eyes were still the same!

(v)
The Reconciliation

Time like the repetitions of a child's piano
Brings me the room again the shallow lamp the love
The night the silence the slow bell the echoed answer.

By no thing here or lacking can the eyes discover
The hundred winter evenings that have gone between
Nor know for sure the night is this and not that other.

318

The room is here, the lamp is here, the mirror's leaning
Searches the same deep shadow where her knees are caught:
All these are here within the room as I have seen them.

Time has restored them all as in that rainy autumn:
Even the echoes of that night return to this —
All as they were when first the earthy evening brought them.

Between this night and that there is no human distance:
There is no space an arm could not out-reach by much —
And yet the stars most far apart are not more distant.

Between my hand that touched and her soft breast that touches
The irremediable past, as steep as stone,
Wider than water, like all land and ocean stretches:

We touch and by that touching farness are alone.

(vi)
The Second Love

In love not love there never are two lovers:
There are but two together with blind eyes
Watching within what ecstasy love suffers.

One, like a shore at which the water rises,
Senses the flooding of a sea to spate
Her naked and lovely longing with its rising.

One, like the flooding of a sea, awaits
The smooth resistance of the gradual shore
To be fallen in shudder of hush from his headlong greatness.

What they remember each of the other more than
Meeting of mouths or even the profound touch
Is their own ecstasy heavy to be borne.

So it is, even with these whose touching
Makes them a moment on a bed to share
What time with all its timid gifts begrudges.

Neither her serious mouth nor pitiful hair
Nor his mouth mortal with the murderous need
Troubles their hearts to tenderness.

                        They stare
Each in the other's face like those who feed
Delight in mirrors: and as though alone
Learn from each other where their love will lead them.

(vii)
THE ROOM BY THE RIVER

They think in each other's arms of the sound of the surf.
(The sound in that street is of barges:
The wake v's out, curves,
Breaks on the bulkhead blurring the water stars.)

They think how the sound of the surf is the sound of forever
Turning upon the returning of time,
Bringing the wave back that has left them,
Taking their knees again with the sea's climbing.

(The sound in that street is the sound of the barges:
One wave breaks along the brackish shore:
Nothing returns. . . .)
                        He rises from her arms to
Dress in silence and go out the door.

320

(viii)
THE REMEMBRANCE

I have forgotten you. There is grey light on my
Hands and I have forgotten you. There is light enough.
There is light enough left to forget your face by,
Voice by, to forget you. As long as the
Light lasts on my hands I forget you.
There needs be some light: a little.
A man remembers by night — even the
Windows barely a sure shape and the
Shadows anything, standing for anything.
Night is never alone, it remembers.
At night the hair mouth eyes —
The eyes — at night they return to us.

Between the night and me this light,
Little enough, a thin cover,
Fragile defense against the meaning dark
Where eyes are always but not seen till night comes.
Now for a little there is light between.

(ix)
THE LATE MEETING

Too cold too windy and too dark
The autumn dawn withholds the bees
And bold among the door-yard trees
The crow cries, the wild foxes bark.

Day alters, seasons alter, we
Walking the wet rut alter too:
The fault of strangeness is with you:
Strangeness is the fault in me.

321

We know each other, not the friend
Each for the other's love once made:
We know the cold, and are afraid
Of new years, now the year will end.

(x)
THE RELEASE

I know where time has departed:
Time has departed thither.
From that unaltering country
Never will time turn.

Tawny and still is that country.
Thither is time gone.
Even the air is motionless:
No leaf may fall there.

Time has left me and gone
To that changeless and unchanged country.
Thither has time departed.
There at a day it stands.

You who stood in that country
You may not ruffle your hair:
You may not move nor may even
The scarf slip from you carelessly.

You are caught in the standing of time.
You may not move nor be changed.
Time's past is still:
Time's stillness has taken you.

This is the winter of time:
This is the water frozen:
The oak mute in the wind:
    Love's memory motionless.

America was Promises (1939)

Who is the voyager in these leaves?
Who is the traveler in this journey
Deciphers the revolving night: receives
The signal from the light returning?

America was promises to whom?

          East were the
Dead kings and the remembered sepulchres:
West was the grass.
        The groves of the oaks were at evening.

Eastward are the nights where we have slept.

And we move on: we move down:
With the first light we push forward:
We descend from the past as a wandering people from
    mountains.
We cross into the day to be discovered.

The dead are left where they fall — at dark
At night late under the coverlets.
We mark the place with the shape of our teeth on our
    fingers.
The room is left as it was: the love

Who is the traveler in these leaves these
Annual waters and beside the doors
Jonquils: then the rose: the eaves
Heaping the thunder up: the mornings
Opening on like great valleys
Never till now approached: the familiar trees
Far off, distant with the future:
The hollyhocks beyond the afternoons:
The butterflies over the ripening fruit on the balconies:
And all beautiful
All before us

America was always promises.
From the first voyage and the first ship there were prom-
    ises—
"the tropic bird which does not sleep at sea"
"the great mass of dark heavy clouds which is a sign"
"the drizzle of rain without wind which is a sure sign"
"the whale which is an indication"
"the stick appearing to be carved with iron"
"the stalk loaded with roseberries"
"and all these signs were from the west"
"and all night heard birds passing."

Who is the voyager on these coasts?
Who is the traveler in these waters

Expects the future as a shore: foresees
Like Indies to the west the ending — **he**
The rumor of the surf intends?

America was promises — to whom?

Jefferson knew:
Declared it before God and before history:
Declares it still in the remembering tomb.
The promises were Man's: the land was his —
Man endowed by his Creator:
Earnest in love: perfectible by reason:
Just and perceiving justice: his natural nature
Clear and sweet at the source as springs in trees **are.**
It was Man the promise contemplated.
The times had chosen Man: no other:
Bloom on his face of every future:
Brother of stars and of all travelers:
Brother of time and of all mysteries:
Brother of grass also: of fruit trees.
It was Man who had been promised: who should have.
Man was to ride from the Tidewater: over the Gap:
West and South with the water: taking the book with **him:**
Taking the wheat seed: corn seed: pip of apple:
Building liberty a farmyard wide:
Breeding for useful labor: for good looks:
For husbandry: humanity: for pride —
Practising self-respect and common decency.

And Man turned into men in Philadelphia
Practising prudence on a long-term lease:
Building liberty to fit the parlor:
Bred for crystal on the frontroom shelves:
Just and perceiving justice by the dollar:

Patriotic with the bonds at par
(And their children's children brag of their deeds for the
    Colonies).
Man rode up from the Tidewater: over the Gap:
Turned into men: turned into two-day settlers:
Lawyers with the land-grants in their caps:
Coon-skin voters wanting theirs and getting it.

Turned the promises to capital: invested it.

America was always promises:
"the wheel like a sun as big as a cart wheel
    with many sorts of pictures on it
    the whole of fine gold"

"twenty golden ducks
    beautifully worked and very natural looking
    and some like dogs of the kind they keep"

And they waved us west from the dunes: they cried out
Colua! Colua!
Mexico! Mexico! . . . Colua!

America was promises to whom?

Old Man Adams knew. He told us —
An aristocracy of compound interest
Hereditary through the common stock!
We'd have one sure before the mare was older.
"The first want of every man was his dinner:
The second his girl." Kings were by the pocket.
Wealth made blood made wealth made blood made wealthy.
Enlightened selfishness gave lasting light.
Winners bred grandsons: losers only bred!

And the Aristocracy of politic selfishness
Bought the land up: bought the towns: the sites:
The goods: the government: the people. Bled them.
Sold them. Kept the profit. Lost itself.

The Aristocracy of Wealth and Talents
Turned its talents into wealth and lost them.
Turned enlightened selfishness to wealth.
Turned self-interest into bankbooks: balanced them.
Bred out: bred to fools: to hostlers:
Card sharps: well dressed women: dancefloor doublers.
The Aristocracy of Wealth and Talents
Sold its talents: bought the public notice:
Drank in public: went to bed in public:
Patronized the arts in public: pal'd with
Public authors public beauties: posed in
Public postures for the public page.
The Aristocracy of Wealth and Talents
Withered of talent and ashamed of wealth
Bred to sonsinlaw: insane relations:
Girls with open secrets: sailors' Galahads:
Prurient virgins with the tales to tell:
Women with dead wombs and living wishes.

The Aristocracy of Wealth and Talents
Moved out: settled on the Continent:
Sat beside the water at Rapallo:
Died in a rented house: unwept: unhonored.

*

And the child says I see the lightning on you.

The weed between the railroad tracks
Tasting of sweat: tasting of poverty:

The bitter and pure taste where the hawk hovers:
Native as the deer bone in the sand

O my America for whom?

For whom the promises? For whom the river
"It flows west! Look at the ripple of it!"
The grass "So that it was wonderful to see
And endless without end with wind wonderful!"
The Great Lakes: landless as oceans: their beaches
Coarse sand: clean gravel: pebbles:
Their bluffs smelling of sunflowers: smelling of surf:
Of fresh water: of wild sunflowers . . . wilderness.
For whom the evening mountains on the sky:
The night wind from the west: the moon descending?

Tom Paine knew.
Tom Paine knew the People.
The promises were spoken to the People.
History was voyages toward the People.
Americas were landfalls of the People.
Stars and expectations were the signals of the People.

Whatever was truly built the People had built it.
Whatever was taken down they had taken down.
Whatever was worn they had worn — ax-handles: fiddle-
    bows:
Sills of doorways: names for children: for mountains.
Whatever was long forgotten they had forgotten —
Fame of the great: names of the rich and their mottos.
The People had the promises: they'd keep them.
They waited their time in the world: they had wise sayings.
They counted out their time by day to day.
They counted it out day after day into history.

They had time and to spare in the spill of their big fists.
They had all the time there was like a handful of wheat
    seed.
When the time came they would speak and the rest would
    listen.

And the time came and the People did not speak.

The time came: the time comes: the speakers
Come and these who speak are not the People.

These who speak with gunstocks at the doors:
These the coarse ambitious priest
Leads by the bloody fingers forward:
These who reach with stiffened arm to touch
What none who took dared touch before:
These who touch the truth are not the People.

These the savage fables of the time
Lick at the fingers as a bitch will waked at morning:
These who teach the lie are not the People.

The time came: the time comes

Comes and to whom? To these? Was it for these
The surf was secret on the new-found shore?
Was it for these the branch was on the water? —
These whom all the years were toward
The golden images the clouds the mountains?

Never before: never in any summer:
Never were days so generous: stars so mild:
Even in old men's talk or in books or remembering
Far back in a gone childhood

Or farther still to the light where Homer wanders —
The air all lucid with the solemn blue
That hills take at the distance beyond change. . . .
That time takes also at the distances.

Never were there promises as now:
Never was green deeper: earth warmer:
Light more beautiful to see: the sound of
Water lovelier: the many forms of
Leaves: stones: clouds: beasts: shadows
Clearer more admirable or the faces
More like answering faces or the hands
Quicker: more brotherly:
                                    the aching taste of
Time more salt upon the tongue: more human

Never in any summer: and to whom?

At dusk: by street lights: in the rooms we ask this.

We do not ask for Truth now from John Adams.
We do not ask for Tongues from Thomas Jefferson.
We do not ask for Justice from Tom Paine.
We ask for answers.

And there is an answer.

There is Spain Austria Poland China Bohemia.
There are dead men in the pits in all those countries.
Their mouths are silent but they speak. They say
"The promises are theirs who take them."

Listen! Brothers! Generation!
Listen! You have heard these words. Believe it!
Believe the promises are theirs who take them!

330

Believe unless we take them for ourselves
Others will take them for the use of others!
Believe unless we take them for ourselves
All of us: one here: another there:
Men not Man: people not the People:
Hands: mouths: arms: eyes: not syllables —
Believe unless we take them for ourselves
Others will take them: not for us: for others!

Believe unless we take them for ourselves
Now: soon: by the clock: before tomorrow:
Others will take them: not for now: for longer!

Listen! Brothers! Generation!
Companions of leaves: of the sun: of the slow evenings:
Companions of the many days: of all of them:
Listen! Believe the speaking dead! Believe
The journey is our journey. Oh believe
The signals were to us: the signs: the birds by
Night: the breaking surf.

Believe

America is promises to
Take!
America is promises to
Us
To take them
Brutally
With love but
Take them.

Oh believe this!

PART FOUR

Colloquy for the States (1943)

There's talk, says Illinois.
                    Is there, says Iowa.
There's talk on the east wind, says Illinois.

Talk about what? says Dakota, says Kansas, says Arkansas.

Can't make out: too far east, says Michigan.

East of the roosters, says Indiana,
                              East of the
Morning crow, says Ohio.
                              East, says York State.

East still, says Connecticut: on east.

It's down east from here, says Massachusetts.

It's east of the quoddy, says Maine, but I hear it.
                                        Hear

335

What? says Texas.
                What can you hear? says Virginia.
Can't be sure, says Maine. Surf on the reefs.
Ice pounding away on the pans in Penobscot.

Listen, says Oregon.
                Scoop your ear, says Kentucky.

Can't tell, says Maine. Too much fog.
Bells on the Old Orchard. Horns at Ogunquit.

Listen, says Mississippi.
                Try to, says Texas.
Lean your lug to the loo'ard, says Massachusetts.

It's tall talk, says Maine. It's tall talking —
Tall as a calf in a fog.
                Call it, says Arkansas.
It's mean talk, says Maine. It's mouthy meaning.

Mean about what? says Nebraska.
                                Mean about us.
What about us? says Kentucky, says Texas, says Idaho.

I gather they don't like us, says Maine.
                                Do
Tell! says Connecticut.
                I vum! says New Hampshire.
I gather we've low ways, says Maine
                                That
So? says Kansas
                Take my seat, says Michigan.

It's how we marry, says Maine. We ain't choosers.
We scrabble them up and we mingle them in. We marry the
Irish girls with the shoes with the quick come-after.

We marry the Spaniards with the evening eyes.
We marry the English with the tiptoe faces.
We marry the golden Swedes: the black Italians:
The German girls with the thick knees: the Mexicans
Lean and light in the sun with the jingling and jangling:
The Chileñas for luck: the Jews for remembrance: the Scots
    girls
Tall as a tall man — silver as salmon;
The French with the skillful fingers: the long loves.
I gather we marry too many, says Maine: too various.
I gather we're bad blood: we're mixed people.

That what they say? says Texas.
              That's what they're saying.
What's in their soup, says Arkansas: what they been eating?

What's in their hair? says Maryland.
                  Aren't they men?
Can't they make it with strangers? says Alabama.

Are they shy? says Missouri.
            Or what? says Montana.
            I gather they're
Bred pure, says Maine: they're superior people.

Have they seen our kids, says York State: the tall girls
The small elegant breasts they have like Egyptians,
The long legs with the delicate slender bones
And the wrists supple and small as a man's three fingers —
The way they walk on the world with their narrow heels?
You can tell them anywhere: tell them in any country —
The height of their heads and the tilt of their heels when
    they walk.
A head higher than most: a hand smaller.

Have they raced our boys, says Michigan — fast as black
    snakes:
Quick on the gun as quail: the sweet striders:
The watchful lads in the lead: dangerous followers:
Strong hearts in the stretch home. Have they beaten them?

I gather they haven't, says Maine. I gather we're mixed
Bloods: they don't take to us.
                Don't they! says Kansas.
Have they seen our towns, says Kansas: seen our wheat:
Seen our flatcars in the Rocky Mountains:
Seen our four-lane highways: seen our planes
Silver over the Alleghenies the Lakes
The big timber the tall corn the horses —
Silver over the snow-line: over the surf?
Have they seen our farms? says Kansas: and who plowed them?
Have they seen our towns? says Kansas: and who planned
    them?

Have they seen our men? says Kansas.
                        Gather not:
Gather we're bad blood, says Maine. They say so.

Who says? says Missouri: who's this saying?

Where from? says Montana: where's he from?

Where from: who? says Georgia.
                    Can't make out.
Way east: east of the Rhine it might be.
The wind veers, says Maine. I don't make out.

East of the Rhine: so that's it, says Montana.

The pure-bloods by the Rhine, says Carolina.

The blood we left behind us, says Wisconsin.

The blood we left behind us when we left:
The blood afraid of travel, says Nevada.

The blood afraid of changes says Kentucky.

The blood afraid of strangers, says Vermont: —
Strange stars and strange women: the two of them.

The blood that never hankered for a strange one: —
A dark one, says Dakota, with strange hair.

Stayed home and married their kin, says Missouri.

Married their cousins who looked like their mothers, says
    Michigan.

So that's all: east of the Rhine! says Wisconsin.

So that's all, says Arkansas: all for that —
All for the pure-bred boys afraid of strangers.

Surf on the reefs, says Maine: ice on Penobscot . . . .

There's talk, says Iowa, ...
                        Talk, says Illinois, ...

Bells on the Old Orchard: horns at Ogunquit . . . .

Clash of corn in the wind, says Illinois, ...

ACTFIVE (1948)

" . . . with no one to whom the duty could be owed and
still to owe the duty — no one here or elsewhere: even the
noble image of ourselves in which we trusted broken and
destroyed."

(i) THE STAGE ALL BLOOD

Whereat — the King unthroned, the God
Departed with his leopards serpents
Fish, and on the forestage Man
Murdered, his wounds like words so many wounds —
Whereat there cometh, audible as sound, a
Silence as if monstrously the sea
That, like a heart, all night upon the beach
Had counted ten had counted ten should
Cease — Whereat there cometh silence like a sound.

And who shall play the hero in the piece?

The empty throne, the bleeding shape,
The gaping sky, the lights that lead
Beyond us and the minutes still to stay —
Who shall speak the couplet for the ending of the play?

Even Nero
Every age must have its hero —
Even the faint age of fear:

Even here
                upon these ruins
                                where the rose
Has no remembrance, where the looking glass reflects
Stars and Orion, clouds and empty air,
Where the shuffling wind
Wanders witless on the bombed-out stair:
Even in this nameless place
Where the chirping of the crickets in the porch effaces
Time and the inscriptions.

Every circle has its center
Where the curve is made and meant.
Every history has one to point its moral
As the annals of the creatures of the coral
Turn upon the surf upon the reef
Or the annals of the tombs within the mound
Upon the amphor where the gold is found.
The flesh has its belief
And the bone its expectation:
Time that turns the wheel of night
Through the iron constellation,
Time that drives the herded stars among the trees,
Turns not on the turning pole but these.

But who will utter the soliloquies
Sole upon the ramparts in these stars
Or hard and bold and thinking with the spill
Of twisted paper on this stair of stone?

Who will play the hero in this story
Where the planet circles in the urn —
Where the stars and petals turn —
Now the far-off figures in the morning air
Are gone and gone the voices in the silver dwelling? —

Now the night has swung the iron gate
And now the stone of God is turned to stone —
Now the King is vanished in his state
And Man is murdered and the flesh the bone
Stand upon the stage alone
And watch and wait?

The God! Oh the God — silver in aspen,
Dissolving in the dolphin's wake,
Discovered in cloud, in a girl's lap,
In a fire of thorns, in a dream, in a boy born on the
Same day at the very hour:
Giver of every good,
Of evils also, of the slaughtered city,
The youth killed by the horse, the girl
Dead on marriage morning in the solemn trees:
Of each sparrow the watch over —
The God that once, within the temple or the grove,
Invisible in beast, in stone, in wood,
In whose Well was all our good,
In whose All was all our Ill,
In whose Will the Well the Ill and All had meaning —
The presence of the God within the flaming on the hill,
Or the voice upon the sea, or the blindness in the dark,
Or the darkness in the mind,
That gave the meaning for the wonder and the fear to find!

The King once — the King's son
Concealed at birth, his consequence made known
By wrenching sword from chock of stone,
Or drawing bowstring that no other,
Or trick turned back on wicked brother —
The King once, the King's son,
That bore the burden for each one,
Shouldered heavy weight of will,
Chose the choice for good or ill,
Wore the burning shirt of pride,
Tore it from his flesh and died:
The King once, the King's son,
In whose rule were all things real,
In whose must the pain the death the dearth had justice —
The statute of the King
That in the anguish of the noose, or the choking of the
    string,
Or the drumbeat in the night,
Or the dead upon the field,
Gave wrong its right!

Man! earth's creature!
Found in plowfield in the winter sleet,
Found among the fishnets on the sand,
At oar, at axe, at forge, on evening street
In every city, found wherever hand
Touched hand, touched earth, touched sea, took food to eat
Or cupped to water in a trough, or lay
Finger in finger on a bed till day —
Man once, time's companion,
Gentled by labor, taught by stone and wood,
By beast and rope, by rain and sun and seed,
To bear and to be born, give need for need,
Live and let live, answer ill with good,

Keep peace, hate war, bind wounds, be patient, love —
Man once in whose love
Peace had hope and fear its intercession —
Man, the sweet humanity of Man
(The charity of flesh)
That in the treason of the wise,
The ambition of the great,
The indifference of the skies,
Gave history its reason!

Who will speak the couplet that can tell —
Act the secret all must share —
Now the stone is stone and in the listening air
No voice will answer from the empty throne:
Now Man is murdered and his sweetness blown
With maggots of the intellectual lies,
His monument the smoke of hate that stands
By day a cloud by night the burning of the lands,
His grave the fallen cities where the flies
Crawl upon his million tangled hands
Upon his million eyes —
Now Man is murdered and, where once he stood,
Armed and in terror, ignorant, rank with blood,
Cruel and desperate, stained with such a stain
As earth nor fire, sea nor the dear rain
Shall wash from heart or hand, his murderers remain.

And I said
Who will give meaning to these broken stones these
Broken bodies violated brains
Corrupted spirits shriveled hearts?

Who will give reason to these ruined cities
Standing and fallen — standing as well as fallen —

Mountainous under the ruptured sky:
Shamed in the shattered innocence of air?

Who will give right to wrongs that death has done us —
That we ourselves have done us worse than death?

Who shall be the hero in the play?
And where, upon what stone or throne or will or
Word or plinth or power shall he stand
To still the world to peace again; to poise
Eternity upon the turning pole
Again: to make us men:
To make us whole?

Who is he that tiptoe in the wings
Takes breath to speak and will not show his face?

On the blond and plunging planet
In the ringling of the sun
Wheels she wheels and he upon it:

On the hull of the downed planet
In the drowning of the sky
Scans the dark and will not die:

He who means what all our time
Writes upon the silver screen
And cannot read and cannot rhyme.

(ii) The Masque of Mummers

The corse is taken off: the scene
Recovers from its sullen light:
A trumpet sounds: the blinds between
The players and the night are drawn.
A dawn of candles is composed,
And, closed behind the solemn doors,
A music marvels with its drums.
The doors swing open and there comes,
Each the Hero of the Age,
A masque of mummers on the bloody stage.

For with us the past is brought down.
With us the divisions, the withdrawals,
The yellow curtain in the bedroom window,
The black screen with the gold dragon dividing
The inward moment from the outward,
The plaster and the lath between the lives,
The dignity of reticence behind the customs,
The customary forms against the meeting of the eyes are
Blown down, blown out,
Scattered in gutters, gutted in ashes, leaving the
Back room with the brick gone and the bed
Naked under the moon, the impress on the pillow:

Leaving the secret heart to crowd
For shelter with the crowd — to lie
Safe and hidden from the sky
In the crypt of light, the loud,
The public night, where none need bear
The staring dark, the marking eye,
The searching heartbeat of the air —
Bombers of the huge despair:

Leaving the secret heart to take
Public shelter from the doom
In the vast and buried room
Where beneath the fallen past
The bulbs burn and the sleepers lie awake.
What do you find
By the smoking tapers
Choked and blind
That light this air? —

What do you find
By the evening papers
Tossed like torches on the stair?

Heroes for the fairy stories!
Deeds and words to keep us warm
Till the wolf puts off his skin
Till the prince takes back his form
Till the talking birds begin.

What do you find
Where the feasting sages
Float their candles
On the stream?
What do you find
By the golden pages
Burning with the holy dream?

Heroes for the infant's dream!
Bedtime comforters
Delicious thumbs
Lights beneath the chamber door
Footsteps where the watching waiting father runs and
    comes: —

The Science Hero with the secret box —
He that finds the key beneath the lake,
Twists the riddle and unlocks
All the golden answers. Take
One! The apple? Right. Take two!
Death? It's very good for you.

The Boyo of Industry!
Him that hists the heavy stone
None but him could heave before —
None can budge but him alone.
Look! Beneath the stone! The sword!

The Revolutionary Hero with the Book,
Cleansed of every feeling — love and
All — who kills the ghost already dead:
Doubles back to overtake
The figure with the future drawn:
Overtakes the past among the bones that will not waken.

                    The Great
Man!
He who wills and all else was!
He in whom the least and lowest
Feel they are and know they can —
Whose immortal photograph
Does not weep and does not laugh,
Does not doubt but always knows:
Whose eternal voice is true
Strong and soothing in the box —
Always knows and always knew:
Hero of the nursemaid night:
Führer of the wetted bed:
Commissar of chill and fright:

Caudillo of the prayers unsaid:
He'll be there whatever comes.
Are the sums too hard for you?
He can do them: never fear!
He'll be there: he'll see you through:
Get you up and tuck you in:
Wipe the error from your chin:
Take your hand and — kindest friend —
Take you with him at the end.

The Victim Hero!
Him we gaze at in the books
Where our time most proudly looks
For the image of its face —
Dog beneath the savage stick
Licking sores of its disgrace —
Shamefulness on every page.
Hero-Victim of the Age!
Citizen who never knows
Why the hurt and why the blows —
Jailed, has never learned the cause:
Sentenced, never knew his crime:
Shot, was ignorant of the laws:
Dying, took for all his pride
Having suffered: having died!
Scapegoat who redeems the time
From every duty, every burden,
Will and purpose, act and word,
Teaching under hurt and blow
All man's courage is to know
Courage not avails him: all
His strength to fail, his will to fall —
Honor to accept dishonor,
Grin before the others, prove

Victim privy to the knife,
Cuckold party to the shame,
Pimp of death in deed and name!

The Visitor!
Immigrant here: king in the old country:
Puts up with anything — cold, dirt,
Dark, hunger, poverty, affront:
Gets his own back later when it hurts
(When the horn blows for the last first:
When the horn blows with the best worst:
When the horn blows and the proud burn)
Escape, says he, the world's sinking!
Take to the church and pull for God!
Return! says he. Turn in and inward —
Find the clew within the clod —
Find within the rod the rue —
Kiss the sod! Mine eyes discern
Jerusalem its shore I think
I see the city on that strand,
I hear their song forevermore. . . .
And leaves us and with delicate hand
Draws back the past as it were veil
And enters where the blessed stand
That hear no more this mortal hail
This desperate hallo from the land
Where seed dies and rains fail.

The State!
Oh the State! Invisible mystery
Visible only to the poor in
Spirit which performs
The miracle of every into all:
Mortal resurrection from the worms,
Fallible redemption from the fall,

Arc to ride the violent flood
Of the lightning and the blood
With the coupled hearts inside,
In the womb where fear can wait,
In the warm where fright can hide,
In the belly of the State. . . .

The I! the
Doctor's darling the big I!
Perpendicular pronoun kept
Perpendicular between the thumb
And finger of minute inspection:
Mirror hero who can come
Where the bridegroom never cometh:
Who can touch himself so near
Dearest touch was never dearer:
Who can look in glass so nigh
All the world becomes the eye
Watching I within the glass.
Theseus of the threadbare puzzle —
Twists from maze to maze to find
The manlike loins, the bull-like muzzle,
Where the blunt and brutal horn
Stabs him through and death is born.

The Crowd!
(Make yourself a part, she says,
Of something larger than yourself!
Spend your sea among the seas!
Lend your face to many faces!
Give your honey to the bees!)
And the Crowd
Coils like slow constrictor on the streets,
Basks on beaches like a summer monster,

Shouts and each one's voice is vast,
Strikes and each one's stroke is victor,
Smells hot, rank, sweet, salt,
Touches at thigh, at flank, at breast, at shoulder,
Holds by the knee, covers with comrade all.
Are none alone are none lonely in crowd is
Left out no one —

           only
The many are all each in the end and
Each as frightened as the other,
Each as wistful for a friend,
Each as lonesome for a brother:

               only
The many added together are not more but
Less than each since each one fears
And all are only each divided
By the fears of all the others —
By the trembling at your side:
By the breathing at your ear.

The Masque removes. The lighted stage
Is darkened and the music stops.
The age is empty as before.
Behind the backdrop where, unseen,
The corse lies naked on a sand
Lapped by the water, the black gulls that tore
The eyes out tear the sinews from the hand.
Sunless the beach is: sunless the dark shore:
Black the cedar on the head of land.
Descending curtains catch and hang. The play
Stands on the empty stage and cannot end.

(iii) THE SHAPE OF FLESH AND BONE
The lights come up. A painted door
Opens on a painted sea
Blue as childhood's. One by one
The colored parasols appear
Delightful in remembered sun,
And under dunes beside the beach
A garden in a far-off year
Lifts silver apples out of reach.
The child beneath the tree is gone
But all the golden birds are here.
The time becomes the time before
As still as morning and as near —
Only that there sounds between
The painted waves upon the shore
The shudder of a surf not seen,
And sounds across the painted wood
A wind not lifted on the leaves,
And sounds beneath the sun the eaves
Dripping their icicles of blood.

Who is he that tiptoe in the wings
Takes breath to speak and will not show his face?

Every age must have its hero:
Even the faint age of fear —

Even here, in this belated place
Deserted by the God, wherein the King
Abandons, and the shape of Man
Lies murdered in his deeds of grace —

Every circle has its center
Where the curve is made and meant. . . .

Every history returns upon its moral
As the annals of the creatures of the coral
Turn upon the turning of the surf upon the reef.

For the flesh has its belief
And the bone its expectation:
Time that turns the wheel of night
Through the iron constellation,
Time that drives the herded stars among the trees,
Turns not on the turning pole but these.

Take the form within the circle,
Take the circle in the form,
Take the stillness at the center
Where the weight of time is borne,
Where the rush of form is spent —

Take the blossom of the laurel,
Or the photograph of Saturn,
Or the pattern of the surf,
Or the circle of the reef,
Or the wheeling of the seasons round the falling of the leaf —
Take the sun returning always to the evenings,
And the stars in their rehearsals,
And the bell his silver verse
With its turning and returning
Like the figures on an urn —

Take the passions in a life
With the pain that turns to rapture turned to pain,
Or the cycles of the war
With the towns that burn again
And the dead that died before —

Find the point in time that turns upon itself
Like the pivot of the thrower's whirling knife
Or the wheeling of the echo of the bell!

Where the word alone is left,
Hard and secret as a shell
That the grinding sea has ground,

There what flesh and bone believe
Shapes the world that whirls them round!

There what flesh and bone — beset
From above: struck from the one side and the other:
Led by folly with its frantic fears:
Taught by hate that shrieks with stoppled ears:
Prayed for by revenge and bloody rage:
Behind, a war that smolders as it dies:
A war before them in their smoldering eyes:
The stench around them of this rotting age —

There what flesh and bone — the marble fountains
Spent, the grace gone, laughter silenced, youth
Spilt on the earth on the salt beach on the mountains,
Pain the constant lot, the daily awakening,
Beauty deprived, quiet taken,
Love a spasm on a bench, the truth
A gun butt and the church a gangster's mask:
Murder by law and falsehood in its state —
There what flesh and bone await
In the late time, in the open obscenity,
Madness private and put on, the rape of
Right from reason, charity from prayer —
There what flesh and bone attend
Shapes the world that shapes its end.

Flesh and bone —
Sojourners here in the light and the next light
And gone some morning and the embers
Cold, the grass trodden;
Strangers in the wheeling light where they alone
Of all that grows and greens do not return
With the turning of the wheel.

The blinded gunner at the ford — the rest
Dead: the rest fallen: none to see:
None to say the deed was well done: no one:
None to praise or to withhold praise: none
Ever to know or guess or speak his name —
The blinded gunner in the beaten cause
Holds the ford behind the fleeing army:
Aims at changes in the water: aims
By the wind's cold on the wound: by the pain: awkwardly. . . .

The responsible man, death's hand upon his shoulder,
Knowing well the liars may prevail
And calumny bring all his days to nothing;
Knowing truth has often been betrayed
By time that keeps it, as the crock taints water;
Knowing nothing suffered or endured
Will change by one word what the worst will say,
What those who listen to the worst believe —
The responsible man: teeth bad: sleep
Difficult: tired tired tired to the heart:
Carries the day to the next day to the next:
Does what must be done: dies in his chair
Fagged out, worn down, sick
With the weight of his own bones, the task finished,
The war won, the victory assured,
The glory left behind him for the others.

(And the wheels roll up through the night in the sweet land
In the cool air in the spring between the lanterns.)

The poor Negro delivers the laundry, refuses the
Extra nickel for carfare. I can walk —
I got my way to walk. . . .

                  The sick bride,
Bedridden, gives her love to the well, comforts the
Happy, makes the town shine with her loss:
Lies all night alone with the one star
Cold in the window, waking and afraid.

The hostage hears the key turn in the lock
Not his but nearer morning after morning,
Hears the footstep stumbling on the stair,
Hears the block door shut, the bolt shot over,
Wonders which one, listens for the volley,
Walks the cell three steps and turn and three,
Smells the urine in the corner, smells
The stale potato smell of dirty stone,
Thinks Tomorrow, turns and thinks and turns:
Will not call out, will not go mad, will not
No matter how long or how many mornings,
No matter whether anyone will know,
No matter whether anyone, no matter . . .

The huge injustice: the intolerable wrong —
The life unmeant: the dying unremarked:
Multitudes mingled together in one death
And none remembered of them all: not one: —
No word or act recovered or put down
In stone or in a poem or recalled
Years afterward in peace in better times —

The eucalyptus fragrant by the water.
The huge injustice! The intolerable wrong!
Death-camp cities where beneath the night
The faceless figures wander without names
Fenced by the barbed and icy stars, and stare
Beyond them at the memory of their lives:
Vastness overwhelming all with its ignorance!

And yet the will endures: the boy dies
Believing in his death and in the others.
The woman tells her son to act the man.
The heart persists. The love survives.
The nameless flesh and bone accepts
Some duty to be beautiful and brave
Owed neither to the world nor to the grave
Nor to the stone God nor the exiled King
Nor Man, the murdered dream, nor anything
But only to the flesh the bone
The flesh that breathes the bone that stands
The eyes the hands and each alone —
Some resolution to be dutiful and good
Owed by the lost child to the dreadful wood.

The flesh that once sang
With the ardor of love
Is dumb and is mute
Where the dog stoops above
Where the dog with his jaws
In the charnel of leaves
Champs it with hate
But the flesh still believes.

The bone that once danced
In the intricate round

Of loving and giving
Is still and is bound.
The spider that stings
And the spider that weaves
Wind it with fear
But the bone still believes.

The flesh and the bone
That danced and that sang —
Fear with its web
And hate with its fang
Bind them in silence
And grind them and grieve
But the flesh and the bone
Still believe still believe.

Abandoned by the guardians and gods,
The great companion of the metaphor
Dead of the wars and wounds (O murdered dream!)
The city of man consumed to ashes, ashes,
The republic a marble rubble on its hill,
The laws rules rites prayers philters all exhausted,
Elders and the supernatural aids withdrawn —
Abandoned by them all, by all forsaken,
The naked human perishable heart —
Naked as sea-worm in the shattered shell —
No further savior standing to come forth,
Nor magic champion with miraculous blade,
Nor help in fight nor succor in the field
(Thou art my Shield! Thou art my Rock!)
No help, no hand, no succor but itself —
The human perishable heart, confused
Weak frightened in the staring face of time —
After so long a shelter shuddering cold,

After so long a slumber sleeping still —
Takes breath to speak and in the iron door
Where once the dreams stood guardian in its place
Stands guard: bears truth: knows fear and will outface,
Unarmed at last before the vast ordeal,
The death behind us and the death before.

The scene dissolves. The closet world
Collapses in enormous night.
The garden where the marble Gods
Kept music and the player Kings
Is gone and gone the golden light,
The careful lawns, the ordered trees,
Where man upon the waste of time
Enclosed his small eternities.
All this has vanished. In its stead,
Minute upon an immense plain
Where vultures huddle and the soft
And torpid rats recoil and crawl,
Gorged with a food that has no name,
And voices in the dark of air
Cry out Despair and fall and fail —
Minute upon an immense plain
The mortal flesh and mortal bone
Are left among the stones to play
The man beneath the moon alone: —
And know the part they have to bear
And know the void vast night above
And know the night below and dare
Endure and love.

from Actfive and Other Poems (1948)

GEOGRAPHY OF THIS TIME

What is required of us is the recognition of the frontiers between the centuries. And to take heart: to cross over.

Those who are killed in the place between out of ignorance, those who wander like cattle and are shot, those who are shot and are left in the stone fields between the histories — these men may be pitied as the victims of accidents are pitied but their deaths do not signify. They are neither buried nor otherwise remembered but lie in the dead grass in the dry thorn in the worn light. Their years have no monuments.

There are many such in the sand here — many who did not perceive, who thought the time went on, the years went forward, the history was continuous — who thought tomorrow was of the same nation as today. There are many who came to the frontiers between the times and did not know them — who looked for the sentry-box at the stone bridge, for the barricade in the pines and the declaration in two languages — the warning and the opportunity to turn. They are dead there in the down light, in the sheep's barren.

What is required of us is the recognition

with no sign, with no word, with the roads raveled out into ruts and the ruts into dust and the dust stirred by the wind — the roads from behind us ending in the dust.

What is required of us is the recognition of the frontiers where the roads end.

We are very far. We are past the place where the light lifts and farther on than the relinquishment of leaves — farther even than the persistence in the east of the green color. Beyond are the confused tracks, the guns, the watchers.

What is required of us, Companions, is the recognition of the frontiers across this history, and to take heart: to cross over.

— to persist and to cross over and survive

But to survive

To cross over.

DEFINITION OF THE FRONTIERS

First there is the wind but not like the familiar wind but long
and without lapses or falling away or surges of air as is usual but
rather like the persistent pressure of a river or a running tide.

This wind is from the other side and has an odor unlike the
odor of the winds with us but like time if time had odor and
were cold and carried a bitter and sharp taste like rust on the
taste of snow or the fragrance of thunder.

When the air has this taste of time the frontiers are not far
from us.

Then too there are the animals. There are always animals
under the small trees. They belong neither to our side nor to
theirs but are wild and because they are animals of such kind
that wildness is unfamiliar in them as the horse for example or
the goat and often sheep and dogs and like creatures their wan-
dering there is strange and even terrifying signaling as it does the
violation of custom and the subversion of order.

There are also the unnatural lovers the distortion of images
the penetration of mirrors and the inarticulate meanings of the
dreams. The dreams are in turmoil like a squall of birds.

Finally there is the evasion of those with whom we have come.
It is at the frontiers that the companions desert us — that the
girl returns to the old country

that we are alone.

VOYAGE WEST

There was a time for discoveries —
For the headlands looming above in the
First light and the surf and the
Crying of gulls: for the curve of the
Coast north into secrecy.

That time is past.
The last lands have been peopled.
The oceans are known now.

Señora: once the maps have all been made
A man were better dead than find new continents.

A man would better never have been born
Than find upon the open ocean flowers
Drifted from islands where there are no islands,

Or midnight, out of sight of any land,
Smell on the altering air the odor of rosemary.

No fortune passes that misfortune —

To lift along the evening of the sky,
Certain as sun and sea, a new-found land
Steep from an ocean where no landfall can be.

JOURNEY HOME

I have wasted my time in my time in many places,
My time in my time and have not found my face.

Imitator of climates and strange skies,
In the mountains alert, in the south a lazy riser,

At the lake hotel I examine the register:
The place and the time and the name of my life are illegible.

Kum is southward of Re and the desert is east of it:
Peach boughs over the walls and the rats feasting.

On the Greasy Grass in the night there was one that knew:
She could not speak my name by name but she knew me.

And where is Jesus that gentle lover?
My life is blown down: the ramblers are over it:

There are poplars growing from the broken hearth.
I have come to the door of my house: I can go no farther.

THE RAPE OF THE SWAN

To love love and not its meaning
Hardens the heart in monstrous ways.
No one is ours who has this leaning.
Those whose loyalty is love's betray us.

367

They are not girls with a girl's softness.
They love not us at all but love.
They have hard and fanatical minds most often.
It is not we but a dream that must cover them.

A woman who loves love cannot give it.
Her part is not to give but take.
Even the great swan by the river —
Her fingers strangle and the feathers break.

PSYCHE WITH THE CANDLE

Love which is the most difficult mystery
Asking from every young one answers
And most from those most eager and most beautiful —
Love is a bird in a fist:
To hold it hides it, to look at it lets it go.
It will twist loose if you lift so much as a finger.
It will stay if you cover it — stay but unknown and invisible.
Either you keep it forever with fist closed
Or let it fling
Singing in fervor of sun and in song vanish.
There is no answer other to this mystery.

THE LINDEN TREES

Tree wanderer! Wheat rider! Wind!
Waylaying the heart in corridors, carrying messages
Picked up in another year and Yes
Yes is the answer Yes and the odor of lindens
Blown over a whole life Listen!
Listen toucher of hair tugger at sleeves
Whisperer under the small moon in the evenings —
Listen wind! I have forgotten that history.
I have forgotten the words and the touch and the startled
Dark of her eyes and her breast in the child's blouse.
I have forgotten the scent of the linden flowers.
Wind! Wind! Why do you lift at my heart?

EXCAVATION OF TROY

Girl do you think
Girl do you think ever
Waking stretching your small
Arms your back arched
Your long legs straight
Out your mouth red
Round in a pout in a half
Yawn half smile
Do you think delicate
Girl with the skin smoother than
Silver cooler than apples
Delicate cool girl

Do you think as your throat
Lifts your breath
Catches ever of
Me
      far back
Buried under the many
Nights layer on layer
Like a city taken a town
Fallen in antique wars and forgotten?

Half awake on your bed the images
Fading from the edge of sleep
As the salt rim of the surf from the wet
Sand do you think of me
As men long landed from the famous ships
Beached by the bright Aegean and the sails brought silver
      down
Of the fallen town
Of the white walls in the sun the cicadas
The smell of eucalyptus by the sea?

THE CAT IN THE WOOD

The cat in the wood cried farewell cried farewell
Farther and farther away and the leaves
Covered her over with sound of the leaves
And sound of the wood O my love O my love
Farther and farther away and the sound
Of leaves overhead when I call to you
Leaves on the ground.

WINTER IS ANOTHER COUNTRY

If the autumn would
End! If the sweet season,
The late light in the tall trees would
End! If the fragrance, the odor of
Fallen apples, dust on the road,
Water somewhere near, the scent of
Water touching me; if this would end
I could endure the absence in the night,
The hands beyond the reach of hands, the name
Called out and never answered with my name:
The image seen but never seen with sight.
I could endure this all
If autumn ended and the cold light came.

WHAT MUST

(i)

We lay beneath the alder tree
Her breast she leaned upon my hand
The alder leaf moved over me
The sun moved over on the land
Her mouth she pressed upon my mouth
I felt the leaf beat in her breast
I felt the sun move in her hair
But nearer than the leaf the sun
I felt the love go deep in me
That has no season in the earth

That has no time of spring or birth
That cannot flower like a tree
Or like one die

          but only be.

(ii)

Take it up in your arms, I said,
Let it lie where it must,
At your side on your breast,
Let it rest:
Love has life not of love
But of us, I said:
Let it lie where it must.

Let it be what it is, she said,
Let it wait as it must,
It will choose soon or late,
Let it wait:
Love has life not of us
But of love, she said,
Let it lie where it must.

(iii)

Lovers who must say farewell
When the road has reached the trees,
Lovers who have all to tell
Before the road runs out of sight
In the green beyond the leaves —
The green cove below the light,
Lovers who must say farewell
When the road has reached the trees,
Touching hand to hand to speak

All their love has ever known,
Find no words to speak and say
Love. . . . Oh love. . . .

                        and, each alone,
Walk together toward the trees
Where the road runs out of sight
In the green beyond the leaves —
The green cove below the light.

POEM IN PROSE

This poem is for my wife.
I have made it plainly and honestly:
The mark is on it
Like the burl on the knife.

I have not made it for praise.
She has no more need for praise
Than summer has
Or the bright days.

In all that becomes a woman
Her words and her ways are beautiful:
Love's lovely duty,
The well-swept room.

Wherever she is there is sun
And time and a sweet air:
Peace is there,
Work done.

373

There are always curtains and flowers
And candles and baked bread
And a cloth spread
And a clean house.

Her voice when she sings is a voice
At dawn by a freshening sea
Where the wave leaps in the
Wind and rejoices.

Wherever she is it is now.
It is here where the apples are:
Here in the stars,
In the quick hour.

The greatest and richest good,
My own life to live in,
This she has given me —

If giver could.

EVER SINCE

What do you remember thinking back?
What do you think of at dusk in the slack
Evening when the mind refills
With the cool past as a well fills in
Darkness from forgotten rains?

Do you think of waking in the all-night train,
The curtains drawn, the Mediterranean
Blue, blue, and the sellers of oranges
Holding heaped up morning toward you?

Do you think of Kumomoto-Ken
And the clogs going by in the night and the scent of
Clean mats, the sound of the peepers,
The wind in the pines, the dark sleep?

Do you think how Santiago stands at
Night under its stars, under its Andes:
Its bells like heavy birds that climb
Widening circles out of time?

I saw them too. I know those places.
There are no mountains — scarcely a face
Of all the faces you have seen,
Or a town or a room, but I have seen it.

Even at dusk in the deep chair
Letting the long past take you, bear you —
Even then you never leave me, never can.
Your eyes close, your small hands
Keep their secrets in your lap:
Wherever you are we two were happy.

I wonder what those changing lovers do,
Watching each other in the darkening room,
Whose world together is the night they've shared:
Whose past is parting: strangers side by side.

TRICKED BY ETERNITY THE HEART

Corruptible if all things are,
Corruption yet has eyes to see.
Dead for a hundred years, the star
Still burns for us above the tree.

Between the cause and the effect,
Time, like the custom of the street,
Teaches our eyes till they expect
What is no longer theirs to meet:

Teaches our eyes until the face
That smiles in mirrors when we smile —
Still young, still fair, still full of grace —
Stands for our aging hearts awhile.

YEARS OF THE DOG

Before, though, Paris was wonderful. Wanderers
Talking in all tongues from every country.
Fame was what they wanted in that town.
Fame could be found there too — flushed like quail in the
Cool dawn — struck among statues
Naked in hawthorn in the silver light.
James Joyce found it. Dublin bore him.
Could have sung with McCormack! Could he? He could.
Did he? He didn't. He walked by the winding Seine.
And what did he eat? He ate orts: oddities:
Oh he was poor: obscure: no one had heard of him:

Rolled on the floor on the floor with the pain in his eyes.
And found fame? He did. Ulysses: Yule Book:
Published to every people even in Erse.
(Molly Molly why did you say so Molly!)
Or the lad in the Rue de Notre Dame des Champs
At the carpenter's loft on the left-hand side going down —
The lad with the supple look like a sleepy panther —
And what became of him? Fame became of him.
Veteran out of the wars before he was twenty:
Famous at twenty-five: thirty a master —
Whittled a style for his time from a walnut stick
In a carpenter's loft in a street of that April city.

Where do they hang out now, the young ones, the wanderers,
Following fame by the rumor of praise in a town?
Where is fame in the world now? Where are the lovers of
Beauty of beauty that she moves among?

THE LEARNED MEN

Whose minds like horse or ox,
Dispassionate in the stall,
Grow great in girth and wax
Beyond the animal,

While mine, like country hog,
Grows leaner as I age,
Chivvied by flea and dog,
Baited by love and rage.

If mind by God was meant
To grow and gain in girth,
Swelling in sweet content,
I cease I have no worth:

But if it was God's will
That mind, no wish refused,
Should waste by wanting still
By God I am well used!

THE TREASON CRIME

Those that by bloody force
Assault oblivion,
Raping by ruse or worse
What should be waited on;

Those that by trick contrive
To break the house of breath,
Looting, while heart's alive,
Heart's last devise of death;

Those who deceive the trust
Each puts in each — that time,
Not we, will say what must —
Theirs is the treason crime.

THE TWO TREES

Oh the maple!
Oaring up
Stream against the
July wind!

But the elm — the elm gives to it
Letting her leaves float out
All Ophelia in the moat of air,
Drowned in summer deep as sun,
Garlands drifting in her hair.

THE SNOW FALL

Quietness clings to the air.
Quietness gathers the bell
To a great distance.
Listen!
This is the snow.
This is the slow
Chime
The snow
Makes.
It encloses us.
Time in the snow is alone:
Time in the snow is at last,
Is past.

THE SPANISH LIE

This will be answered.

The tears were not answered but this will be answered.

The tears of Madrid, of Barcelona, Valencia —
The tears were not answered.

The blood of Guernica, Badajoz, Almería —
The blood was not answered.

The tears are dry on the faces.

The blood is dry on the sand.

The tears were not answered: the blood was not answered.

This will be answered.

Because the men of Guernica do not speak,
Because the children of Almería are silent,
Because the women of Badajoz are dumb,
Are dumb, they have no voices, no voices,
Their throats are stopped with the sand of that place,
They do not speak, they will never speak, and the children,
The children of Almería, they are still,
They do not move, they will never move, those children:
Their bodies are broken, their bones are broken, their mouths
      are —

Because they are dead, are dumb, because they are speechless,
Do not believe,
Do not believe the answer will not come.

Do not believe
Because the blood has not been answered
The lie will not be answered.

Do not believe
Because the tears have not been answered
The lie will not be answered.

Do not believe it.

This will be answered.
This will be answered with
Time.
          There is time.

The dead have time in those cities
In Badajoz, in Guernica, Almería.

They can wait: they have much time.

There is time.
They can wait.

THE YOUNG DEAD SOLDIERS
for *Lieutenant Richard Myers*

The young dead soldiers do not speak.
Nevertheless, they are heard in the still houses: who has not
     heard them?
They have a silence that speaks for them at night and when the
     clock counts.

They say: We were young. We have died. Remember us.

They say: We have done what we could but until it is finished it is not done.

They say: We have given our lives but until it is finished no one can know what our lives gave.

They say: Our deaths are not ours; they are yours; they will mean what you make them.

They say: Whether our lives and our deaths were for peace and a new hope or for nothing we cannot say; it is you who must say this.

They say: We leave you our deaths. Give them their meaning.

We were young, they say. We have died. Remember us.

BRAVE NEW WORLD

But you, Thomas Jefferson,
You could not lie so still,
You could not bear the weight of stone
On the quiet hill,

You could not keep your green grown peace
Nor hold your folded hand
If you could see your new world now,
Your new sweet land.

There was a time, Tom Jefferson,
When freedom made free men.
The new found earth and the new freed mind
Were brothers then.

There was a time when tyrants feared
The new world of the free.
Now freedom is afraid and shrieks
At tyranny.

Words have not changed their sense so soon
Nor tyranny grown new.
The truths you held, Tom Jefferson,
Will still hold true.

What's changed is freedom in this age.
What great men dared to choose
Small men now dare neither win
Nor lose.

Freedom, when men fear freedom's use
But love its useful name,
Has cause and cause enough for fear
And cause for shame.

We fought a war in freedom's name
And won it in our own.
We fought to free a world and raised
A wall of stone.

Your countrymen who could have built
The hill fires of the free
To set the dry world all ablaze
With liberty —

To burn the brutal thorn in Spain
Of bigotry and hate
And the dead lie and the brittle weed
Beyond the Plate:

Who could have heaped the bloody straw,
The dung of time, to light
The Danube in a sudden flame
Of hope by night —

Your countrymen who could have hurled
Their freedom like a brand
Have cupped it to a candle spark
In a frightened hand.

Freedom that was a thing to use
They've made a thing to save
And staked it in and fenced it round
Like a dead man's grave.

PART FIVE

WORDS IN TIME

Bewildered with the broken tongue
Of wakened angels in our sleep —
Then, lost the music that was sung
And lost the light time cannot keep!

There is a moment when we lie
Bewildered, wakened out of sleep,
When light and sound and all reply:
That moment time must tame and keep.

That moment, like a flight of birds
Flung from the branches where they sleep,
The poet with a beat of words
Flings into time for time to keep.

BAHAMAS

Down there in those islands
Vines color of calico
Climb on the coral walls.
The surf falls in flowers.

Down there in those islands
Noon odor of indolence
Sleeps in the naked wind
In the wall's shadow.

Love is by day in those islands.
Love languor of Negresses
Lies in the shuttered rooms:
The blinds tremble.

Love is by day in those islands:
Nights, the slow tread of the sea
Tramples the scent and the flowers,
Stands in the stillness.

Night is the sea in those islands.
The lamp goes out on the balcony,
The leaf returns to its silence,
The sea to the reef.

Down there in those islands
Night is the sound of forever,
Night is the salt on the mouth,
Night is the sea.

OUT OF SLEEP AWAKENED

Long before dawn has silvered the last star
The aged Negro off across the harbor

Cracking his conch-shells on the hollow deck
Has broken the cold brittle coil and wrecked

The rose and secret cavern of the snail.

The shuddering worm, still wincing to the nail

That tore him from the ruin of his shell,
Lies numb and cold and naked where he fell.

Out of what sands, what sea-surge, by what toil
Shall worm rebuild the silver of that coil?

EPITAPH FOR JOHN McCUTCHEON

This is my island. Thirty years ago
I brought my bride here in the yawl to show her

Silence and sea and sun. Silence
And sea and sun were why we bought this island.

There was never enough of the sea, the sun:
Now there's silence here enough for one.

CALYPSO'S ISLAND

I know very well, goddess, she is not beautiful
As you are: could not be. She is a woman,
Mortal, subject to the chances: duty of

Childbed, sorrow that changes cheeks, the tomb —
For unlike you she will grow grey, grow older,
Grey and older, sleep in that small room.

She is not beautiful as you, O golden!
You are immortal and will never change
And can make me immortal also, fold

Your garment round me, make me whole and strange
As those who live forever, not the while
That we live, keep me from those dogging dangers —

Ships and the wars — in this green, far-off island,
Silent of all but sea's eternal sound
Or sea-pine's when the lull of surf is silent.

Goddess, I know how excellent this ground,
What charmed contentment of the removed heart
The bees make in the lavender where pounding

Surf sounds far off and the bird that darts
Darts through its own eternity of light,
Motionless in motion, and the startled

Hare is startled into stone, the fly
Forever golden in the flickering glance
Of leafy sunlight that still holds it. I

Know you, goddess, and your caves that answer
Ocean's confused voices with a voice:
Your poplars where the storms are turned to dances;

Arms where the heart is turned. You give the choice
To hold forever what forever passes,
To hide from what will pass, forever. Moist,

Moist are your well-stones, goddess, cool your grasses!
And she — she is a woman with that fault
Of change that will be death in her at last!

Nevertheless I long for the cold, salt,
Restless, contending sea and for the island
Where the grass dies and the seasons alter:

Where that one wears the sunlight for a while.

THUNDERHEAD

Do not lie there in the darkness silent
Hearing his silence by you in the dark.

That sky could tell you that there must be magic
Waiting as well as working to have miracles —

Thunder in earth for thunder in the air
To bring the flash down and the blinding glimpses.

Rock and loam must smoulder with desire
Before the haycock of the heart is struck on fire.

WHAT ANY LOVER LEARNS

Water is heavy silver over stone.
Water is heavy silver over stone's
Refusal. It does not fall. It fills. It flows
Every crevice, every fault of the stone,
Every hollow. River does not run.
River presses its heavy silver self
Down into stone and stone refuses.

What runs,
Swirling and leaping into sun, is stone's
Refusal of the river, not the river.

THE STEAMBOAT WHISTLE

Woman riding the two mares of her thighs
In July cotton and the Sunday morning
Moseying up the gutter, nudging the cats,
The house-fronts rosy with the feints of heat,
And the Fall River boat going by, its scarlet bunting
Strung across the ending of the street,

When suddenly the crinkled sky was torn
To paper pigeons tumbling from the air
And She we know but have not ever seen
Rose from the river where the streets all end,
Her birds about her, and the silver nervous
Mares of morning, balky in the surf.

STARVED LOVERS

Chrysanthemums last too long for these ravenous ladies.
The flowers they prefer are brief, unfold
At evening filling the cool room then fade,
Budded at pleasure and at pleasure old.

Chrysanthemums stand too still for these starved ladies.
Staring like Vincent's sunlight, bright and still,
They burn until these feasters are afraid
Hunger may leave them and their lives be filled.

The ravenous ladies in the still-starved lives
Strip off the ever-burning leaves with silver knives.

THE OLD MAN TO THE LIZARD

Lizard, lover of heat, of high
Noon, of the hot stone, the golden
Sun in your unblinking eye —
And they say you are old, lizard, older than

Rocks you run on with those delicate
Fishbone fingers, skittering over
Ovens even cricket in his shell
Could never sing in — tell me, lover of

Sun, lover of noon, lizard,
Is it because the sun is gold with
Flame you love it so? Or is
Your love because your blood is cold?

THE TRIUMPH OF THE SHELL
(on a picture by Ellen Barry)

Someone has gathered a shell,
A blue veil, broken
Fragments of shell, sand.
Someone has spoken

saying
The skull of the shell is crowned
With the blue veil of my love
Because of the sea that resounds
In the winding ear of the shell;

saying
The worm is wound in the shell
As the soul in the whorls of time:
Time in its spiral turns,
The worm delights and dies;

saying
The worm with his pushing pride
Went in at the gate of the shell:
That season when he died
Eternity befell;

saying
The skull of the shell is crowned
With the blue veil of my love
Because of my love that resounds
In the winding ear of the skull.

THEY COME NO MORE, THOSE WORDS, THOSE FINCHES

Oh when you're young
And the words to your tongue
Like the birds to Saint Francis
With darting, with dances —
Wait! you say, Wait!
There's still time! It's not late!

And the next day you're old
And the words all as cold
As the birds in October
Sing over, sing over,
Sing Late! Late!

And Wait! you say, Wait!

YOU ALSO, GAIUS VALERIUS CATULLUS

Fat-kneed god! Feeder of mangy leopards!
You who brought me into that one's bed
Whose breath is sweeter than a grass-fed heifer —
If *you* had not willed it, *I* had not willed it —
You who dumped me like a sack of milt
Limp in her eager taking arms as though
Her breast were no more than a bench to lie on,
Listen! Muncher of the pale-pipped apples!
Keeper of paunchy house-cats! Boozy god!
Dump me where you please, but not hereafter
Where the dawn has that *particular* laughter.

THE OLD MEN IN THE LEAF SMOKE

The old men rake the yards for winter
Burning the autumn-fallen leaves.
They have no lives, the one or the other.
The leaves are dead, the old men live
Only a little, light as a leaf,
Left to themselves of all their loves:
Light in the head most often too.

Raking the leaves, raking the lives,
Raking life and leaf together,
The old men smell of burning leaves,
But which is which they wonder — whether
Anyone tells the leaves and loves —
Anyone left, that is, who lives.

THE LINDEN BRANCH

Strophe of green leaves
In the inevitable spiral,
Versical of God,
Of what green sound the body?
Silence of what lyre?
O linden bough, O leaves,
Teach us your intervals:
Our strings are strung so false
We make no music be.
Could we as you be strung
For wind to blow on, we
Might be that song.

AUTUMN

Sun smudge on the smoky water

WHERE THE HAYFIELDS WERE

Coming down the mountain in the twilight —
April it was and quiet in the air —
I saw an old man and his little daughter
Burning the meadows where the hayfields were.

Forksful of flame he scattered in the meadows.
Sparkles of fire in the quiet air
Burned in their circles and the silver flowers
Danced like candles where the hayfields were, —

Danced as she did in enchanted circles,
Curtseyed and danced along the quiet air:
Slightly she danced in the stillness, in the twilight,
Dancing in the meadows where the hayfields were.

THE BURIAL

for Martha Hillard MacLeish

Life relinquishing, by life relinquished —
Oh but the young tart quick beating
Life in your heart, my mother — Oh and sweet —
Where will they put that down among these mingled
Soot-stained grave-stones here? Or do they think
The thirst is gone now and the apple eaten?
Do they think the journeys, like your feet,
Are still? And is it so? The one, the single·
Answer that the bird makes to the hill —
Had your heart, asking, heard it? Was it done?
Life you never finished, did your life
Finish, my mother? Was all suddenly still,
All understood, all answered and all one:
Young girl, old woman, widow, mother, wife?

THE BED

My bed grows narrower as I grow old.
The hurt must on my heart lie, right or wrong.
It has no room but this to turn and toss
That once would sleep beside me the night long.

A MAN'S WORK

An apple-tree, a cedar and an oak
Grow by the stone house in the rocky field
Where I write poems when my hand's in luck.
The cedar I put in: the rest are wild —

Wind dropped them. Apples strew the autumn ground
With black, sweet-smelling pips. The oak strews air,
Summers with shadow, winters with harsh sound.
The cedar's silent with its fruit to bear.

WHAT RIDDLE ASKED THE SPHINX

to the memory of André Gide

In my stone eyes I see
The saint upon his knee
Delve in the desert for eternity.

In my stone ears I hear
The night-lost traveller
Cry *When?* to the earth's shadow: **When? Oh where?**

Stone deaf and blind
I ponder in my mind
The bone that seeks, the flesh that cannot find.

Stone blind I see
The saint's eternity
Deep in the earth he digs in. Cannot he?

Stone deaf I hear
The night say *Then!* say *There!*
Why cries the traveller still to the night air?

The one is not content
With silence, the day spent;
With earth the other. More, they think, was meant.

Stone that I am, can stone
Perceive what flesh and bone
Are blind and deaf to?

                    Or has hermit known,
Has traveller divined,
Some question there behind
I cannot come to, being stone and blind?

To all who ken or can
I ask, since time began,
What riddle is it has for answer, Man?

MUSIC AND DRUM

When men turn mob
Drums throb:
When mob turns men
Music again.

When souls become Church
Drums beat the search:
When Church becomes souls
Sweet music tolls.

When State is the master
Drums beat disaster:
When master is man
Music can.

Each to be one,
Each to be whole,
Body and soul,
Music's begun.

WHAT THE OLD WOMEN SAY

Out there in the fighting
Each day is doubt,
Each night is dread,
Dawn is disaster.

Even at home in the house
If the lock creeps in the socket
The roots of our sleep wake.
We lie listening.

Like flood in a field it comes —
No sound but suddenly
One more stone has vanished,
A dyke drowned.

Never again in our lifetime,
Never will fear end
Or the old ease return to us:
Childhood remembered.

401

Never again will we wait
Content in the dark till our daughters
Off in the evening somewhere,
Laughing, come home.

THE TWO PRIESTS

Man in the West
Man in the East
Man lives best
Who loves life least,
Says the Priest in the West.

Man in the flesh
Man in the ghost
Man lives best
Who fears death most,
Says the Priest in the East.

Man in the West
Man in the East
Man in the flesh
Man in the ghost
Man lives best
Who loves life most,
Who fears death least,
Says Man to the Priest
In the East, in the West.

THE BLACK DAY

to the memory of Lawrence Duggan

God help that country where informers thrive!
Where slander flourishes and lies contrive
To kill by whispers! Where men lie to live!

God help that country by informers fed
Where fear corrupts and where suspicion's spread
By look and gesture, even to the dead.

God help that country where the liar's shame
Outshouts the decent silence to defame
The dead man's honor and defile his name.

God help that country, cankered deep by doubt,
Where honest men, by scandals turned about,
See honor murdered and will not speak out.

God help that country! But for you — for you —
Pure heart, sweet spirit, humble, loyal, true,
Pretend, pretend, we know not what we do.

THE BALLAD OF THE CORN-COB
AND THE LIE

Will Faulkner, Will Faulkner,
You are to blame my friend,
Telling of a maiden
Brought to no good end,
Raped but with a corn-cob,
Raped but with a lie:
They've learned to rape the country
With a corn-cob and a lie.

They've learned to rape the country
Though rape is past their power,
They've learned to have her virtue
Though feeble to deflower:
To soil her lovely thinking,
The freedom of her mind —
They've learned to do it winking
With a corn-cob hid behind.

Will Faulkner, Will Faulkner,
They've learned those lying arts:
They've had her in her freedom
And Oh, it breaks our hearts!
The impotent that could not —
That leered with letching eye,
They've learned to rape the country
With a corn-cob and a lie.

THE DANGER IN THE AIR
a letter to Mark Van Doren

On a day of dry wind
In the summer of fear
I drove a hundred miles to find you.

Off to the north somewhere the woods were on fire.
The smoke tasted of time: the sad odor.
No one knew what country or how far.

You met me at the gate beside your road.
Till the light went
We talked of poems and the men who wrote them —

Great poems, admirable men:
Things enduring and difficult.
When the day ended

I drove down through your lane where the maples lift.
It smelled of well-cured rowan in your field,
It smelled of hearth-fire where the wood-smoke drifted.

ACKNOWLEDGEMENT

". . . I shall not again publicly acknowledge you." Francis
Cardinal Spellman to Eleanor Roosevelt. July 21, 1949.

Prince of the church whose lofty mind
Looks down upon the whole creation —
You who *acknowledge* human kind —
Consider, Prince, your place and nation.

Prince who can acknowledge man
— The word hurts and the spirit winces —
Prince, consider if you can
This land acknowledges no princes!

LIBERTY

When liberty is headlong girl
And runs her roads and wends her ways
Liberty will shriek and whirl
Her showery torch to see it blaze.

When liberty is wedded wife
And keeps the barn and counts the byre
Liberty amends her life.
She drowns her torch for fear of fire.

THE SHEEP IN THE RUINS

for Learned and Augustus Hand

You, my friends, and you strangers, all of you,
Stand with me a little by the walls
Or where the walls once were.
The bridge was here, the city further:
Now there is neither bridge nor town —
A doorway where the roof is down
Opens on a foot-worn stair
That climbs by three steps into empty air.
(What foot went there?)
Nothing in this town that had a thousand steeples
Lives now but these flocks of sheep
Grazing the yellow grasses where the bricks lie dead beneath:
Dogs drive them with their brutal teeth.

Can none but sheep live where the walls go under?
Is man's day over and the sheep's begun?
And shall we sit here like the mourners on a dunghill
Shrilling with melodious tongue —
Disfiguring our faces with the nails of our despair?
(What dust is this we sift upon our hair?)
Because a world is taken from us as the camels from the man
      of Uz
Shall we sit weeping for the world that was
And curse God and so perish?
Shall monuments be grass and sheep inherit them?
Shall dogs rule in the rubble of the arches?

Consider, Oh consider what we are!
Consider what it is to be a man —
He who makes his journey by the glimmer of a candle;

407

Who discovers in his mouth, between his teeth, a word;
Whose heart can bear the silence of the stars — that burden;
Who comes upon his meaning in the blindness of a stone —
A girl's shoulder, perfectly harmonious!

Even the talk of it would take us days together.
Marvels men have made, Oh marvels! — and our breath
Brief as it is: our death waiting —
Marvels upon marvels! Works of state —
The imagination of the shape of order!
Works of beauty — the cedar door
Perfectly fitted to the sill of basalt!
Works of grace —
The ceremony at the entering of houses,
At the entering of lives: the bride among the torches in the
        shrill carouse!

Works of soul —
Pilgrimages through the desert to the sacred boulder:
Through the mid night to the stroke of one!
Works of grace! Works of wonder!
All this have we done and more —
And seen — what have we not seen? —

A man beneath the sunlight in his meaning:
A man, one man, a man alone.

In the sinks of the earth that wanderer has gone down.
The shadow of his mind is on the mountains.
The word he has said is kept in the place beyond
As the seed is kept and the earth ponders it.
Stones — even the stones remember him:
Even the leaves — his image is in them.
And now because the city is a ruin in the waste of air

We sit here and despair!
Because the sheep graze in the dying grove
Our day is over!
We must end
Because the talk around the table in the dusk has ended,
Because the fingers of the goddesses are found
Like marble pebbles in the gravelly ground
And nothing answers but the jackal in the desert, —
Because the cloud proposes, the wind says!

Listen, my friends, and you, all of you, strangers,
Listen, the work of man, the work of splendor
Never has been ended or will end.
Listen! We are neither weak nor few.
Where one man does what one can do,
Where one man in the sun alone
Walks between the silence and the stone,
We are not yet too weak nor yet too few.
One finger in the dust can trace the circle,
Can begin the work,
Large in the level morning of the light
And beautiful with cisterns where the water whitens,
Rippling upon the lip of stone, and spills
By cedar sluices into pools, and the young builders
String their plumb lines, and the well-laid course
Blanches its mortar in the sun, and all the morning
Smells of wood-smoke, rope-tar, horse-sweat, pitch-pine,
Men and the trampled mint leaves in the ditch.

One man in the sun alone
Walks between the silence and the stone:
The city rises from his flesh, his bone.

EZRY

Maybe you ranted in the Grove —
Maybe! — but you found the mark
That measures altitude above
Sea-level for a poet's work.

Mad if you were or fool instead
You found the bench-mark in the stone —
Horizon over arrow-head —
Alder and dock had overgrown.

These later and more cautious critics
Think themselves high if they look down
From Rome's or England's steeple — spit
On fools below them in the town:

Not you! Although the absolute sea
Is far down from the Muses' Wood,
You gauged the steep declivity,
Giddy with grandeur where you stood.

THE RENOVATED TEMPLE

Ma'am, you should see your house!
Remember where the pillars stood, the douse
Of sea-surge smashing clean across the porches,
Everything open, the wet windy torch,
The blind man shouting things of gods and girls

Above the wave sound in the smoky swirling —
Things about Troy, the horse-trick and those troubles?

The place, Ma'am, is a private club —
Never a shout in the house or a girl either:
Only those pimply boys who breathe
Sour as cooky dough. Where once the surge,
Curtains: mirrors where the windows were.

It's a neat place, Ma'am. They've stuffed the hawk
And hung the oars up varnished and they talk:
God, how they talk! — about the members and their stations,
About the house rules and the regulations,
About their battles with the mice and spiders —
They talk of anything but what's outside.
The coal-fire tinkles and the tea-cup lulls.

It's not like Dante's time with all those skulls
And shrieks and pitch-pots and old putrid years
Dug up from Hell to dress the chandeliers,
Or Villon's, dragging dead men in to hang,
Or Baudelaire's when all the roof cats wrangled —
Shakespeare's of the Fierce Dispute —
It's not like that. It's neat, Ma'am, and they know their duty:
Neat as a catechism.

                    Still, they thumb
Their eyes and wonder why you never come.

POET'S LAUGHTER

"Why do I live among green mountains?"
Said Li-tai Po. "I laugh and do not answer."

You laughed a long time back, Li Po,
And men laugh with you still — but do they know
Better than him you laughed at long ago
Just why you lived among green mountains?

THE SNOWFLAKE WHICH IS NOW
AND HENCE FOREVER

Will it last? he says.
Is it a masterpiece?
Will generation after generation
Turn with reverence to the page?

Birdseye scholar of the frozen fish,
What would he make of the sole, clean, clear
Leap of the salmon that has disappeared?

To *be*, yes! — whether they like it or not!
But not to last when leap and water are forgotten,
A plank of standard pinkness in the dish.

They also live
Who swerve and vanish in the river.

CROSSING

At five precisely in the afternoon
The dining car cook on the Boston and Albany
Through train to somewhere leaned and waved
At the little girl on the crossing at Ghent, New York —
The one with the doll carriage.

                             Who understood it best?
She, going home to her supper, telling her Pa?
The Negro cook, shutting the vestibule window,
Thinking: She waved right back she did? Or I,
Writing it down and wondering as I write it
Why a forgotten touch of human grace
Is more alive forgotten than its memory
Pressed between two pages in this place?

THE REEF FISHER
for K. MacL.

Plunge beneath the ledge of coral
    Where the silt of sunlight drifts
    Like dust that settles toward a floor —
    As slow as that: feel the lifting
Surge that rustles white above
    But here is only movement deep
    As breathing: watch the reef fish hover
    Dancing in their silver sleep
Around their stone, enchanted tree:
    Stoop through the wavering cave of blue:

413

Look down, look down until you see,
Far, far beneath in the translucent
Lightlessness, the huge, the fabulous
Fish of fishes in his profound gulf:
Grip your stickled spear to stab
And sink below the shadowy shelf —

But fear that weed, as though alive,
That lifts and follows with the wave:
The Moray lurks for all who dive
Too deep within the coral cave.
Once tooth of his has touched the bone
Men turn among those stones to stone.

HYPOCRITE AUTEUR

mon semblable, mon frère

(1)

Our epoch takes a voluptuous satisfaction
In that perspective of the action
Which pictures us inhabiting the end
Of everything with death for only friend.

Not that we love death,
Not truly, not the fluttering breath,
The obscene shudder of the finished act —
What the doe feels when the ultimate fact
Tears at her bowels with its jaws.

Our taste is for the opulent pause
Before the end comes. If the end is certain
All of us are players at the final curtain:
All of us, silence for a time deferred,
Find time before us for one sad last word.
Victim, rebel, convert, stoic —
Every role but the heroic —
We turn our tragic faces to the stalls
To wince our moment till the curtain falls.

(2)
A world ends when its metaphor has died.

An age becomes an age, all else beside,
When sensuous poets in their pride invent
Emblems for the soul's consent
That speak the meanings men will never know
But man-imagined images can show:
It perishes when those images, though seen,
No longer mean.

(3)
A world was ended when the womb
Where girl held God became the tomb
Where God lies buried in a man:
Botticelli's image neither speaks nor can
To our kind. His star-guided stranger
Teaches no longer, by the child, the manger,
The meaning of the beckoning skies.

Sophocles, when his reverent actors rise
To play the king with bleeding eyes,
No longer shows us on the stage advance
God's purpose in the terrible fatality of chance.

No woman living, when the girl and swan
Embrace in verses, feels upon
Her breast the awful thunder of that breast
Where God, made beast, is by the blood confessed.

Empty as conch shell by the waters cast
The metaphor still sounds but cannot tell,
And we, like parasite crabs, put on the shell
And drag it at the sea's edge up and down.

This is the destiny we say we own.

(4)
But are we sure
The age that dies upon its metaphor
Among these Roman heads, these mediaeval towers,
Is ours? —
Or ours the ending of that story?
The meanings in a man that quarry
Images from blinded eyes
And white birds and the turning skies
To make a world of were not spent with these
Abandoned presences.

The journey of our history has not ceased:
Earth turns us still toward the rising east,
The metaphor still struggles in the stone,
The allegory of the flesh and bone
Still stares into the summer grass
That is its glass,
The ignorant blood
Still knocks at silence to be understood.

Poets, deserted by the world before,
Turn round into the actual air:
Invent the age! Invent the metaphor!

THE INFINITE REASON

(1)
Rilke thought it was the human part
To translate planet into angel —
Bacteria of mortal heart

Fermenting, into something rich and strange,
The orchard at home, the sky above Toledo:
Sight into soul was what we lived to change.

The key, he told us, was the angel's need,
Not our necessity — and yet
No angel answered for *his* heart to feed.

(2)
The truth is nearer to the true than that.
The truth is, the necessity is ours.
Man is creature to whom meaning matters.

Until we read these faces, figures, flowers,
These shapes averted from us that all vanish,
Everything vanishes — a swarm of hours

Swirling about a bonfire that began
When? Why? To end where? And for what?

(3)
Miser of meanings in the stars, O man

Who finds the poem moonlight has forgotten!
Eternity is what our wanderers gather,
Image by image, out of time — the cut

Branch that flowers in the bowl. Our father,
Thou who ever shalt be, the poor body
Dying at every ditch hath borne Thee, Father.

(4)
Our human part is to redeem the god
Drowned in this time of space, this space
That time encloses.

From the Tyrrhenian flood

The floated marble, the cold human face!

THEORY OF POETRY

Know the world by heart
Or never know it!
Let the pedant stand apart —
Nothing he can name will show it:
Also him of intellectual art.
None know it
Till they know the world by heart.

Take heart then, poet!

DR. SIGMUND FREUD DISCOVERS
THE SEA SHELL

for Harry Murray

Science, that simple saint, cannot be bothered
Figuring what anything is for:
Enough for her devotions that things are
And can be contemplated soon as gathered.

She knows how every living thing was fathered,
She calculates the climate of each star,
She counts the fish at sea, but cannot care
Why any one of them exists, fish, fire or feathered.

Why should she? Her religion is to tell
By rote her rosary of perfect answers.
Metaphysics she can leave to man:
She never wakes at night in heaven or hell

Staring at darkness. In her holy cell
There is no darkness ever: the pure candle
Burns, the beads drop briskly from her hand.

Who dares to offer Her the curled sea shell!
She will not touch it! — knows the world she sees
Is all the world there is! Her faith is perfect!

And still he offers the sea shell . . . .

                                   What surf
Of what far sea upon what unknown ground
Troubles forever with that asking sound?
What surge is this whose question never ceases?

REPLY TO MR. WORDSWORTH

(1)
The flower that on the pear-tree settles
Momentarily as though a butterfly — that petal,
Has it alighted on the twig's black wet

From elsewhere? No, but blossoms from the bole:
Not traveller but the tree itself unfolding.
What of that stranger in the eyes, the soul?

(2)
Space-time, our scientists tell us, is impervious.
It neither evades nor refuses. It curves
As a wave will or a flame — whatever's fervent.

Space-time has no beginning and no end.
It has no door where anything can enter.
How break and enter what will only bend?

(3)
Must there be elsewhere too — not merely here —
To justify the certainty of miracles?
Because we cannot hope or even fear

For ghostly coming on the midnight hour,
Are there no women's eyes all ardor now
And on the tree no momentary flower?

THE SIGNAL

Why do they ring that bell
Twelve times in the steeple?

> To say the hill has swung —
> Houses and church and people,
> All of them fast asleep —
> To this place in time where the bell
> Tilts to its iron tongue
> Twelve times in the steeple.

Houses and hill don't care
Nor sleepers fast asleep.

> But the steeple says to the star:
> Here in the night we are,
> Hill and houses and men.
> Andromeda's shivering light,
> Orion's distant flare,
> Here we are in the night,
> Here we go by again.
> We go by you again says the bell,
> Again, says the bell, again. . . .

WITH AGE WISDOM

At twenty, stooping round about,
I thought the world a miserable place,
Truth a trick, faith in doubt,
Little beauty, less grace.

Now at sixty what I see,
Although the world is worse by far,
Stops my heart in ecstasy.
God, the wonders that there are!

WHY THE FACE OF THE CLOCK IS NOT TRULY A CIRCLE

Time is not gone,
Time does not go,
Time can be found again
Old men know
If you travel a journey.

Paris again
And that scent in the air,
That sound in the street,
And the time is still there
At the end of the journey.

Turn at the door
Climb the stone stair —
What fragrance is that

In the dark, on the air,
At the end of the journey?

Time does not go:
Time keeps its place.
But oh the brown hair
And oh the bright face!
Where? By what journey?

VICISSITUDES OF THE CREATOR

Fish has laid her succulent eggs
Safe in Saragossa weed
So wound and bound that crabbed legs
Nor clattering claws can find and feed.

Thus fish commits unto the sea
Her infinite future and the Trade
Blows westward toward eternity
The universe her love has made.

But when, upon this leeward beach,
The measureless sea journey ends
And ball breaks open, from the breach
A deft, gold, glossy crab extends

In ring-side ritual of self-applause
The small ironic silence of his claws.

THE WOOD DOVE AT SANDY SPRING

Dove that lets the silence answer
Time after time the asking voice,
Trusting stillness as sweet dancer
Trusts to the music all her choice,

Dove that lets the music fall
Note after note into the silence,
Dove, ah dove, we also call:
Shall we learn silence in a while?

ST. PHILIP'S CHURCH IN ANTIGUA
for John Cowles

I think these empty pews are not deserted
Even though the ocean wind
Sings to itself as though they were,
And the blinds rattle. Here in the West Indies

Women, when they learn that lonely music,
Learn to hide their heart-beats from each other.
There might be kneeling women in these pews
Although the wandering wind touched nothing.

I think dead English women come here.
This church was all they had of England —
This and the hymn-tunes and the prayers:

424

They never called the island home,
But here, however the wood blinds might swing
And the wind cry, all the house was theirs.

FOR THE ANNIVERSARY OF MY MOTHER'S DEATH

You think a life can end?
Mind knows, nor soul believes
How far, how far beyond
The shattering of the waves,
How deep within the land,
The surge of sea survives.

There is no least sea sound
Along these inland coves
Where the last waters ground,
Yet something, lapsing, leaves
Slow silver on the sand:
The wave still lifts. It lives.

Those surgings never end
Where salt sea water moves.
Not even, locked in land,
Is sea-beat still: it laves
The last, far-off, profound
Dark shore and deepest caves.

POETICAL REMAINS

What will our reputations be?
Whole things? Constructions
Resisting time (that sea!)
With the rock's persistent luck?

I doubt it. We leave behind
An anthological rubble:
Mind mingled with mind,
Odd and even coupled.

But poetry thrives that way.
Out of the tumbled coral
One exquisite spray,
Ivory, tipped with ore.

MY NAKED AUNT

Who puts off shift
Has love's concealment left.

Who puts off skin
Has pain to wind her in.

Who puts off flesh /
Wears soul's enormous wish.

Who puts off bone
Has all of death for gown.

None go naked who have drawn this breath
Till love's put off and pain and wish and death.

POET

for Ernest Hemingway

           There must be
Moments when we see right through
Although we say we can't. I knew
A fisher who could lean and look
Blind into dazzle on the sea
And strike into that fire his hook,
Far under, and lean back and laugh
And let the line run out, and reel
What rod could weigh nor line could feel —
The heavy silver of his wish,
And when the reel-spool faltered, kneel
And with a fumbling hand that shook
Boat, all bloody from the gaff,
A shivering fish.

CAPTIVITY OF THE FLY

The fly against the window pane
That flings itself in flightless flight,
So it loves light,
Will die of love and die in vain.

Prisoner of the open wall
Where freedom is but turning round,
Still is it bound:
Love barred, there is no way at all.

My heart against the hard rib bone
Beat like a fly and would not be:
It had gone free
But that the shining world so shone.

SHIP'S LOG

What islands known, what passages discovered,
Rocks seen from far off to leeward,
Low, a few palms, odor of sandalwood,
The whole thing blue with dusk. . . .

Mostly I have relinquished and forgotten
Or grown accustomed, which is a way of forgetting.
The more I have travelled the less I have departed.
I had foreseen the unicorn, the nose-rings.

Once in my youth I bailed ship and launched her
As a blue-jay bolts from an apple-tree.
Now I go but have not gone:
Troy is Ithaca again but farther.

Only the young, on a first voyage, facing the
Whole horizon of the sea
Depart from any country. The old men
Sail to the sea-beach they have left behind.

SHIP OF FOOLS

                       shoaled on this shingle,
Beached by the ebbed age, grounded. . . .

If you want spectacles, WE are a spectacle!
The living lot, the generation,
Poking around in pools on the mudflat,
Kicking at clams, cokes, condoms,
Dead fish, minute animalcula,
Ear cocked to the long, withdrawing
Gurgle out of a ketchup bottle
Sucked by the descending silt. . . .

Where are the fountains of the deep, the fountains?
Where are the springs of the sea to enter them?

The ship fast and the fools everywhere!

Fools off in the muck to the eastward
Waiting for history to flood
On the date set by the Central Praesidium:
A tide in the affairs of men
Fixed by the water-works, a fraudulent
Season of the sea. . . .

                              Fools
Off to the west in the place opposite
Damning the possibility of tides,
Screaming there are no tides in this ocean,
Pooling the past in shallow foot-prints,
Impounding the used brine. . . .

429

                    Fools
And the ship fast, the hull careened,
The planks warped by the sun, the beautiful
Carved curve of the stern in the caked
Ooze and the Minoan prow
Dribbled by roosting birds. . . .

                        Four thousand
Years of that sea-wandering brought to
This!
         Stalled!
                    Stinking of sulphur!
Gas out of guts in the muck like voices
Blathering slanders in the house of
State, and the obscene birds, the black,
Indecent, dribbling, obscene birds,
Their mouths filled with excrement, shrieking,
Fouling the figure of the prow. . . .

The springs of the sea, O God, where are they?

Where shall the slavered eyes be washed with
Salt, the ears with salt, the tongues
Washed with the sea-salt?

                        On what tide
Rising to what fresh wind, what cries
Of morning seagulls, shall the ship move;
Stir in her stench of ooze and lift
And on the cold sea, on the cleansing water,
Lean to her course?

            Where are the fountains?

REASONS FOR MUSIC

for Wallace Stevens

Why do we labor at the poem
Age after Age — even an age like
This one, when the living rock
No longer lives and the cut stone perishes? —

Hölderlin's question. Why be poet
Now when the meanings do not mean? —
When the stone shape is shaped stone? —
Dürftiger Zeit? — time without inwardness?

Why lie upon our beds at night
Holding a mouthful of words, exhausted
Most by the absence of the adversary?

Why be poet? Why be man!

Far out in the uttermost Andes
Mortised enormous stones are piled.
What is man? Who founds a poem
In the rubble of wild world — wilderness.

The acropolis of eternity that crumbles
Time and again is mine — my task.
The heart's necessity compels me:
Man I am: poet must be.

The labor of order has no rest:
To impose on the confused, fortuitous
Flowing away of the world, Form —
Still, cool, clean, obdurate,

Lasting forever, or at least
Lasting: a precarious monument
Promising immortality, for the wing
Moves and in the moving balances.

Why do we labor at the poem?
Out of the turbulence of the sea,
Flower by brittle flower, rises
The coral reef that calms the water.

Generations of the dying
Fix the sea's dissolving salts
In stone, still trees, their branches immovable,
Meaning
       the movement of the sea.

AT THE LINCOLN MEMORIAL

✤

Slow Potomac, tarnished water
Silent already with the sense of sea
And still the stain upon you of those raging reaches,
Ravaged Shenandoahs and the toppled elm —
Hold us a little in your drifting thought,
O soiled, sad river! We,
We, too, forefeel; we too remember:
Greatness awaits us as it waits for you
Beyond the sea-fall on those shuddering beaches . . .

And the shame pursues.

✣

We bring the past down with us as you bring your
Sodden branches,
Froth on your yellow eddies and a few
Blind flowers floating like a dead bird's wing:
All that defiling refuse of old wrong,
Of long injustice, of the mastered man,
Of man (far worse! far worse!) made master —
Hatred, the dry bitter thong
That binds these two together at the last;
Fear that feeds the hatred with its stale imposture;
Spoiled, corrupted tramplings of the grapes of wrath . . .

We bring the past down with us, the shame gathers
And the dream is lost.

✣

Think of us, river, where your eddies turn
Returning on the purpose of the stream
And the gulls scream!

Think beyond there where the surges burn
Bright on their beaches and the waters live,
Think of us, river!

Is this our destiny — defeated dream?

✣

Within that door
A man sits or the image of a man
Staring at stillness on a marble floor.
No drum distracts him nor no trumpet can
Although he hears the trumpet and the drum.
He listens for the time to come.

"As to the policy I 'seem to be pursuing' . . .
I would save the Union . . .
My paramount object in this struggle is to save the Union . . ."

The trumpet's breath,
The drummer's tune —
Can drum and trumpet save the Union?

What made the Union — held it in its origins together?
"I have often inquired of myself
what great principle or idea it was . . .
It was not the mere matter of the separation from the mother-
    land
but something in the Declaration giving liberty
not alone to the people of this country
but hope to the world . . .
It was that which gave promise
that in due time
the weights should be lifted from the shoulders of all men."

To save the Union:
To renew
That promise and that hope again.

❦

Within this door
A man sits or the image of a man
Remembering the time before.
He hears beneath the river in its choking channel
A deeper river rushing on the stone,
Sits there in his doubt alone,
Discerns the Principle,
The guns begin,
Emancipates — but not the slaves,

434

The Union — not from servitude but shame:
Emancipates the Union from the monstrous name
Whose infamy dishonored
Even the great Founders in their graves . . .

He saves the Union and the dream goes on.

♣

Think of us, river, when the sea's enormous
Surges meet you on that morning shore!
Think of our destiny, the place
Named in our covenant where we began —
The rendez-vous of man,
The concourse of our kind, O kindred face!

And you,
Within there, in our love, renew
The rushing of that deeper flood
To scour the hate clean and the rusted blood,
The blind rememberance!
        O renew once more,
Staring at stillness on that silent floor,
The proud, lost promise of the sea!

Renew the holy dream we were to be!

Songs for Eve (1954)

1. WHAT EVE SANG

Space-time

Is all there is of space and time
But is not all. There is a rhyme
For all of space and all of time.

I heard it on that Eden night
The branching tree stood dark alight
Like willow in the wind, so white
Its unknown apples on the night:

I heard beyond that tree a tree
Stir in silence over me.
In space and time, eyes only see,
Ears only hear, the green-wood tree:

But Oh! I heard the whole of time
And all of space give ringing rhyme

And ring and ring and chime and chime
When I reached out to touch and climb
In spite of space, in spite of time.

2. WHAT EVE SAID

Eve said:
From tree to tree
Will journey be;
The one, she said,
Alive and green,
The other dead,
And what's between,
Eve said,
Our lives mean.

Eve said:
With tree began
That traveller, man;
With tree, she said,
Will journey end.
That tree, though dead,
Its leaves will spend,
Eve said,
World without end.

Eve said:
The first is his
Whose world this is:
The last, she said,
Blossomed and blown

Though wood be dead,
Is mine, my own.
Eve said:
O my son! O my son!

3. WHAT ADAM SAID

My life began
Not when I was moulded man
But when beneath the apple tree
I saw what none but I could see:
Adam flesh and Adam bone
And Adam by himself alone.

That day he sees
His own two hands, those mysteries —
His flesh, his bone and yet not his —
That day man knows himself, and is.

4. WHAT THE GREEN TREE SAID

Wakening is forbidden
To all in space and time —
Star and stone, bird and beast.

Wakers see what sleep has hidden.
Wakers will no longer rest
In space and time as they were bidden.

5. EVE'S EXILE

Eden was an endless place,
Time enough for all of space
And space for all that time to pass.

We lived in time as fishes live
Within the lapsing of the wave
That with the water's moving move.

We lived in space as hawk in air:
The place we were was everywhere
And everywhere we were, we were.

Fish and hawk have eyes of glass
Wherein the skies and waters pass
As in a glass the images —

They mirror but they may not see.
When I had tasted fruit of tree
Fish and hawk, they fled from me:

"She has a watcher in her eyes,"
The hawk screamed from the steep of skies,
Fish from sea-deep where he lies.

Our exile is our eyes that see.
Hawk and fish have eyes but we
Behold what they can only be.

Space within its time revolves
But Eve must spin as Adam delves
Because our exile is ourselves.

6. EVE ANSWERS THE BURDOCK

What did I eat when I ate apple?
What did I eat in the sweet
Day, in the leaves' dapple?
Eve.

What did I know when I knew apple?
What did I know in the new
Night, in the stars' stipple?
Eve.

7. WHAT THE VINE SAID TO EVE

Man is the leaky bung
That lets the ferment in:
The wine were sweet and young
But for your sin.

But for your fault the wine
Were sweet as water is:
No taint of taste, no sign,
No promises.

But for your sin no tongue
Had tasted, salt as blood,
The certainty among
These grapes of God.

8. THE FALL!

                    said Eve;
That Fall began
What leaves conceive
Nor fishes can —
So far a flight
Past touch, past sight.

Get down, said Eve
Upon your shins,
Upon your shanks,
And pray reprieve,
And give God thanks
For Eden sins.

The Fall! she said —
From earth to God!
Give thanks, said she, for branch, for bole,
For Eve who found the grace to fall
From Adam, browsing animal,
Into the soaring of the soul!

9. EVE'S NOW-I-LAY-ME

To separate myself from space
I gave the water pool my face:
To separate myself from time
I gave the stars my soul to climb.

10. ADAM IN THE EVENING

Beauty cannot be shown
But only at remove:
What's beautiful is known
By opposites, as love.

Counter, the mind can see.
When first Eve disobeyed
And turned and looked at me,
Beauty was made.

That distance in the blood
Whereby the eyes have sight
Is love — not understood
But infinite.

11. EVE IN THE DAWN

Time created out of clay.
That animal with whom I lay.

Like she of wolf or lion's she
In season he would tumble me,

Yet touched me never till he took
The apple from my hand and Look!

Look! he said, your eyes that see
My eyes have images of me!

That night until the next of day
We touched in love and loving lay:

We were awake then who had slept.
Our bodies out of Eden leapt

Together to a lifted place
Past space of time and time of space

That neither space nor time had made.
There first we laughed, were first afraid.

Was it Adam, only he,
Bred that flowering branch of me
Whereon shall hang eternity?

12. EVE'S CHILD

Does anyone know, says Eve, that fable
Women in their dotage tell
Of girls covered by gods, unable
Afterward to call the babe?
What pipped and tapped in Leda's shell
Laid by the shoal there in the fable?

The soul that comes from God, one says,
And one remembers him as swan
Because the swan has feathery ways,
And one as bull, so brisk the blaze,
But none remembers him as man.
It was a man took me, Eve says.

444

Women, when a child is found,
Make the sea sound: Hush! Hush!
Does anyone know why they make that sound?
Our blood is salt as the sea around,
Our body, at each beginning, fish:
Hush! says Eve, when a child is found.

13. ADAM'S JEALOUSY: EVE'S ANSWER

Cover that infant's mouth and eyes,
Said Adam, softly where it lies:
The soul that lurks, the soul that flies,
Will enter where it clucks and cries.

Hold close, said Adam, in the leaves,
That struggling girl who first conceives.
The souls are fluttering at the eaves:
They enter flesh when flesh believes.

The invisible souls, now Eden's lost,
Hunt, he said, the chosen host
To house them, body sick with ghost.
I fear the souls, said Adam, most.

Adam, Adam, there are none
Enter flesh but flesh and bone.

Flesh and bone have wonder done
And wonder, bone and flesh are One.

14. ADAM'S RIDDLE

> Raddle me riddle,
> I'll spell you the word:
> Two are together
> And still there's a third
> Mingles to meddle
> Beneath the green tree:
> One is its father,
> One is its mother. . . .
>
> What's born of three?

15. THE SERPENT'S RIDDLE

> Riddle me raddle,
> I'll tell you another:
> The worm is its father,
> The apple its mother,
> It couples astraddle
> But thinks it is moth
> That on heavenly wing
> Can fly and can fling.
>
> What is it? . . . And why?

16. EVE'S RIDDLE

Raddle me riddle
Or weep if you'd rather.
Adam's its father,
Eve is its mother,
Yet where in the middle
There grows the green tree
Eve must take apple
Before it can be.

What is it? Ah me!

17. THE BABE'S RIDDLE

Riddle me raddle
And tell me the weather:
What wakes in a cradle
As light as a feather
And fallen from where?
What clings to its mother,
Its hand in her hair,
But stares at that other?

What knows its own father?

18. EVE'S REBUKE TO HER CHILD

Who said you were bred
Not of flesh and of bone
But of somebody flown
From a place in the sky
Had no thew and no thigh
And no pelt and no poll?
Who told you that lie
About body and soul?

You think it was I,
Not that girl in the tower,
Was had by a shower
Of gold from the sky?
We do what we can!
There was none lay with me
But was made like a man
As a man ought to be.

You came by the soul
As you came by the skin
Where the raging strikes in
And the wrestlers must roll.
If you'd rather be more
You can brag if you'd rather:
Make your mother a whore,
Have a ghost for a father.

But O, the noon day
And O, the green tree!
Body of me
In the fern where we lay!

The flight that was flown
From the place in the sky —
The flesh and the bone
Made those wings that could fly.

19. WHAT THE SERPENT SAID TO ADAM

Which is you, old two-in-one?
Which is which, old one of two?
When the doubling is undone
Which one is you?

Is it you that so delights
By that woman in her bed?
Or you the glimmering sky afrights,
Vast overhead?

Are you body, are you ghost?
Were you got or had no father?
Is this you — the guest? — the host?
Who then's the other?

That woman says, old one-of-two,
In body was the soul begun:
Now two are one and one is you: —
Which one? Which one?

20. WHAT THE LION SAID TO THE CHILD

The flesh they say is stronger
And brisk with brutal blood;
The spirit mild and meekly made and good:
And spirit shuns the fight but should no longer,
For the flesh must be withstood,
So fell its lust, so foul its hunger.

If those that teach were fewer
And truer what they taught
A child might learn what fight is really fought
And which is lamb, which lion, of those two.
A child might learn, when prey is caught,
Flesh is not the fierce pursuer.

21. EVE QUIETS HER CHILDREN

Eve, our mother, care and keep!
We who call you cannot sleep.

Wake then! Weep!

Eve, our mother, all the rest
Sleep about us, bird and beast.

Waking's best.

All things other turn and twine
Like gnats in atmospheres of wine.

Eden's sign!

Stars that circle in their sleep
Silver solemn statutes keep.

Stars! Time's sheep!

Suns and moons and nails and claws
Sleep out time's revolving laws.

Time! Time was!

Eve, our mother, what was wrought
Broke the sleep when we were got?

Sleep's green tree was cut, was cut.

Eve, Eve, who are we,
Born to wake and waking see?

Wake and see!

22. THE SERPENT'S CRADLE SONG

You are the children of Eve by the apple.
By the pip of the apple she came to conceive.
Adam, that cuckold, never begot you.
You are the children of Eve
By the apple.

Adam was hot
In the heat of the day,

And he lay in her lap
And she gave him his way,
But the pip of the apple
I taught her to eat
(Tart? — sweet!)
Was quick in her womb.
When Adam came knocking
The inn had no room.

Said the king to the cock:
When the day comes to bloom
Be quiet for once!
I must sleep in the tomb.
Said the king to the huntsman:
Quiet your horn!
Let the day begin dumb:
There is sleep to be born.
But the pip of the apple
Was quick in his blood:
Eve's children can sleep
But not well — not for good.

23. EVE TO THE STORM OF THUNDER

Who teaches child that snivelling guilt
For space rejected and time spilt?
Tell me, how was Heaven built?

Space and time I disobeyed:
It was so that he was made,
Little man so fast afraid.

Had I not, in wonder's awe,
Disobeyed the lion's law,
Voice and hand were shriek and paw.

Had I not, for wonder's sake,
Broken law no leaf may break,
Lids were closed that now awake.

Only when I disobeyed
Was the bliss of Eden stayed —
Bliss of sleep in that thick shade.

Was it shame and was it sin,
Shameful out and shameless in,
So in waking to begin?

How else can heavenly thunder shake
The heart but if the heart awake?

24. EVE OLD

The taste of time is sweet at first,
Then salt as tears, then tame as water:
Time to the old tastes bitter, bitter.

No child of mine may quench his thirst
However deep he drink of time,
Sweet or bitter, salt or tame.

Because my tongue that apple durst

453

His tongue shall want what time is not—
Not tame, not bitter, salt nor sweet:

Because my tongue that apple durst
Eternity shall be his thirst.

25. EVE'S FIRST PROPHECY

God who made the garden green
Made the apple tree to lean
And glitter in that shine and sheen.

The apple tree will fall away.

Straight of bole and strict of bough,
Sons of mine will shape and hew
Tree that Eden never knew.

The dry tree branch will swing and sway.

All to this my sons are born:
To hew and shape and raise that tree,
And stand beneath in scorn, in scorn . . . .
And on it bear eternity.

The apple tree shall fall away.

The dry tree branch shall swing and sway.

26. EVE'S SECOND PROPHECY

This sun at last will stand and stare
And blaze and burn its planets out,
And all God's works of skill and care
Will strew the starry sky about,
Yet hearts remain what once they were.

When nothing lives of all this light
But, somewhere between star and star,
A greater darkness on the night
Where once our glimmering signals were,
What heart has seen will still be sight.

Eden's tree will wither up,
And char and in its ashes drift,
But not one leaf will wilt or drop
From that dry tree my children lift
To bear the heart's rebellious hope.

27. EVE EXPLAINS TO THE THRUSH
WHO REPEATS EVERYTHING

(1)

On the first tree,
The green tree,
Mystery
Created me.

On first tree grew
Whereby I knew,

Struck by that wonder's wonder through:
Stricken and knew.

    Apple eaten of that tree
    Animal I ceased to be.

On the last tree,
The dry tree,
Eternity
My fruit shall be:

    On last be hung
    Whereby my tongue
    Shall sing and all the stars among
    Meaning be sung.

      Apple eaten of that tree
      Time itself shall cease to be.

(2)

Green tree,
Time's tree,
Mystery.

    By time was made
    The sheen, the shade,
    The fruit that in my mouth betrayed
    All that time made.

      Apple eaten of that tree
      Eve I was — and Eve might be.

Dry tree,
Man's tree,
Eternity.

By man, his hand,
That tree shall stand,
And hold so still time's stars — so stand
The world will end.

> Apple eaten of that tree
> Eve and thrush shall cease — and be.

28. WHAT THE WIND SAID TO THE WATER: WHAT THE WATER REPLIED

Man, like any creature,
Dies where two days meet:
Dead, by time is eaten.

> *Sea worm leaves behind*
> *Shell for wave to find:*
> *Man, the shell of mind.*

Like any creature, man
Lives by luck and vanishes:
The chance wind takes the candle.

> *No creature leaves behind*
> *Huck or shell or rind*
> *Obdurate as the mind.*

Life is luck, death random.

> *Tell me, what is man*
> *That immortal order can?*

PART SIX

HURRICANE

Sleep at noon. Window blind
rattle and bang. Pay no mind.
Door go jump like somebody coming:
let him come. Tin roof drumming:
drum away — she's drummed before.
Blinds blow loose: unlatch the door.
Look up sky through the manchineel:
black show through like a hole in your heel.
Look down shore at the old canoe:
rag-a-tag sea turn white, turn blue,
kick up dust in the lee of the reef,
wallop around like a loblolly leaf.
Let her wallop — who's afraid?
Gale from the north-east: just the Trade . . .

And that's when you hear it: far and high —
sea-birds screaming down the sky

461

high and far like screaming leaves;
tree-branch slams across the eaves;
rain like pebbles on the ground . . .

and the sea turns white and the wind goes round.

THE SHIP IN THE TOMB

Cheops, to sail eternity,
built him a ship, a real one, sea-
worthy, solid cedar, gear
complete to the last metaphor;

even a heavy-weather prow
to breast the spiritual surge and throw
the foam of fiery stars about.
Cheops was wise. He knew. Without

the shape of actual ship the notion
founders in that kind of ocean.

Consider the Idea of God. Before
God was God forevermore
how was immortality made known?
By stone.

Even the Idea must start
in stone, surmount the stone by art,
surmount the art by Angelo,

leave Angelo upon his Sistine ceiling . . .
and so
          go.

Even the Idea demands
the work of hands,
the shape to feel.

CREATOR

The world was made by someone else,
not God. The moist, inexplicable bees,
the crystal stones, the painted shells,
the lights beyond the swarming Pleiades —

God knows nothing of these things.
We found him in the burning bush
above the desert where he sings
as flames do, trilling in their fiery hush.

He told us where the end was, knew
the way to reach it, showed the path:
there men like marigolds, he said, come true
and understand their lives and live their death.

We help each other through the blind
tall night beneath the infinite spaces:
God looks before and we behind
but somewhere else that other unknown face is.

THE BOATMEN OF SANTORIN

The boatmen on the bay of Santorin
where the world blew up about the time of Minos
sit with their hands on their oars inviting the tourists.

Visit the myth! Visit the fable!
Visit the drowned volcano where the world
blew up about the time of Minos!

The sea sings. The sun shines.
Visit the end of the world! they shout at you.

And all at once on the bright blue
tourist sea, suds of pumice,
floating shoals of gray decaying stone,
grate at the wooden oars.

                              We float here
feathering death at our oar-blades.

THE PEEPERS IN OUR MEADOWS

The way at night these piping peepers
suddenly and all at once are still —
too suddenly, too all together, to have dropped asleep
at God's sweet will.

Things stop like that: altogether.
Nations falter, great art fails,

ages of poetry draw Periclean breath;
then death prevails.

What stills these peepers in our midnight pond?
Do wings go over? Skulkers come?
Or are they silenced by that silence out beyond?
Struck dumb?

WAKING

The sadness we bring back from sleep
like an herb in the mouth . . .

                              sage?

                                    rosemary?

like a fragrance we can neither lose nor
keep . . .

              woodsmoke?

                         oak-leaves?

like the closing
softly of a distant . . .

                    distant? . . .

                               door . . .

                                          Oh
like earth on our shoes from an unremembered journey . . .
What earth?

              What journey?

                    Why did we return?

AUTOBIOGRAPHY

There was a landscape in my childhood
over opposite — against:
another world than this one, wild
and hence.

There was another time, an earliness:
the sun came up out of Eden, out of the Odyssey —
freshness like the fragrance of a girl
or god.

What do I know of the mystery of the universe?
Only the mystery — that there was a mystery:
something opposite beneath the moon
to this.

But I who saw it — who was I?
And who am I who say this to you? All
I know now of that world, that time,
is false.

REVOLUTION OF THE CHILDREN

Leafless Dodder, Rabbit's Silk,
wind-sown on some farmer's acre,
cut for fodder, fed for milk,
crazes a city's children. Something
odder, dafter, dizzier than cow
sniggers in the school-bus laughter,
capers at the picture show,

when Leafless Dodder, Rabbit's Silk,
scents the city's sanitary milk.

Girls in scants and boys in beards
offer to make love to flowers,
Jesus dances, music showers,
words and weirds sing songs together,
heifers in their lolling herds
leave the green alfalfa, feed
on gossamer of Rabbit's Silk,
on thistle down of Dodder seed.

Let ordinances close the town
to Dodder seed, that thistle down,
to gossamer of Rabbit's Silk —
there'll still
         be milk.

BLACK HUMOR

The jangle of the jeering crows
has somehow crossed into my dream
to scream and circle there. I seem
in sleep to understand the crows.

Evil is in the world, they scream.
Something on the garden path
salt as blood and cold as death
has fallen from the air, the dream.

I find it with the daylight, too:
cold upon the path, to gather
drops of silence from the dew,
one inscrutable, black, bleeding feather.

BOY IN THE ROMAN ZOO

TO THE FLAMINGOS

                        Ravished arms,
delighted eyes — and all the rest,
parental cautions and alarms,
treacherous sidewalks and his best
blue suit forgotten. He has seen
heaven upon the further shore
and nothing in the null between
has mere existence anymore.
Those shapes of rose, those coals of ice,
command him as love never has
and only they can now suffice.
Forgotten is the child he was,
unguessed the man he will be. One
moment, free of both, he'll run
toward the flamingos in the sun.

SEEING

BY NIGHT

What did you see, Cromarty, by the house
or where the house once was?

                A tree.

I know it hurts. I have to ask you.

I said I saw a tree.

              What kind of
tree?

      A pear tree.

             Look here, soldier!
Look! We drop a flare. You see . . .
what do you see?

           A pear. A tree . . .

I told you I was sorry . . .

          . . . tree
bloom in the night.

           And that was all?

No. I saw a petal fall.

Think! You haven't long, Cromarty.

I thought! Good God, I thought! I thought,
Christ! I'd never seen a tree!

And that was all . . . ?

(2)
<small>AT THE SATURDAY CLUB</small>

Harlow: Our generation discovered the universe.

Robert: That's why we're lost.

Harlow: Men before us
thought in beginnings and ends, all of them.
Nobody knew that time is a circle,
that space is a circle, that space-time
closes the circle.

Robert: They weren't lost.

Harlow: They didn't know they were lost but they were:
they were wrong.

Robert: And we're right and we're lost.

Harlow: When you're right
you can't be lost: you know where you are.

Robert: You know where you are when you're lost.

Harlow: Where?

Robert: Lost.

470

(3)

Why are you moving your lips, said the Emperor I Tsung.

I am blessing the prophets, said Ibn Wahab the traveler.

Where are the prophets, said the Emperor I Tsung.
        I do not see them.

You see them, said Ibn Wahab the traveler:
        you do not recognize them but you see them.

I see a man in a boat on a great ocean, said the Emperor I
        Tsung.

That, said Ibn Wahab the traveler, is Noah.
        who swam on the world when the Flood drowned it.

I see a man in the fields, said the Emperor I Tsung:
        he is wandering.

That is Abraham, said Ibn Wahab the traveler:
        he is wandering everywhere looking for God.

I see a man on a tree, said the Emperor I Tsung.

That, said Ibn Wahab the traveler, is Jesus.

What did he do, said the Emperor I Tsung:
        did he swim on the world? Did he wander everywhere?

He died, said Ibn Wahab the traveler.

Why do I weep, said the Emperor I Tsung.

You have recognized Jesus, said Ibn Wahab the traveler.

(4)
AT THE DARK'S EDGE

Sister tree,
deaf and dumb and blind, and we
have ears to hear, have eyes for sight,
and yet our sister tree can find,
fumbling deaf and groping blind,
the field before her and the wood behind,
what we can't . . .
                    light.

COMPANIONS

The flowers with the ragged names,
daffodils and such,
met us on the road we came,
nodded, touched.

Now, the golden day gone by,
we walk the other road:
they throng the evening grass beside,
touch us . . .
                    nod.

SURVIVOR

On an oak in autumn
there'll always be
one leaf left at the top of the tree
that won't let go with the rest and rot —
won't cast loose and skitter and sail
and end in a puddle of rain in a swale
and fatten the earth and be fruitful . . .
                                        No,
it won't and it won't and it won't let go.
It rattles a kind of a jig tattoo,
a telegrapher's tattle that *will* get through
like an SOS from a struggling ship
over and over, a dash and a skip.

You cover your head with your quilt and still
that telegrapher's key on Conway hill
calls to Polaris.

                I can spell:
I know what it says . . . I know too well.
I pull my pillow over my ear
but I hear.

GREAT CONTEMPORARY DISCOVERIES

The Writers: We die.

The Readers: Aie!

The Writers: We disappear from the
                    bed, the bedroom, from the chair:
                    nothing remembers us.

The Readers: Perhaps a mirror
                    found on a closet shelf long afterward? —
                    Whose? Hers? Tinkle of memory . . .?

The Writers: We leave no memory.

The Readers: A son? A daughter?

The Writers: They too die, one first then the other:
                    the house sold, the furniture carted off,
                    different flowers.

The Readers: God then: God will remember us.

The Writers: How can God remember us? Think of the
                    earth, that boneyard — a man's tooth by a
                          jackal's —
                    Olduvai of indistinguishable bones!

The Readers: Nevertheless we have lived. We leave our lives.

The Writers: What is a man's life! An absurdity —
                    extinguished unintelligible cry.

The Readers: Absurd? Our lives?

The Writers: Because we die.

The Readers: But Sirs! But Sirs! That's why we love them.

The Writers: Why?

The Readers: *Because we die!*

The Writers: Aie!

SPRING IN THESE HILLS

> Slow May
> deliberate in the peach tree,
> lighting the pear blossoms, one first then another,
> sullen almost sometimes,
> comes,
> delicately through the thaws of snow
> to scatter
> daffodils like drifting flaws
> of sunlight on these winter hills.

OBSERVATIONS OF P. OVIDIUS NASO ON THE INCIDENCE OF SEX IN THE CONTEMPORARY NOVEL

What have they done to you, all-conquering love? —
you who taught the lecherous birds to preen and even
men to walk like men for pride of love —
what have they done to you?

And who are these,
these nudest, lewdest, noisiest, their naked buttocks
scarcely skirted and their breasts tipped up to tease —
these who set upon you with their silver scissors,
clip your famous arrow, cut
your bowstring, tell you what your mother is
and walk off whistling?

Show me, you,
all-conquering triumphant captain, what
precisely you propose to do!

LA FOCE

Close the shutters. Let the ceiling fly
dance around the chandelier
in silent circles with inaudible small cry
in celebration of my seventieth year.

Why grow older in a Tuscan spring
where everything,
follies and flowers, loves and leaves,

476

grows younger and the loam conceives
and even the slow venerable sun
splashes in the water spills
and hills
invent again the new
first blue?

Close the shutters. Tuscan noon.
A hen upon the barley ground
tells the welkin what her industry has found
and heaven answers. All must run,
Yeats tells us, backward to be new begun
as does the silver bullion of the moon.

Only one small circling fly
remembers that the world goes by
and we go with it
                he and I.

OLD MAN'S JOURNEY

The deep-sea salmon far at sea,
fierce with silver, scoured with salt,
flailing toward eternity,
returns as we do — our too human fault.

Remembrance of the brown Tobique,
the gravel shoal, the succulent mud,
the inchling sleepers cheek to cheek
somehow infects his restless blood,

477

and seasons after, in the deep,
cold, farthest ocean flood, he sees
the pebbled rift, the pools of sleep,
the rippling shallows under rippling trees,

and turns and puts his journey by
and climbs from sea to stream to brook to die.

Only in Dante's Hell does Ulysses
sail on and on to always farther seas.

TYRANT OF SYRACUSE

This stranger in my blood, my skin,
can I command him? Will he stand
when I say stand? Come out? Go in?
Do anything?
              And yet if he,
snake in his brittle grass, command
I jump I tell you! Haw or Gee
I take his orders, come awake
when he wakes, sleep when he sleeps, love
what pleases him and for his sake
not mine. He's master, lord thereof,
Tyrant of Syracuse who hears
whatever's spoken in the cave.
                        Sometimes,
pacing the silence in a fit of work,
a half-made poem humming in my ears,
hammering its pattern in my mind,
I'll know he's listening in that room behind,

478

stirring a little in his place to smirk
and nod as though he'd shaped the rhymes . . .

he! that fumbler! dumb and blind!

WHERE A POET'S FROM

                                        Where he's born?
Settles? Where the papers claim him?
Carl Sandburg, born in Illinois,
died in Flat Rock, Carolina, in Chicago famous —

where was Sandburg from? Chicago?
People knew where Frost was from
in spite of San Francisco — from New England.
What town or what proud county knew this other coming?

He lived around: he lived in Kansas,
Chicago on the Old West Side,
Michigan, Nebraska — in Wisconsin.
Where was Carl from in the Carolinas when he died?

His tongue might tell: he talked "Peoria" —
O as in Oh or Low, the way
the railroad trainmen on the Illinois
called it in those cool reverberating stations.

His sound might say: he said "Missouri" —
a stumbled M and an S and an OO
long as a night freight off across the prairie
asking the moon for answers and the sound goes through and
    through.

Where was Sandburg from, old poet,
dead in Carolina in his great repute?
"Peoria," he said, "Missouri," the neglected names
that now, because his mouth has spoken them, are beautiful.

MARK'S SHEEP

Mark's sheep, I said, but they were only
stones, boulders in the uncropped grass,
granite shoulders weathered to the bone
and old as that first morning where God was.

And yet they looked like sheep — so like
you half expected them to startle,
bolt in a leap because some tyke
had barked, because a bluejay darted —

dart of shadow under blue of jay —
or someone shouted by the water trough,
slammed a car-door, drove away,
or squirrels quarreled, or a gun went off,

or just because they must: that terrified
impulse to be somewhere else
browsers and ruminators seem to share
as though they knew, they only, the sky falls

and *here* is dangerous (as of course it is).
But Mark's sheep never startled from the grass.
They knew their place, their boulders' business:
to let the nights go over, the days pass,

let years go, summer, autumn, winter,
each by itself, each motionless, alone,
praising the world by being in it,
praising the earth by being stone.

CUMMINGS

"He was sitting watching the sunset."
Marion Cummings, September 2, 1962

True
poet who could live and die
eye to eye

The rain ends, the sky slides
east a little as our skies here do
this time of year and lets the sunset through . . .

or not the sunset either but a blue
between the hills and what the cloud still hides
that promises
                a poet's blue

I should have known, my friend, you'd watch it too
eastward across New Hampshire where the night
found you in that glimpse of light

The cloud lifts and the rift of blue
blazes and the sun comes through

HEMINGWAY

"In some inexplicable way an accident."
Mary Hemingway

Oh, not inexplicable. Death explains,
that kind of death: rewinds remembrance
backward like a film track till the laughing man
among the lilacs, peeling the green stem,
waits for the gunshot where the play began;

rewinds those Africas and Idahos and Spains
to find the table at the Closerie des Lilas,
sticky with syrup, where the flash of joy
flamed into blackness like that flash of steel.

The gun between the teeth explains.
The shattered mouth foretells the singing boy.

EDWIN MUIR

The memory of Edwin Muir is green
as garden parsley when the first hard frost
blackens the asters and the rose is lost —
snow in all the garden paths between.

"Strophe of small leaves
in the inevitable spiral,
versicle of God . . ."

still lyre.

482

Aie, how they sang in their youth together,
trill of Hesiod in the spring,
Pindar in the showery weather,
all those lovely poets . . .

how they sing!

WILLIAM ADAMS DELANO

The supple haft, the helve,
outlasts the brutal stick.

The brittle honey wax
outburns the tallow wick.

The man with ardor quick,
the man by grace refined,

though girth and thew he lack
and live but by the mind

can still outcount by twelve
the Grand Climacteric

and where the great decay
and where the gross decline

grow nobler day by day:
reveal the pure design.

RUE CARPENTER

Some for their looks,
some for their powers,
some like Rue Carpenter
for bowls of flowers.

Some for an age,
some a few hours,
some like Rue Carpenter
as long as flowers.

BROOKS ATKINSON

Brooks Atkinson, that quiet man
who kept the torches of Parnassus
steady as New England can
(or could) behind his steel-rimmed glasses,

Brooks Atkinson who loved the tongue
well consonanted and well voweled
(Actors who mouthed it should be hung,
writers who blurred it, disemboweled),

Brooks Atkinson who hated hue
and cry and mode and art-in-fashion,
and never wrote a wrong review
to show his wit or wave his passion

or imitate the *dernier cri*
or scratch for academic plaudit

but saw the plays there were to see
and searched his soul and made his audit

and kept alive for thirty years
of Venus in a pouting sweater,
Ares in skirts and art in tears,
the taste for good, the hope for better,

Brooks Atkinson, the role complete,
the task performed, the judgment certain,
prepared to vanish from his seat
unnoticed at the final curtain.

Wrong for once. The faithful man
who guards the honor of the muses
never vanishes, never can:
they keep his fame for their sweet uses.

APRIL IN NOVEMBER

Even in spring, even in first
spring when the tree can put forth again
mending its broken branches with new green,
even in spring there is ruin enough from these tempests,
whirling tornadoes from God knows where, violent and
unforetellable sudden descent of the wind on the
white leaves and the gasp and the branches threshing . . .

Unwished, unexpected visit of loveliness.

Now, this later season of the year

there is no healing green, the bare
bole stands broken for the world to see.

Unseasonable tempest: naked tree.

HOW THE RIVER NINFA RUNS THROUGH THE RUINED TOWN BENEATH THE LIME QUARRY

to remember Marguerite Caetani

Italy breaking her bones for bread
eating her stones

But the Nymph, O the Nymph in her crisp cresses
clattering over the cobbles on slippery
heels where the little palazzi were and the churches
ages ago, ages ago . . .

O but the Nymph in her cool cresses
jigging with midges in the slants of sun
nobody's shadow now, nobody's shadow . . .

chattering under the bridges nobody's shoes . . .

O but the Nymph in her crisp cresses
cracking her knuckles in time with a tune
nobody knows anymore now, nobody . . .

chuckling her fables
over and over again and then
when the dynamite kicks at the sky and the quarry . . .

Italy breaking her bones for bread
eating her stones

. . . shudders and tumbles . . .

O but the Nymph! — how she hushes and humbles
just for a heart's beat and is dumb . . .

. . . Nymph in the ruin of time . . .

                                    and then laughs again.

CONTEMPORARY PORTRAIT

This woman mask that wears her to the bone
they say for certain is her soul's disguise:
such holes are cut in colored cloth for eyes
where the live lid winks beneath the painted one.

The eyes are hers, the mouth is not her own.
The mouth smiles soft, remembers well, complies,
laughs, lifts a little, kisses — these are lies
when at the lid the tragic look is shown.

Whether her soul in fear has made this mask
for easier wandering beneath our moon
or time has tricked her so, they never ask:
they know the false face hides the honest one.

And yet it's certain, when she comes to die,
this is the face that death will know her by.

PITY'S SAKE

For pity's sake
never give the heart away!
Sell it, barter it for marbles, play
the ponies with it, let it break,
but never give the heart away
for pity's sake.

When pity gives what pride should take
love becomes a hand to hold,
a comfortable knee, a shoulder
made to cry on in the cold
and by and by
a nastier faleshood than a lie.

Go out, my dear, too old to play,
but never give the heart away
for pity's sake.

NOVEMBER

A drop on the window, once, twice.
A blasted rose at the end of a brier.
Sparrows in the weeds like mice
and the cat indoors beside the fire.

Love, old love and old desire,
let the puddles skin with ice;
pile the bed up higher, higher . . .

Time at the window, once, twice.

HOTEL BREAKFAST

On a stale morning
in a miserable winter town in Illinois
neither of us ever heard of,

sipping a sticky cup of some
(not tea, not coffee, cocoa?) tepid brew
you surely, of all living, never knew,

the napkin reeking of its dead cigars
(scent of yellow roses was your warning),
suddenly,
        across the table,
                you.

The plastic prisms of the chandelier
shiver with laughter from another year,
another country, Oh, another life;
the cold sun crawls along the butter knife.

I tremble, heartsick with a mortal fear —

What brings you here?

RAINBOW AT EVENING

Rainbow over evening, my
Iris of the after-sky,
show me, now the gales are by,
where the gold is.

489

When the rain
crazed the whirling weather vane
I never wondered. I knew then.
Gold was where the heart could find.

Now the heart is out of mind
in this late light your seal has signed,
show me, *arc-en-ciel*, bright bow,
where the gold is hidden now.

ARRIVAL AND DEPARTURE

The train slows down,
   the town appears,
      persons in
the *Place 'la Gare*
   sit in Sunday
      hats and stare,

Sunday sunshine
   stalks the cats.
      The engine sighs.
Across the square
   a window opens:
      heavy hair

Falls all gold
   from sill to air.
      The engine jerks,
the *Place* withdraws,

490

                    the staring faces
                    turn away.

        (They go: we stay.)

                    The window opens:
                    heavy hair
        falls all gold
            from sill to air . . .

                    Our journey to the
        world stopped there.

LATE ABED

        Ah, but a good wife!
        To lie late in a warm bed
        (warm where she was) with your life
        suspended like a music in the head,
        hearing her foot in the house, her broom
        on the pine floor of the down-stairs room,
        hearing the window toward the sun go up,
        the tap turned on, the tap turned off,
        the saucer clatter to the coffee cup . . .

        To lie late in the odor of coffee
        thinking of nothing at all, listening . . .

        and she moves here, she moves there,
        and your mouth hurts still where last she kissed you:

                        491

you think how she looked as she left, the bare
thigh, and went to her adorning . . .

You lie there listening and she moves —
prepares her house to hold another morning,
prepares another day to hold her loves . . .

You lie there
thinking of nothing
watching the sky . . .

"THE WILD OLD WICKED MAN"

Too old for love and still to love! —
Yeats's predicament and mine — all men's:
the aging Adam who must strut and shove
and caper his obscene pretense . . .

And yet, within the dry thorn grove,
singer to singer in the dusk, there cries
(Listen! Ah, listen, the wood dove!)
something conclusion never satisfies;

and still when day ends and the wind goes down
and not a tree stirs, not a leaf,
some passion in the sea beats on
and on . . .
                    (Oh, listen, the sea reef!)

Too old for love and still to long . . .
for what? For one more flattering proof

492

the flesh lives and the beast is strong? —
once more upon the pulse that hammering hoof?

Or is there something the persistent dove,
the ceaseless surges and the old man's lust
all know and cannot say? Is love

what nothing concludes, nothing must,
pure certainty?

      And does the passionate man
most nearly know it when no passion can?
Is this the old man's triumph, to pursue
impossibility — and take it too?

PART SEVEN
NEWLY COLLECTED
POEMS

PREFATORY NOTE

At his death in April 1982, Archibald MacLeish left a goodly number of poems that had not been gathered into a book, and more that had never been put into print. Some of these were the work of his late years, written after the new poems comprising Part One of the present book were published in the 1976 edition. Others had appeared earlier in periodicals but were passed by when he came to assembling choices for a book. This was apparently inadvertent in at least one instance. Five poems originally published in Paris in 1927 were brought to the poet's attention many years later by R. H. Winnick, editor of *Letters of Archibald MacLeish*; MacLeish told Winnick that he considered them as good as anything he was writing at that time, and that their omission from any collection was an oversight. A few poems that make their first appearance in this edition were evidently of too private a nature to be brought out during his or his wife's lifetime.

It was the poet's custom to write in a bound notebook, usually of an inexpensive sort he could pick up in a local store. When he had done a first draft he moved on to the next page in the notebook to try a second draft, and continued so until he had achieved a poem that satisfied him. Sometimes he put a date at the end of a draft. When he did not find that his "hand's in luck" with a poem, he went on to a fresh poem and a different idea. A work that had been left as unfinished might be taken up again months or years later in another notebook and brought to final form.

The poems that were among his papers at the farm in Conway, Massachusetts, which was his home for many years, ranged from casual verses and fragments to carefully finished lyrics. Of those, twenty-nine have been chosen as deserving a place in this volume. They are arranged approximately in chronological order, since they do not represent the work of one period but rather the span of the poet's life.

MacLeish wrote in a small hand that is not always easy to decipher. For suggestions that have helped to establish chronology and resolve uncertainties about the reading of words or phrases I am grateful to William Heyen, William MacLeish, Richard Wilbur, and R. H. Winnick. In the preparation of these poems for press, punctuation has been supplied in a few instances where it seemed obviously to have been overlooked in the penciled draft. Where MacLeish did not give the work a title, the one now provided is set in brackets. On pages 523 and 524 are notes explaining the provenance of certain poems.

The responsibility for the selection of poems that are newly added to this edition is mine, as the poet's literary executor. They are presented in the belief that they will reward old and new readers of Archibald MacLeish.

Richard B. McAdoo

[RUMOR AND SIGH]

Rumor and sigh of unimagined seas,
Dim radiance of stars that never flamed,
Fragrance of petals never strewn from trees, —
Meaning of words unsaid and never named;

So from a silence I have made you songs,
So from a starless night a rose of stars.
Can you not hear how all the stillness jars
With music, and the darkness throngs?

THE LOVER APOSTROPHIZES
THE POETS

You, you within whose minds the moon
leaves incommun-
icable words
and the night birds
memories
briefer than they —

tell, tell me, O retell me these
and I
when I have heard you say,
when you are silent, will remember how
our mouths met
and will remember, will remember why —
what now
I have forgotten — why
she could so soon
forget.

CATHEDRAL

Perpendiculars
Stemmed upward, blossoming,
Bend over from a sky of stone.
Stars,
Stars larger than the moon in heaven, swing
Circles of blue and crimson through the blown
And frozen branches of a granite tree.
A slanting rope
Of light unravels fraying into dark:

As of a bee
Mumbles across the gloom and echoes grope
After it following. A sullen spark
Rings from reluctant bronze and smouldering
Flares up and falls.
Silent, an imminence of walls
Leans on the world with overreaching wing.

[TO BE UNWOUND]

To be unwound
yard by yard
by year by year by year
by the counter-clockwise revolutions
of a certain number of tons of earth and rock
and so forth
turning round and round
in the middle of nothing at all —
to be unwound
to the bare
spool
and beyond it —
this,
being the understood and agreed determination of man,
the unappealable sentence,
the doom,
is regarded
generally
without the slightest amazement.

PHILOSOPHICAL ALOOFNESS

I do not demand for myself a window
on the top floor
from which you can see to Connecticut
and the people on the street below you
resemble themselves.
I do not demand the difficult serenity
of the perpendicular view.
It will be enough for me
to walk myself — but on the other side of the street
regarding with the detachment of obliquity
the business of rotating in an empty sky.
As for my soul,
let her hire an office for the conduct of her insolvent affairs
as high as she pleases.
She will not surmount
the giggle of the moon on the roof,
the snigger of the white stars.

VERNISSAGE

On the opening day of the automobile show the well-
Known President of the French Republic complete
In high hat demountable collar and bell
Hung body (with senators) rose from the royal seat
In the Grand Stair and moved on vibrationless feet
Down the Triumphal Aisle to the gradual swell
Of the brass band while the all but inaudible beat
Of his sleeveless valves rose in the air and fell.

The automobiles were however indifferent. The more
Expensive models preserved their decorum but four
Citroëns coughed. There were giggles, cat-calls, guffaws.
Even the shiny black cylindrical tall
Top hat of the chief of state of the Gall-
ic People failed to impress. There was no applause.

BIRTH OF EVENTUALLY VENUS

Cast up by the sea
By the seventh wave
Beyond the sea reach
In the rubble of weed and
Wet twig
The not yet amphibious
Animalcula
Gasps and wiggles on the beach
Gathering her long gold hair about her
And gazing with pure eyes
Upon the unknown world

POEM

Who of us all have seen
Nakedness?

Leaning above the wash stones by the river
The skirt pulls close at the knee, the breasts show

That, or an arm withdrawn as the door closes

503

But the bare thighs are animals lying in leaves,
The belly is secret as tigers running in sun ripple

Who among us have seen these nude girls
                              more than we've seen
The wind's shape under the silk in the doorway?

PROJECT FOR AN AESTHETIC
SUB-TITLE: MOONLIGHT OF A MAN

Mr. and Mrs. Longfellow Little who
Disapproved of Picasso (having — the catalogue erred —
Permitted themselves the emotions appropriate to
The *Gouache of a Nude* while beholding the *Sketch of the Word
Prone with Bananas*) who disapproved
of Picasso (and not that Picasso was Modern and not
That Mr. and Mrs. Little were slow to be moved
By Good Work — provided they recognized what

It was they were moved by — but how could one tell if one ought
To admire a thing unless one could say of it This is
A glass, This is a girl? How could one love
What might or might not be Important?) Mr. and Mrs.
Little who disapproved of Picasso bought
A Still Life. One knew what a Life was *of*.

POEM DEDICATED TO THE ADVANCEMENT OF AVIATION . . .

But that's all different now. They've got it fixed.
They give the prizes to Authentic Artists.
They put no Colley Cibbers in their lists.
They know the Homers and the Hacks apart.
(You tell the works of Homer by the blurbs)
They know the bum ones from the Edna Ferbers
And Miss Millay's Own work from what's not hers.
They never get the salt and sugar mixed —

They know too much. And when all's done and said,
When all the lady novelists and neat
She-poets are (if worms still be) worm's meat
And names in magazines, i.e., are dead,
No unknown kid will get their laurel stem.
By Yee! They'll have no Keatses crowding them!

[LET US DESTROY]

Let us destroy the forests all
And set the wild land free
That the naked moon may walk on the hill's shoulder
And the earth be seen.

Let us light in the green valleys a conflagration
That shall burn the willows away from the wet springs
And leave the water to shine in the sun like a metal
And the moon to ring.

505

Let us make of the sunset grass and the flowers
And all the liked and lovely garments of earth
A great flame in the air till the naked body
Of life come forth.

[SPRING]

Spring happens in one land only.
In England bluebells under the trees like
Skies sidewise are not spring, nor primroses:
False sun from a dark day. Spring is the
Blue in New England with great clouds over mountains;
Large sunlight everywhere full of well-being
And the world opening outward like wide doors
And a woman's body mild with moist warmth
And lying in bed in an aired room and by daylight,
The world outside all altered with green leaves and
High and bright and forever like mornings in childhood.

THE LITTLE BOY IN THE LOCKED HOUSE
for Charles 9¾ McLaughlin

Call and shout!
Call and shout!
Once you're in
You can't get out!

You can't go back
By crack in door.
No board will lift,
No stiffened latch
Uncatch and give.

You can't get through.
No ruined wall
Will fall apart.
Your heart may pound
Like sound of heel
On hollow floor:
There's no trap door.

You can't go down
By rounded drain
Or ancient well.
No cellar stone
Will groan and shift.
Lift up the hearth:
Beneath the sill
There still is earth.

You won't go up
By cupboard stair.
You'll force no latch
On attic doors.
You'd never dare!
(There's someone there.)

You can't get out!
. . . Call and shout:
Once you're in
You can't get out!

You can't get out!
The only way
To pick the locks —
The only trick
Is this: to stay!

To say the sun's
Within the room:
To say the moon's
Within the pane:
To say the rain's
Along the sill:
To say the hills
Are in the door.

To say you're in
And wish to stay!

SUMMER OF THE YEAR

All day long it has prepared to rain.
Now at dusk it is cold as late autumn.
The song sparrows creep in the ragged grass like mice
Eating the crab-grass seed. The wind is caught
In a tangle of fallen vines on the brick wall.
There is one butterfly, blue, at the end of a briar,
Swinging, swinging, swinging in the wind.
It is not yet August and the wind says winter, winter.

[OLD AGE]

Old age — to live in your life
as a man in his home town, when Interstate
Ninety cuts through Parsons' orchard, slices
Florence's Lunch in two, demolishes
seven elms — all that was left of them —
kills the maple by the Tap and Die,
bulldozes Totman's woods — pines, birches,
coons and Tittleman Brook and the thrushes — all of it —

to live in your life like a man in his own town
when you can't remember where the church was, coming from
Pumpkin Hollow over the underpass west of it
or how to get down to the store from River Road
now they've rerouted it east instead of north
or how to get home again even —
                              like the story:
Hey Rube! How do you get to Deerfield?
Well, I'll tell you — I wouldn't start from here.
You can't get home from here.
                              When you're old.

NICHOLAS NABOKOV HEARD LENIN SPEAK

Fourteen I was — a boy in a good school.
It was one of those April days when the ice on the Neva
drifts down and grounds and the air fogs.
They shoot cannon at intervals, one a minute,
hoping the reverberations will free the ice.
He spoke in the white fog in the intervals —

a high, sweet voice like the voice of an officer.
He was saying dangerous simple things
in a gentleman's voice between the cannon
Quietly
     the river rising.

AVANT GARDE

The caravan of the aforesaid sages,
marching forever toward the coming age,
never arrives. Upon a certain morning,
peering for palm trees through the usual thorns,
one, the foremost, finds a dusty fumet
gray in its grass-ring; studies it, presumes
something or someone has been there before —
a mounted man — in any case a horse.

Once in each generation as they journey
riders halloo, the camels kneel, the sages
gather in solemn circle, poke, sniff, rage,
remount, jerk rein; an ass brays and they turn.
Not one of them considers that the spoor
might have been theirs when last they marched the beat.
They're scholars, masters of the learned mind;
they know the future must be back behind.

And all this time, across some other desert,
single, without a camel or a fez,
a boy from Charleville in the April mud
has found the future floating in a puddle.

WHISTLER IN THE DARK

George Barker, British poet,
writes a eulogy of Dylan Thomas,
calls him whistler in the dark
and great because the dark is getting darker.

Is it? Was the dark not always darker?
Have we not always had these silver whistlers?
Listen! . . .
            That's Chaucer like a bobolink.

I think it's not the darkness, Mr. Barker,
makes for whistling well. I think
perhaps it's knowing how to whistle.
Listen! . . .
            That's Dylan trilling like a lark.

LIVE IN THE WORLD

Live in the world as men live in a
tight town, their own watchmen,
warning the dark off with their tolling bells
at midnight and their cries and candles.

There once were towns like that. The longest days
they'd pasture shadows underneath the leaves
like sheep but keep good dogs to bark at them,
and when the long nights came they shut them down,

lit wicks, lit kindling, lit a driftwood log
and slept by embers so no dark got in
but what the cat brought. Let me live
by embers too and bells against the wind.

DYING IN *THE NEW YORK TIMES*

On the same page of *The New York Times*
there died
of natural causes in Basel, Switzerland,
Karl Barth, Protestant theologian,
        and,
in the Far East, of electricity — a grounded
wire — Thomas Merton, monk.

Of the words of Karl Barth *The Times* recalled,
"Man can give himself to isolation but even
in isolation he must demonstrate the im-
possibility of playing the individual over against
God."

Nothing about the impossibility of playing God
over against the individual without
(finger to finger on the Sistine ceiling)
the individual over against — without
Karl Barth in Basel, Switzerland, writing on his knees.

Of the words of Thomas Merton, monk, *The Times* remembered
"We cannot arrive at the perfect possession of God in
this life and that is why we are traveling and in darkness."

Nothing about the perfect possession of
Man in this life — Saul
on the road to Damascus — Thomas Merton, monk,
traveling in the Far East and in darkness
and then no longer traveling, no longer dark,
total incandescence of the seeking man.

NURSERY RHYME

Don't cry, my lad,
don't knock, don't shout.
Once you're in
you can't get out.

You can't go back
the way you came:
it's choked by something —
horror? shame?

You can't go on:
the other door
is years beyond
with years before.

You can't go up:
the attic stair
creaks at night —
there's Someone There.

So don't, my dear,
don't cry, don't shout.

513

Turn your prison
inside out.

Tell the sun,
the moon, the star,
they're in; you're out.
They'll be.
                    You are.

KINDS OF FIRE

Flame, that flower with no root that rises
petal by petal in its bright disguises,
dies, leaves nothing, substance nor surmises,

flame, they say another —
sister is it? brother? —
burns as bright as you do, flares and flashes,

dies . . .

    but not to nothing:
dies to ashes.

OLD PHOTOGRAPH

There she is. At Antibes I'd guess
by the pines, the garden, the sea shine.

She's laughing. Oh, she always laughed
at cameras. She'd laugh and run
before that devil in the lens could catch her.
He's caught her this time though: look at her
eyes — her eyes aren't laughing.

There's no such thing as fragrance in a photograph
but this one seems to hold a fragrance —
fresh-washed gingham in a summer wind.

Old? Oh, thirty maybe. Almost thirty.
This would have been the year I went to Persia —
they called it Persia then — Shiraz,
Bushire, the Caspian, Isfahan.
She sent me the news in envelopes lined in blue.
The children were well. The Murphys were angels:
they had given her new potatoes sweet as peas
on a white plate under the linden tree.
She was singing Melisande with Croiza —
"mes longues cheveux." She was quite, quite well.
I was almost out of my mind with longing for her . . .

There she is that summer in Antibes —
laughing
            with frightened eyes.

THE BIG BANG AND THE EVENING STAR

There were signs in the sky when we were children:
signals off beyond the wood, the hill:
One —
the one we waited for — was after sunset,
faintly pulsing in that perfect blue
so secretly we knew it knew.

Now it is we who know.
They are only
sparks, these stars — cinders of the past —
fragments of the vast disaster
twenty billion years ago
when everything was blown to nowhere leaving
nothing but these dying
embers that with dawn are
gone.

And yet,
there still are evenings even now when we forget
what all those certainties of ours have settled:
evenings when a single star,
faint in that sunset blue but farther,
signals that we are not lost and not alone —
that we are seen and known,
and we believe it.
And our lives
are true for that one heart-beat — are our own.

OVERSTAYING

We used to walk here in the woods, we two,
laughing at time the way young lovers do —
laughing and talking of our new-born son.

And when we're dead, you'd say, and gone . . .

So we go first?

       It's not in nature to outlive
the life you've borne, the breath you've given.

But we're entitled, surely, to our day.

Provided there's no talk of overstaying!

Agreed. So when we're dead and gone? . . .

He'll have it all; the farm to run,
the house to keep, the brook, the timber.

And walk here talking of us.

       As we talk of him.

Laughing at us?

      Oh a loving laughter.
You have the right to laugh if you live after.

You have the right to silence if you die before.

Oh la! He'll keep our silence for us, never fear. . . .

Now we walk here in the late last year,
the wood hushed and the daylight almost done.
We do not speak. We keep the silence for our son.

ACROSS THE RIVER AND
UNDER THE TREES

How time goes racing now when there's no need to —
when there's so little farther left to go:
over the river — under the trees. Time ought to lead us
slow now . . . slow!

No need to race the days so — Sunday, Monday.
Yesterday was April: now it's May.
Time ought to stop a little just at sundown —
stand there — stay:

stay there by the roadside while the evening
hangs one star beyond the moon
and nothing stirs or breathes. Then leave us
soon. Ah . . . soon.

EPIGRAPH

This old man is no one I know
even if his look is mine —
or was when he first wore it in the jacket
photograph that advertised his book.

Everyone seems to know him: I don't know him.
People stop him at the post office to talk:
they don't stop me when I go walking.
I've lived here fifty years but they don't stop me.

It's him they want to see: the writer.
What I am they've never figured out —

only that I take to wood-lots evenings
crazing all the door-yard dogs.

Must be out for honey, way they see it —
lining up the late, last homeward flights
for bearings on a bee-tree somewhere.
Maybe I am but not their kind of honey.

I wonder, when they come to dig his grave
and find me lying in it, will they guess
whose death he died of, his or mine? —
Whose life I lived? —
                    Who wrote this line?

PHOTOGRAPH ALBUM

I used to see my life in front of me
on beyond the aunts and uncles,
farther than the first black boots,
the grown-up underwear, the tapered
trousers with the buttoned fly.
When God received me in the Baptist Church
in Evanston, Illinois, the reverend
dry in his trout-fisher's pants, the soprano
aching as the waters closed,
I saw my life go on before me
pure and singing as a bird
and all the way home on the C and NW
washed sins, washed sins.

In those days I was sure of meeting.
My life would wait for me beside

the evening somewhere on a fallen
tree-trunk and we'd sit and stare
and wonder at each other. Every
gravestone joins an ended life
to what once lived, love and bones
together in the dark at last.
Well, I'm here now at the fallen tree —
here, at least, in Conway, Massachusetts,
a small room in the woods, a pine
table and a painted chair.
Where is my life? Not waiting for me.
Not ahead now, certainly. But where?
In a cardboard box in a timbered attic?
Photographs of Paris? Persia?
Glencoe, Illinois? New Haven?

"Il ne reste que vos photos," Cocteau said,
quoting an advertisement doubtless,
giggling as usual. Limoges.
Spring of nineteen-eighteen sometime.

RETURN TO THE ISLAND

Years ago in the night
there were words in the sound of the wind,
words in the sound of the sea.
I would wake in the night and know
that they spoke to me.

Now in the night the words
cry in the sound of the wind,
cry in the sound of the sea.
I wake and I know they speak
but not to me.

Page 499. This poem was written in the early 1920s. It is printed with the permission of the Collection of American Literature, the Beinecke Rare Book and Manuscript Library, Yale University.

Page 500. "The Lover Apostrophizes the Poets" was a focal point of a dialogue in verse written by MacLeish under the title "Conversation Lugubre" and sent as a letter to John Peale Bishop dated June 3, 1924.

Page 500. "Cathedral" appeared in the *North American Review* of September 1924.

Pages 502 through 505. The five poems beginning with "Vernissage" appeared first in a 1927 issue of *transition*, in Paris, and were reprinted in *Poetry*, November 1980, under the heading "Five Poems from the 1920's."

Page 506. Charles McLaughlin, son of a friend of Archibald and Ada MacLeish living in Cambridge, Massachusetts, asked for a contribution to his *Coolidge Hill Gazette*, which was produced in the winter of 1938–39. The poet had evidently indicated to the editor, who was nine years old going on ten, that he contemplated further revisions, for the editor wrote, "We like your Peom [*sic*] very much and we hope your improvements will be as successful as the Peom is now." The poem is republished with the kind consent of Mr. McLaughlin, who is editor-in-chief of the Frederick Law Olmsted Papers and professor of history at The American University.

Page 509. Numerous drafts of "Nicholas Nabokov Heard Lenin Speak" appear in MacLeish's notebooks, beginning in 1934 when he and Nabokov were working together on the ballet "Union Pacific." This last version was written in 1973.

Page 511. "Whistler in the Dark" was reproduced in manuscript facsimile by the *Paris Review*, Summer 1974. In a letter to the editor who had asked for the manuscript to illustrate the poet's way of working, MacLeish wrote:

> Will this do as a manuscript? It doesn't show corrections but it shows me as a pencil man and, worse still, a slave to the eraser. (Black Wing pencils have erasers which eradicate as clean as time.)
>
> As for the lines themselves — they went into a notebook and never came out again because Dylan's death was too great a loss and George Barker's piece was too deeply felt to fool with it in a tone like this one.
>
> But that's all in the past now. People die too absolutely these days — disappear like pencil marks to an eraser — black wing.

Page 513. This later version of the poem beginning on page 506 was written thirty-five years afterward.

Page 515. The photograph evidently dated from 1926, the year that MacLeish went to Persia as secretary of a League of Nations commission, leaving his wife and children in France.

Page 517. The MacLeishes' oldest child, Kenneth, named for the poet's brother who had been killed in Belgium in 1918, died in the summer of 1977 and was buried at Conway.